WITHDRAWN

DUANE J. MACMILLAN is a member of the Department of English at the
of Saskatchewan.

MARSTON LAFRANCE was a member of the Department of English at C
University from 1963 until his death in 1975. His colleagues remember h
teacher intensely loyal to his students and to the intellectual functions of t
versity, as well as a critic with great sensitivity to the craft of language. H
writing was vigorous, flexible, lucid, and precise. He was a stoic for most
although the basic *humanitas* of the man softened what otherwise might ha
mere grim endurance. This tribute to him focuses on stoicism in Americar
ture. The strain is evident in both the tension in the works of various impo
American writers and in the philosophical vein of stoicism which runs thro
several genres, over long periods of time.

Of Henry David Thoreau's *Civil-Disobedience* (1849), LaFrance said: '1
seems to me to be the best available statement of a distinctive philosophical
tion – the assertion of a moral self-reliance – which is found throughout Am
literature ... a peculiar strain of cussedness which seems to me to be an esse
property of the American mind.' That 'strain of cussedness' is explored in v
ways in this book. These are essays which provoke and advance scholarship
critical insight. Strict philosophical rigour is sometimes 'strained' in favour o
unity, but the essays, in their juxtaposition, suggest that the stoic theme in
American literature is a fruitful subject for exploration.

EDITED BY DUANE J. MACMILLAN

The Stoic Strain in American Literature

Essays in Honour of Marston LaFrance

University of Toronto Press
TORONTO BUFFALO LONDON

CALVIN T. RYAN LIBRARY
KEARNEY STATE COLLEGE
KEARNEY, NEBRASKA

© University of Toronto Press 1979
Toronto Buffalo London
Printed in Canada

Illustrations: Patrick Hayman, London

Library of Congress Cataloging in Publication Data

Main entry under title:

The stoic strain in American literature.

CONTENTS: Johnston, G. For Marston LaFrance.
– Buitenhuis, P. The stoic strain in American
literature. – Stern, M.R. Towards Bartleby the
scrivener. [etc.]
1. American literature – History and criticism –
Addresses, essays, lectures. 2. Stoics in
literature. 3. LaFrance, Marston. 4. Authors,
American – 20th century – Biography. I. LaFrance,
Marston. II. MacMillan, Duane J., 1937–
PS121.S76   810'.9   79-523
ISBN 0-8020-5441-2

GEORGE JOHNSTON

For Marston LaFrance

North you came and for a while felt free
as though you might have left bigotry
behind. No such luck. North has bigots too.
But having made your move you stayed
and we shall remember you: your jaw
set for standards and sparing no one, least
yourself. Neither shall we forget
the head you let be handsome, grudgingly;
the sweetness that pierced your harumph;
the teacher and scholar that you were, whose good opinion
was dear; your craftsmanship, loyalty,
old-fashioned things, guarding which
we guard your memory, and ourselves.

Contents

For Marston LaFrance v
GEORGE JOHNSTON

Preface xi

The Stoic Strain in American Literature 3
PETER BUITENHUIS

Towards 'Bartleby the Scrivener' 19
MILTON R. STERN

Walt Whitman and Stoicism 43
GAY WILSON ALLEN

Henry James: 'The Voice of Stoicism' 63
MUNRO BEATTIE

A Reading of Frank Norris's *The Pit* 77
RICHARD ALLAN DAVISON

The Mock-Heroics of Desire: Some Stoic Personae in the Work of
William Carlos Williams 97
ROGER B. SALOMON

Death and Birth in Hemingway 115
MELVIN BACKMAN

His '*Magnum O*': Stoic Humanism in Faulkner's *A Fable* 135
DUANE J. MacMILLAN

Saul Bellow and the Example of Dostoevsky 157
DANIEL FUCHS

The Moviegoer and the Stoic Heritage 179
LEWIS A. LAWSON

Marston LaFrance: A Tribute and Memorial Bibliography 193
TOM MIDDLEBRO'

Notes 199

Notes on Contributors 221

Whatever is in any way beautiful hath its source of beauty in itself, and is complete in itself; praise forms no part of it. So it is none the worse nor the better for being praised.
(Marcus Aurelius Antoninus, *Meditations*, IV, 20)

Preface

Marston LaFrance (1927–75) was a stoic for most of his life, although the basic *humanitas* and *caritas* of the man softened what otherwise might have been mere grim endurance. He was 'not careless in deeds, nor confused in words, nor rambling in thoughts' (Marcus Aurelius Antoninus, *Meditations*, VI, 51); and he clearly believed that life was for the living. Of Henry David Thoreau's *Civil Disobedience* (1849) Marston states in some unpublished notes: 'It seems to me to be the best available statement of a distinctive philosophical position – the assertion of a *moral* self-reliance which is found throughout American literature. And the position is moral, neither intellectual nor practical except so far as it is actively put to use ... *Civil Disobedience* is the best attempt I know to define a peculiar strain of cussedness which seems to me to be an essential property of the American mind.' That 'strain of cussedness' is explored in various ways by the contributors of this book. We have not only attempted to honour Marston LaFrance; we have also essayed to posit a forward-reaching, vital testimonial which will provoke and advance scholarship and critical insight. Strict philosophical rigour is 'strained' in favour of some degree of unity; but the essays, in their juxtaposition, suggest that the stoic theme in American literature is a fruitful subject for exploration.

Peter Buitenhuis provides a useful introductory essay on the vein of stoicism which LaFrance identified, while concurrently noting the 'strain' which the editor suggests may prove useful to further scholarship. Milton R. Stern reviews published criticism and finds that an insistence on stoicism is negatively useful on at least two counts: it implies that Melville may have been dealing with deeper philosophical and psychological concepts of 'the victim' than has often been thought; and it provides direction for future readings of 'Bartleby the Scrivener.' Fresh insights into the stoicism of Walt Whitman are offered by Gay Wilson Allen through a re-examination of much primary material and Frances Wright [D'Arusmont]'s *A Few Days in Athens* (1822): Allen concludes that Whitman tried to conquer the fear of death 'not with stoic indifference, but with faith in the purpose of death.' Munro Beattie examines the stoic qualities in Henry James and, in tracing that theme through James's works, deftly humanizes the author in a refreshing way seldom found in the standard biographies. Frank Norris's *The Pit* is examined from a structurist point of view by Richard Allan Davison who suggests that only characters who adhere to stoic or Christian principles and virtues survive or die with dignity. This essay develops further the 'strain' or stress of the stoic theme in American literature, an idea which was introduced in Peter Buitenhuis's overview of the literary tradition in the United States. Roger Salomon observes the similarity of concepts, attitudes, and behavioural patterns (as opposed to stringent 'systems of beliefs') between the stoic humanism of Cervantes and certain personae in the works of William Carlos Williams, especially in terms of the environment of the mock-heroic. Melvin Backman analyses a significant portion of the Hemingway canon in such a way as to emphasize the stoicism inherent in the traditional 'Hemingway code': Backman concludes that 'locked within the hurt self, the Hemingway hero is not able to make the kind of authentic relationship to others or to a divine power which would give purpose to life and sustain the human spirit in its struggles.' Faced with such reality in his own life, Hemingway could no longer stoically endure and he committed suicide. William Faulkner's *A Fable* is examined by Duane MacMillan, who argues that Faulkner sees man's ability simply to endure and to create his own self-sufficiency as finally more stoic than Christian, and Christian only to a coincidental degree. Daniel Fuchs traces the stoic strain through the major works of Saul Bellow by means of detailed comparisons with those of Dostoevsky. Lewis A. Lawson carefully traces the stoic heritage in American letters from historical colonial evidence through the 'strain' of the Civil War and the Reconstruction Era into modern times. In a superb analysis of Walker Percy's *The Moviegoer* Lawson convincingly demonstrates 'the continuing vitality of stoicism in the South.' Finally, the stoic balance of this volume is struck by the poetic portrait and tributes to Marston LaFrance by George Johnston and Tom Middlebro'. Middlebro' has also thoughtfully and carefully compiled the memorial bibliography.

The editor's task has been an extremely pleasant and rewarding one. I thank each and all contributors for their kindness, patience, and co-operation, which they have unflinchingly extended to an untried hand. This book has been published with the help of subventions from Carleton University, where Marston LaFrance is greatly missed as both a teacher and an administrator, and the University of Saskatchewan, and a grant to University of Toronto Press from the Andrew W. Mellon Foundation; their help is sincerely appreciated. Marie Ann LaFrance kindly granted permission to quote from Marston's lecture notes: for this privilege and for a thousand silent encouragements over the years I am eternally grateful. Special thanks must go to Mr Patrick Hayman, London, England, for accepting and so brilliantly executing my commission to illustrate *The Stoic Strain in American Literature*. Finally, I thank Professor D.R. Cherry, Dean of Arts and Science, and Carlyle A. King, Professor Emeritus University of Saskatchewan, for their encouragement, assistance, and advice; Professors Claud A. Thompson and David F. Hiatt for reading the manuscript; Mrs J.L. McConnell and Mrs D. Young for hours of typing services; and Miss Jean Jamieson, Humanities Editor, University of Toronto Press, who helped immeasurably to bring about *The Stoic Strain in American Literature*.

DUANE J. MACMILLAN
Saskatoon, Saskatchewan
November 1977

THE STOIC STRAIN IN AMERICAN LITERATURE

PETER BUITENHUIS

The Stoic Strain
in American Literature

Complacency is a delusion in a world where nothing but death is final, where no ideal can
ever be possessed because man has to reckon with externalities beyond his control, a
stoic's world in which a continuous present poses a continuous demand upon man's moral
and physical endurance.
(Marston LaFrance, 'Stephen Crane's Private Fleming: His Various Battles,'
in *Patterns of Commitment in American Literature*, edited by
Marston LaFrance [Toronto 1967], p 124)

To attempt to introduce a theme such as this is to run straight up against its knotted
complexities. In the first place, to summarize stoic tenets would take an extended
essay, since the school began in the third century BC and flourished until the beginning of the second century AD. Its proclaimers included men as diverse in temperament and life styles as Zeno, Cleanthes, Chrysippus, Epictetus, Seneca, and Marcus
Aurelius. It was a philosophy which, according to R.D. Hicks, 'provoked fierce
opposition and was continually modified by pressure from without and within.'[1] In
the second place, American writers who can be said to have stoic elements in their
work came by the philosophy in a variety of ways, at the extremes of which are
Emerson, who made a careful study of it, and Hemingway, who probably knew little
or nothing of the philosophy through books.

And yet, it is possible to outline crudely a system of stoic belief which remains
more or less constant, and constitutes its core down through the ages. Some of these
tenets have entered the stream of what Aldous Huxley has called the Perennial
Philosophy, that which is transmitted not only through books, but also by human
example and experience. Such an outline must include the following elements: an
emphasis on personal courage and endurance, the control or suppression of emotion, the curbing of sexual and other bodily appetites, indifference to pain, suffering,
and death, the acknowledgment of the kinship of men, the distrust of pleasure, the
maintenance of imperturbability, devotion to duty and to an ideal of virtue. It is an

individualistic philosophy, appealing to those who lead and to those who are scepti-
cal of the efficacy of group action. It is a philosophy without illusions, with debts to
the cynics, but with less of the cynic's contempt for conventional morality. Stoic
philosophy, Hicks points out, began in a period of storm and stress,[2] and it has
continued to be largely true that it has had most appeal at times of crisis in religious
or ethical belief, or when one social or political system is giving way to another.
Marston LaFrance's statement, quoted above, provides as good a summary as I
have seen of the central concern of the stoic attitude, and it is applicable not only to
Crane, but also, in various degrees, to many American writers.

I shall attempt to outline, then, the times which gave rise to stoicism in American
literature and its effects on some of its chief proponents. Other contributors to this
volume will no doubt flesh out what I have to say.

It is curious that there appears to have been no systematic study of the stoic strain
in American literature in general, or in certain specific literary periods, or even in
many individual authors.[3] New England evangelical Protestantism was not a fertile
seedbed for stoic ideals, even though the conditions of the wilderness were often
productive of stoic virtue. William Bradford found need of it in leading the early
settlers in Massachusetts when he wrote:

> In these hard and difficult beginnings they found some discontents and murmurings arise
> amongst some, and mutinous speeches and carriages in other; but they were soon quelled
> and overcome by the wisdom, patience, and just and equal carriage of things, by the
> Governor and better part, which clave faithfully together in the main.[4]

The powerful belief in Providence, the doctrine of revelation, and the various
enthusiasms generated by periodic evangelical revivals, particularly Jonathan Edwards's Great Awakening, kept the stoic ideal pretty much at bay.

The decline of the age of faith and the rise of the age of enlightenment brought
about the revival of stoic ideals. This can clearly be seen in that central document of
the eighteenth century, Pope's *Essay on Man*. Benjamin Franklin typified many of
the ideals of the age and it is in his work that we find clear traces of stoicism,
particularly in his *Autobiography*.

Franklin's early trials and misfortunes schooled him well in stoic behaviour, and
his reading in Plutarch, Shaftesbury, and the eighteenth-century rationalist tradition
lent philosophical depth to his thought. Stoic philosophy had always stressed self-
discipline, and the careful regulation of one's behaviour; it also frequently embodied
proverbial wisdom into its thought. For example, Marcus Aurelius laid out in sche-
matic form in book VIII of *The Meditations* rules for the good life. Franklin was
carrying on an honourable tradition when he set out on 'the bold and arduous
project of arriving at moral perfection.'[5] His precepts provided a model of stoic

behaviour, although perhaps geared more to self-interest than to the good of the state, a value often emphasized by earlier stoics. Most to be marked in Franklin's list of twelve virtues – the thirteenth, humility, was only added later on the advice of a Quaker – is Franklin's emphasis on the control of passion. Emotion is to play little or no part in the conduct of life. Every endeavour is to be made to control and direct such an unruly factor to good ends.

Such a schematized list of moral virtues led naturally to Franklin's famous and influential *Poor Richard's Almanac*, which is a kind of combination of proverbial wisdom, stoic principles, and deistic religion. It was a useful guide for a country which had an abundance of land and resources: no doubt it indirectly aided the rise of material prosperity in the Colonies and later the emerging nation.

In the long and bitter War of Independence there was need for stoic virtue. George Washington came to represent the ideal leader in adversity and he also provided an example of the Roman virtues that had considerable influence on revolutionary and early federal political, artistic, and architectural, as well as literary, expression. Philip Freneau was perhaps the most representative author of the period, and he was early schooled in adversity by having to face the problem of literary authorship in an age of revolution, political turmoil, and cultural deprivation. In 'To an Author' he outlined the problems of authorship, and in 'The House of Night' he presented a picture of despair and death which is lightened only by the concluding stoic stanzas of reflection:

> What is this Death, ye deep-read sophists, say? –
> Death is no more than one unceasing change;
> New forms arise, while other forms decay,
> Yet all is Life throughout creation's range.[6]

Freneau was among the first to praise the native Indians for stoic virtue, as in 'The Indian Burying Ground.' This, of course, became a central theme of James Fenimore Cooper's *Leatherstocking Tales*. Deriving many of his traits from that race, Natty Bumppo became the first significant stoic hero in American literature. Fearless, tireless, resourceful, indifferent to fatigue, suffering, hunger, and the presence of death, Natty shows by his example the way to cope with the wilderness and to establish personal freedom based on conformity to nature and proud individualism.

It is, however, a fact that the Perennial Philosophy of stoicism can be adapted to many ends. Emerson changed the direction of stoic thought in American literature towards a more contemplative and analytic form. For him it was a response to the loss of his own orthodox Unitarian Christianity – a deliberate rejection of the faith of his forefathers. Emerson was well read in the stoic philosophy, and it is clear that the stoic code of behaviour as well as its thought appealed to Emerson's reserved and unemotional nature.[7] His most characteristic, and most extreme, essay, 'Self-Reliance,' is full of stoic maxims. Moreover, Emerson's style has been influenced by the crispness and dogmatic clarity of stoic philosophy, particularly, I think, that of Marcus Aurelius. Take, for example, this paragraph from book X of the *Meditations*:

> The residue of life is short. Live as on a mountain. It matters not whether here or there, everywhere you are a citizen of the city of the world. Let men see and witness a true man, a life conformed to nature. If they cannot bear him, let them make away with him. Better that, than life on their terms.[8]

The aphoristic sentence form, the disregard of public opinion, the moral certainty, the constant appeal to nature, are all typical of late stoic thought.

Such a philosophy was a practical one for Emerson, met, as he frequently was, with economic and personal problems, yet it led to a kind of aloofness and isolation. His concept of friendship was, in particular, a stoic one, as he wished to limit his friendship to the wise and good and was constantly aware of how personal relationships could interfere with the integrity of the self. And yet, typically, Emerson went beyond the stoics in proclaiming the essential isolation and priority of the self. In his essay 'Friendship' he writes: 'Let us even bid our dearest friends farewell, and defy them, saying "Who are you? Unhand me: I will be dependent no more." '[9] Emerson took the stoic philosophy to extremes, as he did so many other ideas, and in the end took it out of this world into the transcendental world in which he had his most profound being. The transcendentalist's Nature is not only that physical world which serves man, but, overridingly, that mystical realm in which Emerson, like the English romantics, encountered the Godhead. Ultimately, that weird and wonderful mixture in Emerson of the stoic philosopher, the Hindu sage, and the Yankee peddler made him totally individual and non-definable.

It has often been said that Thoreau lived the life which Emerson merely theorized about, and this is particularly true of the way in which Thoreau put to work the ideal of stoicism in his daily life at Walden Pond. Emerson was the stoic of the drawing room while Thoreau was, as George Eliot remarked in an early review, 'a stoic of the woods.'[10]

Thoreau wrote near the beginning of *Walden*:

> To be a philosopher is not merely to have subtle thoughts, nor even to found a school, but so to love wisdom as to live according to its dictates, a life of simplicity, independence, magnanimity, and trust. It is to solve some of the problems of life, not only theoretically, but practically ... How can a man be a philosopher and not maintain his vital heat by better methods than other men?[11]

Deliberately simplifying everything, and striking out against the main current of American materialism, Thoreau made of his life an assay of the essentials. What could be dispensed with? is his recurring question in *Walden*. One by one, frills, possessions, and even apparent necessities, go by the board. And his intention in this exercise was not merely the one so often practised by stoic philosophers in classical times – the retreat from the temptations and the toils and troubles of the city to the country, but an endeavour to find the forms in which a man could best live according to the terms which he himself defined.

This course of action was in radical opposition to what the vast majority of Americans in his time thought was right and proper. Instead of making money, he chose almost to do without it. Instead of seeking success, he chose obscurity. Instead of supporting his community, he ridiculed it. Instead of worshipping God in the church, he created his own sanctuary in the woods. Instead of seeking to uphold the ideal of citizenship, he chose to explore what it was to become a citizen of the world of nature. And there is a kind of passion in this enterprise which reveals itself not only in the extraordinary rigour of his life, but also in the purity and clarity of his prose:

> I wanted to live deep and suck out all the marrow of life, to live so sturdily, and Spartan-like as to put to rout all that was not life, to cut a broad swath and shave close, to drive life into a corner, and reduce it to its lowest terms, and, if it proved to be mean, why then to get the whole and genuine meanness of it, and publish its meanness to the world; or, if it were sublime, to know it by experience, and be able to give a true account of it in my next excursion.[12]

In order to render this account Thoreau observed closely, recorded accurately, and reflected profoundly on all that he did. He bore all extremes of climate and diet with equanimity and observed his own reactions to experience with as much clinical detachment as he observed the battle of the ants or the behaviour of the ice on the pond. He did not live without passion; rather, he refined passion to a pitch of intellectual keenness which has seldom been surpassed. I think that our only reservation about the man is a slight chill that his personality and his rigour evoke. There was something so essentially stoical about his whole life that it was in the end, slightly more, or less, than human.

These qualities in Emerson and Thoreau both fascinated and infuriated Herman Melville and led to the fine satirical sketches of the philosopher, Plotinus Plinlimmon, in *Pierre* and Mark Winsome and his Thoreauvian disciple, Egbert, in *The Confidence Man*. It was the dreaming, mystical, transcendental side of Emerson that Melville ridiculed, as can be seen in the Masthead chapter of *Moby-Dick* where Ishmael falls into a reverie and forgets his precarious perch.

> In this enchanted mood, the spirit ebbs away to whence it came; becomes diffused through time and space; like Cranmer's [sic] sprinkled Pantheistic ashes, forming at last a part of every shore the round globe over.

It is in such a mood that man loses his hold on reality and his grip on the nature of things:

> And perhaps, at mid-day, in the fairest weather, with one half-throttled shriek you drop through that transparent air into the summer sea, no more to rise forever. Heed it well, ye Pantheists![13]

Melville also parodied the Yankee Peddler aspect of Emerson, as he did of Thoreau, but he still retained an admiration for that serene and stoic side of Emerson's character.

He certainly tended to put a touch of stoicism into his heroes or into some character to act as a counterbalance to the romantic excesses of his major figures. This is particularly true of *Moby-Dick* in which Ishmael counterbalances Ahab's monomania, isolation, and wild excesses of feeling with stoicism, serenity, and friendship. This is made quite explicit in the chapter called 'A Squeeze of the Hand,' in which Ishmael, squeezing the sperm, is led to reflect that man must always lower 'his conceit of attainable felicity; not placing it anywhere in the intellect or the fancy; but in the wife, the heart, the bed, the table, the saddle, the fire-side, the country ...'[14] Stoic man settles for the middle way and for achievable happiness; the romantic hero strives always for greatness or for revenge, and fails. It is the perceived bond between men, so much emphasized in the stoic ideal of friendship, that in the end seems, symbolically, to save Ishmael. Where Captain Ahab is an *isolato*, Ishmael, after his initial suspiciousness, and prejudice, becomes a fast friend of Queequeg. Their joint interdependence is symbolically illustrated in the chapter called 'The Monkey Rope.' As the voyage continues, their friendship grows just as Ahab's isolation increases. In the end, Ahab's monomaniacal quest results in the destruction of the ship with all hands but Ishmael, who is saved by the coffin that Queequeg had fashioned for himself.

Melville's whole life and art can be interpreted as one long quest for some kind of certainty in a world of change and illusion. *Pierre* and *The Confidence Man* particularly are voyages into total ambiguity, so that any philosophy which provided at least a code of conduct was welcome to Melville. Yet he was always aware that excess of any idea could lead to failure.

That strange tale 'Bartleby' can be read as a commentary on stoicism. Bartleby may be the ultimate stoic – a man who has reduced his bodily needs almost to zero and who has his emotions so totally under control that he never expresses them, or even appears to feel them. His demeanour is always the same, his wants minimal. He bears whatever befalls him with the utmost composure. He is in complete control of his own destiny, and he wants for nothing. This may be taken as a description of a stoic, and yet, of course, it is stoicism reduced to absurdity. Bartleby has severed the essential tie which binds man to his fellow men and to the essence of life itself. He has come, it is reported, from the Dead Letter Office in Washington and, apparently, has lost all ability to communicate, except with his incantatory saying: 'I would prefer not to.' In the end, after his removal from the lawyer's office, and his being deposited in the Tombs, he prefers not to live at all, and dies, curled up in the foetal position.

It may be that Melville was commenting on the impossibility of an individual, particularly a writer, for Bartleby is a scrivener, ever retreating into a solipsistic, stoic world and surviving. When Melville did officially shut up shop and retreat into the Custom House, he still went on writing poetry and, most importantly, *Billy Budd*. In that novella Melville uses a stoic hero, Captain Vere, as a foil for the impulsive and tragic Billy and perhaps, also, as another commentary on the limitations of the stoic vision. Vere's behaviour is uniformly grave and serious; his bravery is unquestioned: and he is, in many respects, the ideal Roman gentleman. He believes implicitly in the necessity for order and discipline, and in the naval law which insists upon obedience and subordination, particularly in times of war. He believes, therefore, that he has no choice when the moment comes for the judgment of Billy's killing of the master-at-arms.

Billy Budd seems to profit by the example of the fatherlike Captain Vere in meeting his own death so bravely and stoically. His last words ring out, '"God bless Captain Vere!"' And these words seem to have been the strongest trial that the captain has to face. Melville's essential ambiguity is most clearly expressed at this moment in the story because Vere's reaction is described in the following terms:

> Captain Vere, either through stoic self-control or a sort of momentary paralysis induced by emotional shock, stood erectly rigid as a musket in the ship-armorer's rack.[15]

Captain Vere retains his stoic composure until his end, which comes after he is shot by a French sailor during a naval engagement. His final remark is ambiguous, but probably reveals an acceptance of death and a celebration of goodness: '"Billy Budd. Billy Budd."'

That watershed in American history and literature, the Civil War, brought about a series of political, social, and cultural conditions which led to the emergence of stoic traits in a good many American writers. The war certainly deepened the stoic sense that Walt Whitman had earlier derived, in part at least, from his study of Epictetus. Sholom Kahn has fully documented this aspect of Whitman's work, largely by discussing his earlier poetry. The stoicism was reinforced by Whitman's experience in the war, as can be seen in such *Drum Taps* poems as 'The Centenarian,' 'A March in the Ranks Hard-Prest,' 'The Road Unknown,' and 'The Wound-Dresser.'

In 'The Centenarian' the old soldier recalls the stoic figure of Washington crossing the river after his defeat at the Battle of Brooklyn Heights in 1776: 'As resolute in defeat as other generals in their proudest triumphs.'[16] Washington is the example on which the Union soldiers should model their behaviour. And so they do – the soldiers in the field as Whitman perceives them in many poems, and the wounded and dying in 'A March in the Ranks' and 'The Wound-Dresser.' Walt himself dresses the wounds 'with impassive hand,' but the stoic attitude stops far short of suppressing emotion and of curbing appetites, sexual or otherwise. Nevertheless, stoicism sustained him through the most testing period of his life, and enabled him to come through to the serenity and grandeur of the last *Drum Taps* poems and 'When Lilacs Last in the Dooryard Bloom'd' – in which Lincoln takes his place in the ranks of stoic heroes.

A writer whose best work emerged from Civil War experience is Ambrose Bierce. His work anticipates that of Stephen Crane, but his attitude towards stoicism was more complex than that of his successor. Bierce saw too much of war to believe in the universal efficacy of stoicism. His most ironic tale is 'Parker Adderson, Philosopher.' Adderson's philosophy is stoicism. A captured Federal spy, he answers the interrogation of a Confederate general with cool and witty insouciance as he looks forward to his death at dawn the following morning. The general, on the other hand, shudders at the idea of death. The boot is exchanged, however, when the general decides to have the spy shot at once, and not wait until morning. Adderson's stoicism disappears; he goes berserk, kills the provost-marshall, and gravely wounds the general. He is dragged to his death 'begging incoherently for life,' while the general dies smiling sweetly, and saying: 'I suppose this must be death.'[17]

Stoic bravery comes in for equally rough treatment in 'A Son of the Gods,' in which the brilliant conduct of a lone officer, sent out to see if the enemy is concealed in force behind a wall, inspires the troops so much that they rush against orders into attack. Many are killed and wounded, and the brave, insouciant act goes for nothing. There are many similar ironies in Bierce's fine war stories. In one only does stoicism serve an individual's purpose. In 'One Officer, One Man' Captain Graffenreid, long eager to see battle, becomes deathly afraid when he does because he is forced to lie under fire next to the dead body of a private. At the end of the engagement, in which his company is not called upon to fight, he glances down at his sword: 'Foreshortened to his view, it resembled somewhat, he thought, the short heavy blade of the ancient Roman. The fancy was full of suggestion, malign, fateful, heroic!' He falls on the sword and dies. The story is nonchalantly concluded by the general's dispatch: 'Owing to the enemy's withdrawal from my front to reinforce his beaten left, my command was not seriously engaged. My loss was as follows: Killed, one officer, one man.'[18]

The war, then, gave rise to a more complex awareness of the nature of stoicism than had hitherto prevailed. The sense of complexities grew in the troubled peace that followed it. One of the best portraits of the age is to be found in *The Education of Henry Adams*. In that work Adams goes with merciless clarity into the forces which inhibited his political, intellectual, and artistic life and he admits in the chapter 'The Dynamo and the Virgin' his complete inability to deal with the power released upon the world by science and technology. His refuge in such a world without guideposts lies in his theory of force and in a stoic resignation in which he could accept, with an ironic and caustic wit, everything that happened in fulfilment of his gloomiest predictions. Since many of the springs of his emotional life had been dried up at the death of his wife, stoic disdain of passion fitted well with his attitude. Like the old Roman philosophers, he retired from the follies and the preoccupations of men to speculate in tranquillity among his books.

Henry James's stoicism can be traced to some of the same roots as that of Henry Adams. He, too, was revolted by the rapacity, materialism, and corruption of post–Civil War America and he was also schooled in disappointment when his work failed to receive popular acceptance. C.B. Cox has traced the development of the stoic attitude in James from an early review of the work of Epictetus to Strether's remarks in *The Ambassadors* concerning the 'tin mould' in which consciousness is formed.

In some important particulars James's stoicism was a necessary reaction to the facile optimism of American culture. With heroes as widely different as Christopher Newman of *The American* and Maggie Verver of the *The Golden Bowl* he traced the emergence of a sense of complexity of tragedy in human life and the consequent necessity of developing a certain stoicism. The criticism has many times been levelled at James that he deals with characters from a class whose wealth removes them from the problems that face the mass of people. But I believe that Cox is quite right when he concludes that 'to the Jamesian heroes and heroines, rigid self-control and consistent moral behaviour are of more importance than health, riches, and prosperity.'[19]

Mark Twain faced similar social, political, and artistic questions, but was not able to work his way towards the kind of stoicism which was of such value to James's later career. Bitterness and pessimism in the face of man's folly and corruption gained the upper hand, and though, as in a story like 'The Man that Corrupted Hadleyburg,' Twain's blackness of vision could be camouflaged by an uproarious humour, the humour becomes clouded more and more by the darkness of Twain's later years.

What is, perhaps, most remarkable about Stephen Crane's work is that he was able to arrive at a stoic stance at such an early point in his career. Marston LaFrance has finely documented the growth of Henry Fleming's consciousness in *The Red Badge of Courage* and has concisely summed up the necessity imposed upon Fleming in that novel:

> Fleming is not the undiscovered Achilles of his grand illusions; he is just another lad who has to learn to be a man. And to be a man in Crane's world is to perceive the human situation as it is, accept it, and remain personally honest in fulfilling the commitments such a perception demands of the individual.[20]

Many of Crane's later heroes had to go through similar kinds of testing experiences in order to discover their humanity and to come to grips with the nature of the universe. The clearest example of this is the correspondent in 'The Open Boat.' I have described this elsewhere as an existential story,[21] and I should have to add that stoicism is an important constituent of the existentialist philosophy, particularly as it was practised by Albert Camus. The emphasis in both philosophies is on discovery of one's self through experience and self-trust, as it was indeed for Emerson in 'Self-Reliance,' but stoic and existential ideals insist on the limitations which the individual must discover, and not the infinity which Emerson sees in man's potential.

Clearly, as we move into the modern period, we find that the appeal of stoicism remains strong. Theodore Dreiser called the last of his trilogy on Frank Cowperwood, the financier, *The Stoic*. The novel was not quite completed at the time of his death in 1947, and it is possible that he might have articulated more fully the philosophy in his reworking of it, but it is clear that Dreiser's definition of the heroic in the American character is bound up with the self-reliant, self-determining, dominant, and tranquil bearing of Cowperwood as he triumphs over every obstacle except that of death. Only one persistent strain in *The Stoic*, as in the other two novels of the trilogy, interrupts the steady progress of Cowperwood towards financial and social domination, and that is his overmastering sexual drive. In his stumbling and half-articulate way Dreiser was, perhaps, groping at the limitations of the stoic philosophy when dealing with a man of heroic proportions like Cowperwood.

In order to have risen so far and to have gained so much power and wealth Cowperwood needed not only reason but also passion. The passion reinforced and drove his ambition while his reason worked out elaborate schemes for financial takeover and control of many operations. The concomitant to this drive was the overflow of his passion into an overwhelming love for beauty, which took the form partly of art but mostly of women. In the last three decades of the nineteenth century, during which the Cowperwood saga is set, his free-ranging behaviour with many women is an impediment to his social, and sometimes to his financial, success.

Ostracism is one of the highest barriers that Cowperwood has to climb in his ruth-less march to success. But the passion makes him more truly human than he would otherwise have been, and this Dreiser illuminates in the closing pages of the trilogy. After having heard the doctor's diagnosis that he might have only a year to live, Cowperwood reflects on the fact that his much-looked-forward-to relationship with his young ideal woman, Berenice, would not, in all likelihood, be long enjoyed. 'For once he could not contemplate the fatal processes of life with his usual equanimity. Actually he could only consider the poetic value of this hour, and its fleetingness, which involved sorrow and nothing but sorrow.'[22]

The real stoic, in reflecting on the transience of life and love, can assimilate that to his scheme; but Cowperwood is all too human and too frail to be able to do this. He seeks to leave behind him monuments in the shape of his great art collection housed in a mansion which is to become a museum. He also plans a hospital to be named after him. The end of the novel is full of ironies as Dreiser shows that these dreams, too, are human folly. In the extensive litigation about the will after Cowper-wood's death the art collection and house are sold, and the hospital is never built. Cowperwood, in many ways, does not live up to the stoic ideal. Dreiser's title, therefore, is probably more than a little ironic. I believe that he intends to show that the materialistic nature of American culture works against the achievement of such an ideal.

The stoicism of the heroes of Ernest Hemingway is a much more pragmatic philosophy. Hemingway works less with theories of human behaviour than he does with the twisted texture of experience. His heroes are always projections of various aspects of his own life. And the definitive part of that life was Hemingway's time in the front line during the Great War, when he discovered that 'All is vanity.' The Hemingway hero's behaviour after such experience is a compound of the British stiff upper lip and Emersonian self-reliance. This is an ideal for the most part realized by Jake Barnes in *The Sun Also Rises*, conveyed by Jake's laconic behav-iour and speech and by his amusedly ironic attitude towards the gaiety and folly of Paris in the post-War period.

Only two things can break through Jake's stoical behaviour. One is the appeal of the natural world as it is shown in the Burguete fishing episode. During this time Jake's guard is temporarily down and his vulnerability, not to say his sentimentality, is revealed. The other is in his love for Lady Brett Ashley. Jake is, of course, physically unable to consummate that relationship and Lady Brett's nature is such that her love for him cannot be fulfilled on a platonic or non-physical plane. As has often been pointed out, Jake Barnes's wound represents the broken, impotent con-dition of western man after the catastrophe of the Great War. That huge parade of violence and destruction followed by the mindless hedonism of the 1920s seems to symbolize the destruction of a society and its meaning. In contrast is the virile, ritualized, stately behaviour of the bullfighter, Romero. Jake can only pay tribute to Romero's style, which is beyond him, and then maintain his honour by helping Lady Brett give Romero up. Jake is the man without illusions either about his culture or about himself, and the closing words in the novel indicate his clearsighted stoicism. Brett says, 'We could have had such a damned good time together.'

'Yes,' Jake replies. 'Isn't it pretty to think so?'[23]

In *A Farewell to Arms* Frederick Henry's progress towards the stoic ideal is constantly interrupted by the appeal of passion. The novel's main thrust seems to be towards an attitude in which the hero can make his farewell not only to a destructive and utterly useless war, but also to a dependence on romantic and sexual love. Death is as arbitrary in the one field as in the other, and Henry has to come to the bitter realization that all human desires are vanity. I believe that Hemingway is showing that dependence on sexual love is ultimately as unsatisfactory as dependence on patriotism or physical courage and that the only possible way to encounter life adequately is through a recognition of the limitations of human desires and ideals and stoic resignation in the face of what is bound to be continual disappointment in life.

This philosophy is worked through in a variety of forms in subsequent novels and stories and is realized in its purest and simplest form in *The Old Man and the Sea*. In this novella a man's illusions and possessions are stripped from him one by one as Santiago goes through trials which are similar to those of Job. Somewhere within the sources of his being he finds the strength to go on to be ultimately self-reliant in the face of everything that man and nature can do to destroy him. After the sharks begin to attack the marlin, Santiago says, 'But man is not made for defeat ... A man can be destroyed but not defeated.'[24]

A similar strain of stoicism can be seen in the work of William Faulkner and its origin can be traced to sources similar to those in the work of Hemingway. Faulkner, too, was concerned with the breakdown of a civilization as seen in the holocaust of the Great War and after. *A Fable* is precisely a fable about the destruction of civilized values and the near impossibility of transformation through a second coming. In the light of such a breakdown, especially in Faulkner's South, one of the few appropriate responses is a stoic resignation. Of course, most of Faulkner's characters are unable to reach such an ideal, although many attempt it. Quentin's attempt at stoic acceptance in *The Sound and the Fury* breaks down and ends in obsession and suicide. Joe Christmas in *Light in August* is continually frustrated in his attempts to cope stoically with the world and he is driven and hunted to his death. The older generation of Sartorses or Compsons in the historical parts of Faulkner's novels seems to have been able to achieve a stoic dignity, but for the later members of those generations it seems to be impossible. Perhaps only in Dilsey, the black servant of *The Sound and the Fury*, is a stoic ideal partly realized. Her experience comprehends and assimilates the endless follies, jealousies, and evils of the human condition, and she is yet able to carry on. As she says after the Easter church service, 'Never you mind ... I seed de beginnin, en now I sees de endin.'[25]

For a variety of reasons post-modern writing has shown, on the whole, little evidence of the emergence of a stoic philosophy. I imagine that Freudianism in particular has demonstrated that the philosophy does not correspond too well to complex human reality. Modern popular as well as high culture places little premium on the inhibition of expression and downplaying of emotion. Expressionism, impressionism, surrealism, abstractionism, and most other modern movements in the arts and literature emphasize the expression of the impulse, the random, and the instinctual, with a corresponding playing down of the rational mind. In part, too, the classical and renaissance division between reason and passion has broken down under the scrutiny of modern psychology. It is notable that existentialism, which had such a powerful vogue in the years after the Second World War, has suffered a decline. For example, the absurd, which figures so significantly in existential philosophy and fiction, becomes in a book like *Catch 22* merely ridiculous. It is even rarer to find now in philosophy any convincing defence of individualism or self-reliance. One of the most thoughtful of modern American writers has put the situation concisely. Robert Pirsig writes in *Zen and the Art of Motorcycle Maintenance*:

> It's been necessary since before the time of Socrates to reject the passions, the emotions, in order to free the rational mind for an understanding of nature's order which was as yet unknown. Now it's time to further an understanding of nature's order by reassimilating those passions which were originally fled from. The passions, the emotions, the affective domain of man's consciousness, are a part of nature's order too. The central part.[26]

There can be no doubt, however, that for a long time in the history of American literature stoicism was a potent force in the work of many major and minor writers. Stoicism was viable and appealing in a culture which emphasized individual enterprise, the conquest of nature, and the necessity of a curb on the emotions. It was also valuable in a culture which faced a succession of challenges to orthodoxy. Although its original roots were usually literary, through the classical learning of writers, later forms of stoicism arose, it seems to me, much more out of a reaction to dominant forces of optimism, progressivism, millenarianism, and the other doctrines of material and spiritual success which permeated American life from the Enlightenment onwards. Stoicism came with a healthy dose of scepticism against popular ideas, a scorn of the rabble, and an individualistic desire to hew out the face of reality in clarity and honesty from the dull rock of American bourgeois life. It has constituted a kind of continuing critique of commonly accepted attitudes and ideas and has therefore been a continual source of originality and vitality in the culture. Few of America's great writers have been able to resist its appeal, and many have depended upon its philosophical strength to sustain them through long bitterness and disappointment. It must be recognized, then, that the stoic strain of the title of my essay and of this volume is a strain in both senses of that word – a strain which has tested and often proved the mettle of the writers who both felt and adopted it.

MILTON R. STERN

Towards
'Bartleby the Scrivener'

When Ishmael asserted that the changefulness of life 'requires a strong decoction of Seneca and the Stoics to enable you to grin and bear it,' he was offering a jocular way to handle the shock and horror that accompany the discovery of our human oneness in our common, mortal victimization by the conditions of life. 'Bartleby the Scrivener' is a tale of that discovery, not by seafarers in the vastness of natural force and space, but by landlubbers in claustral immurement.

Some critics are tempted to find stoic heroism in the pallid law-office clerk and to dismiss the lawyer-narrator as merely a wicked victimizer. Other critics more wisely sense a more complex connection between the two men. When I follow the lead offered by a view of Bartleby as stoic hero, I find that treating the tale as an example of Bartleby's stoicism results in oversimplifications and dead ends that do not account for tone and imagery. The insistence on stoicism is negatively useful because it leads to the conclusion that Melville was playing with other, deeper aspects of victimization than grinning and bearing it. Attempts to heroize Bartleby with ideological particularity diminish the dimensions of this perennially fascinating tale, so central among Melville's works. All such attempts seem to arise from the readers' desires to identify and secure Melville within their own rather than his contexts. A review of 'Bartleby' criticism is a useful approach to critical caveats which define the directions that future readings might usefully take.

Melville made mirrors. No other writer in English since Shakespeare has assumed so many protean shapes, and so invitingly, for his readers. 'Bartleby' especially is one of the weird pieces in which readers find whatever they came to seek. The ideological possibilities of 'Bartleby' are enormous: the seer of psychiatric, political, literary, metaphysical, or religious positions is sure to find in the tale a paradigm for his own advocacy. So, a critic reading critics becomes like Ishmael contemplating water as the mirror of the self: 'And still deeper the meaning of that story of Narcissus, who because he could not grasp the tormenting, mild image he saw in the fountain, plunged into it and was drowned. But that same image, we ourselves see in all rivers and oceans. It is the image of the ungraspable phantom of life; and this is the key to it all.' What image could be more tormenting and mild than that of the tormenting, mild Bartleby? The critical literature concerning 'Bartleby' exposes the process of interpretative criticism as very often a narcissistic operation in which each reader sees the tale as a mirror of the Gestalt within his own mind.

But the story itself is a fixed thing; it undergoes no more revision by Melville. Though each reader shifts it, unlike water it does not shift itself. Some Gestalts fix more of the story's details than do others. If much criticism is foolish, not all criticism is useless. And each critic knows that although he too will find the key to it all in a version of his own vision, there are priorities of value to be found in a criticism of the criticism; some visions are better than others.

The political Gestalt of Leo Marx's 'Melville's Parable of the Walls,'[1] for instance, remains a valuable mirroring because it illuminates more details within the story than does a set of literary parallels like Egbert S. Oliver's 'A Second Look at "Bartleby,"'[2] which sees the pallid scrivener as a type of Thoreau. When we move beyond the story to the references the criticism furnishes, Marx provides a more usably wide focus: his Gestalt expands rather than contracts the area within which the story exists. For all its gratuitous contumaciousness, an essay like Kingsley Widmer's 'Bartleby and Nihilistic Resistance'[3] fixes many more details in a brilliantly suggestive and useful mirror than does the pendantically narrow angle of vision of works like Mario L. D'Avanzo's 'Melville's "Bartleby" and Carlyle,'[4] which, in effect, makes Carlyle the ghostwriter of 'Bartleby.'

When George Bluestone commented on the making of his film out of the tale, he provided pertinent caveats for critics precisely because he had to specify details in order to recreate them in another medium, and therefore had to examine closely the components of his own Gestalt. His activities led him quickly to a concentration on what was usable for translation, and this process led him, in turn, to an important conclusion about the puzzling scrivener: one cannot specify in event, in historical or literary parallel, or in psycho-biography, exactly what made Bartleby the way he was. Bluestone realized that his film would lose power if it attempted to show the cause of Bartleby's depression precisely because in this area Melville provided no usable details. The film would have to centre on what Melville did provide, which was the effect of whatever it was that turned Bartleby into Bartleby: 'To explain the malaise is to explain it away.'[5] In accounting for the criticism available to him in 1962, when he made the film, Bluestone summed up his findings as follows: 'Critics have seen ... ["Bartleby"] as a tale (1) of exorcism, in which Bartleby figures as a surrogate for Melville, the artist protesting the killing demands of hack work; (2) of psychosis, a classic case of depression, or catatonic schizophrenia,[6] with overtones of homosexuality; (3) of the alter ego, Bartleby as a projection of the death-urge in the Lawyer, a kind of early 'Secret Sharer'; (4) of social criticism, a critique of industrial America symbolized by an implacable Wall Street. Certainly there are overtones of all these.'[7] There is, however, another category at least as important as any that Bluestone has listed, and that is the Gestalt in which the tale is seen as a metaphysical treatise in which man is a homeless wanderer in a universe of indifference, meaninglessness, and absence of moral point or purpose. This last critical vision often merges with Bluestone's first and fourth categories, and provides one of the few general areas of critical agreement.

When we look at the criticism that appeared up to the time of Donald M. Fiene's bibliography,[8] which includes work published through 1965, and add to it a few pieces published later, we become aware that the 'Bartleby' mirror attracts and reflects more water-gazers in certain areas than in others.[9] When many disparate individuals begin to fix the tale into one or two dominant shapes, and especially when those shapes encompass and account for the greatest number of details in the tale, the cumulative effect is to make criticism a useful act as it incrementally defines areas of agreement and, more important, the areas that are problematical and require more and new attention. Accumulated criticism spotlights the points at which we must try to shift our own Gestalts and begin anew with a basic experience of the details in question.

Those who see Bartleby as a type of the writer living in but alienated by a heartless bourgeois society join at many points with those who see the tale as a metaphysical and psychological examination of the terrible loneliness that results from a vision of the universe as empty of meaning: Bartleby becomes the typal figure who repudiates established society, its shallow vision of human experience, and its concomitant easy beliefs. For both groups of readers the lawyer and Bartleby represent conflicting opposites: the lawyer represents the establishment, the unexamined life, the surface vision with its facile hopes; and Bartleby is his rebellious, stoic victim. Depending upon the critic's Gestalt, the lawyer represents (1) the selfish capitalist society; (2) the repressive world of law and order; (3) the world of rationality, (3a) the world of self-deceiving rationalization, (3b) the world of genteel consciousness; (4) the world of orthodoxy; (5) the world of surfaces; (6) all of the above. Bartleby represents (1) the man who will no longer conform to the standards of the capitalist world; (2) Christianity, or Christliness, or – sometimes – Christ; (3) the unconscious, (3a) the hidden recognition of the world as meaningless chaos, as the absurd, (3b) the lawyer's conscience, (3c) the world of preferences, will, and revolution; (4) the stoic tragic view; (5) the defeated stoic writer-artist-rebel; (6) the heroic stoic writer-artist-rebel; (7) the defeat of the stoic human will; (8) the stoic triumph of human will; and (9) any of the above that are not too obviously mutually contradictory.

Many of those who see Bartleby as a redemptive challenger of the lawyer see him as a type of Christ,[10] while those who see him as a passive or defeated challenger may make him a type of the absurd itself.[11] The view of him as Christ is as much a catch-all as any other category, ranging from a rather rigid and silly assertion that the lawyer is Jehovah, Bartleby is Christ, Turkey is Michael, Nippers is Lucifer, and Ginger Nut – the poor little kid – is Raphael (see John Gardner, note 9), to Bruce Franklin's much more useful and suggestive considerations of the mythic possibilities within the tale (see note 9). It is also possible to see Bartleby as Christ, even though passive and defeated, if one sees him as an 'emasculated' Christ (see William Stein, note 10). But whether he is seen as active or passive, almost all critics agree that he typifies the principle of *non serviam* in whatever world he is said to inhabit.[12] The line of logic leads critics from the *non serviam* relationship Bartleby maintains with his employer to a speculation about Bartleby as a kind of *doppelgänger* or, at least, a conscience for the lawyer. Here too there is a range of opinion, from Bartleby as the embodiment of the principle of the English Court of Chancery, 'the Keeper of the King's Conscience,' to Bartleby as the lawyer's hidden deathwish.[13]

Three firm agreements emerge from the welter of hermeneutics, propaedeutics, and ephemera. One is that Bartleby becomes the repudiator of the civilization and vision that the lawyer stands for. The second is that Bartleby cannot be defined except through a definition of the lawyer. The third is that the lawyer, at least at the beginning of the story, is the bad guy. I delay discussion of the first until I look at Bartleby a bit later in this essay. The second should be obvious, by virtue of the narrative method, without any critical aids. The third is fixed through a series of self-revelations that every critic who has examined the lawyer has noted.

The revelations always cited are the lawyer's 'conviction that the easiest way of life is the best'; that he never suffers any real involvement in his law cases to invade his peace; that he loves the 'cool tranquillity' of his 'snug retreat' as he does 'a snug business among rich men's bonds, and mortgages, and title-deeds'; that he is considered to be an 'eminently safe man'; that he loves being associated with John Jacob Astor, that he loves Astor's name, which 'hath a rounded and orbicular sound to it, and rings like unto bullion'; that he is proud that John Jacob Astor has named the lawyer's two grand points as prudence and method; that he is greedy about the Court of Chancery and is upset only when easy income from the Master's office is denied him through dissolution of the court – *that* invades his peace if equity and justice do not; that he uses people – his clerks – selfishly, putting up with their vagaries not out of any really compassionate humanity but only out of his sense that they are 'most valuable' to him; that he is concerned only with the appearances of things and desires decorum and seemliness at all human costs; that he tolerates Bartleby at first not out of real compassion or fraternal feeling, but because to humour Bartleby 'in his strange wilfullness, will cost me little or nothing while I lay up in my soul what will eventually prove a sweet morsel for my conscience'; that he betrays and abandons Bartleby while mouthing pious and/or legalistic rationalizations for refusing responsibility and running away. In short, the lawyer reveals in every way that he is a smug and heartless man of small vision and hypocritical Christianity, that he is a respectable, bourgeois cannibal, a conformist to all the surfaces, gentilities, selfishnesses, and human enormities of established values, law, and order. He is mindless of pain, soulless to real suffering, compassionless to any possible vision that sees the establishment's world as a lie. Whether he discloses his consciousness as a factor of political, economic, social, metaphysical, or psychological reality, he is a shallow and complacent man of easy optimism.

In detailing the lawyer there is critical agreement that the world he rules dooms human activity to a walled-in (almost all critics, especially since Leo Marx, have specified the imagery of the walls: that need not be done again) round of alternating acquiescence and frustration (almost all critics have noted the complementary ante- and post-meridian changes in the behaviour and personalities of Turkey and Nippers: that need not be done again). People struggle between desire and submission in the lawyer's world – if Bartleby's opting-out is characterized by 'I prefer not to,' Turkey's key phrase is 'with submission, sir' – and spend half their lives conforming to their lot and half their lives raging against it. Yet, the established world is inhabited by people whose very vision is walled-in for, despite their longings for freedom from their hated rounds of monotonous sameness in which everything and everyone is a copy and a repetition, they uphold the system: what they aspire to is the lawyer's top-dog position in the walled-in world. The narrator is interested only in containing and repressing the periods of resentment in which people do not engage in profit-making labour for the boss, in which they turn against the symbols of their monotonous lives (Turkey blots his papers in steaming fury, Nippers grinds his teeth and fights with his hated desk), and in which people have no real individuality – no real names, but only nicknames – but merely alternatingly duplicate each other with fits that differentiate them only so that they reflect each other. The lawyer wants to see all activity and appearances buttoned up into law, order, decorum, and profitable routine: everyone is to spend his life copying the law indeed. Whenever the lawyer confronts Bartleby in a serious showdown, he buttons things up. 'I buttoned up my coat, balanced myself, advanced slowly towards him ...' 'What shall I do? I now said to myself, buttoning up my coat to the last button.' The buttoning is itself an enactment of a contemporary slang phrase, 'button up,' meaning 'shut up,' 'shape up.' The phrase, like the action, is one of repression, suppression, conformity.

If the walled-in workers yearn, like Nippers, 'the truth of the matter was, Nippers knew not what he wanted. Or, if he wanted anything, it was to be rid of his scrivener's table altogether.' However, Nippers thinks that the way to be rid of his table is by taking on even more of the same, by succeeding, like the lawyer, by continuing the system, not by opting-out of or by destroying it. His twin vices of ambition and indigestion (Turkey's twin characteristics are, similarly, submission and insolence), are indicators of his impatience with how far he has come in a system in which he too wants to be a lawyer. His ambition 'was evinced by a certain impatience at the duties of a mere copyist, an unwarrantable usurpation of strictly professional affairs, such as the original drawing up of legal documents.' Thus Turkey, also, when presented with a token of status – fittingly, the lawyer's cast-off coat 'which buttoned straight up from the knee to the neck' – becomes insolently and snobbishly restive not with the world he lives in but merely with his position within it. And Ginger Nut, the little son of a carter, also plays at being a lawyer with his little desk in the corner. In sum, the ordinary population, in its fits and frustrations and frenzies and alternations, acquiesces, with submission, sir, to the values of the world epitomized by the lawyer. Melville's metaphors for the populace, like Shakespeare's, never give us a picture of a revolutionary mass with class consciousness despite several wistful critical attempts to find in Melville a major literary neo-Marxian voice.

Given the nature of the world's common inhabitants, the snug lawyer becomes even more the enemy of human freedom when he blandly and civilly views the inhabitants of his world not as people but in the way he first views Bartleby – as 'a valuable acquisition.' Committing the unforgivable sin of reducing people to things, he thinks that, like any acquisition, people can be bought. Twice, while trying to get Bartleby out of his life, he gives him money. Commercializing all human relations, he is yet smug enough to feel that Bartleby's 'perverseness seemed ungrateful, considering the undeniable good usage and indulgence he had received from me.' He 'trembled to think' of what might happen to his world if the implications of 'prefer' were to become the basis of human conduct – button up, boy. Contemplating Bartleby's incredible and fantastic plight, the lawyer allows 'necessities connected with my business' to 'tyrannize over all other considerations.' He congratulates himself that his assumptions about Bartleby's departure will get rid of Bartleby in a seemly and decorous way: he can do something that nags at his conscience, but is satisfied as long as appearances and the *status quo* remain undisturbed. He indulges in 'sweet charity's sake' only as a guarantee of his own safety – he continues to buy human beings and human actions. He is constantly concerned that Bartleby is 'scandalizing [his] professional reputation,' and even in the Tombs he tries to placate his conscience by attempting to talk Bartleby into enjoying the sky and the grass – in prison. In sum, that is the case against the lawyer-narrator, and up to this point almost all critics agree.[14]

A quantitative overview of the criticism suggests that this, too, is ground that need not be gone over yet once more, and can be taken as a given in the tale. But just beyond this agreement lies one of the rocks upon which criticism splits, and that is the question of whether or not the narrator changes. Some see that modifications must be made in the condemnation of the lawyer.[15] Generally, the arguments favouring the proposition that the lawyer undergoes a change of vision insist (1) that there is no possibility of salvation for Bartleby, no matter how great his lonely integrity may be, and that there is a possibility of salvation for the narrator, whose increasingly pained awareness of what Bartleby might be gives him a new sense of the connectedness of all humanity no matter how smug and shallow he was at the beginning; (2) that when all is said and done, it is a vast act of sentiment to see Bartleby as a rebel-hero only, for he effects no rebellion. All he does is to commit an ultimate withdrawal. So, too, it is dangerous to see Bartleby as stoic hero for, as we shall see, it is questionable at best that there are positive moral values shoring up Bartleby's bearing of his burden and, in any event, Bartleby does not in any positive way indicate how life may be borne. Just the opposite, in fact. But the narrator comes to feel the agony of the world at last: Melville is as much the lawyer as he is Bartleby, and to divide him into allegiance to only one aspect of himself is to over-simplify Melville's sense of reality by substituting a straw-man for the narrator who actually exists in the story. (3) For all that is wrong with the lawyer, Bartleby, finally, is socially irresponsible: he leads only towards death. All arguments that would modify the agreement about the initial self-presentation of the narrator de-pend upon the narrator's sympathetic acts and thoughts concerning Bartleby, upon the tone of the narratorial voice when the lawyer describes the Tombs and mur-murs, 'with kings and counselors,' upon the section presenting the Dead Letters Office, and upon the tone of the narrator's final cry, 'Ah Bartleby! Ah humanity!'

Those who see the narrator as unredeemable and a total villain all denigrate as maudlin the lawyer's feelings when he begins to react deeply to Bartleby; they dismiss the epilogue as the 'thick Victorianism' of an attempt to furnish a liberal 'hard times' explanation for Bartleby, and refuse to see the narrator's last cry as anything but 'a last sentimental gesture.'[16] It is significant, for instance, that the most uncompromising view of the lawyer as villain not only sees him as 'incapable of moral regeneration' but fails to deal with or even mention the narrator's final cry.[17] The Dead Letters epilogue is seen suddenly and somehow as 'Melville's' rather than as the narrator's, for to attribute sensitivity and pained compassion to the narrator would ruin the thesis of unmixed villainy. In fact, all views of the narrator as un-changing villain sweep away every instance in which Melville makes the narrator's villainy problematical without ever distinguishing in terms of tone between the nar-rator's moments of smugness and his moments of pain.

Well, I find that there is no arguing about tone. If there is any one aspect of literary art that is crucial to comprehension it is tone, and of all aspects of art it is the one most encysted by the Gestalt in which the reader sees the parts. As just one more critic I can only assert that a quick juxtaposition of parts will establish tone. Read the opening passages through the Turkey and Nippers episodes. Then immediately read the entire Sunday morning sequence detailing the narrator's 'over-powering stinging melancholy' as distinct from the mere sentimentality of 'a not unpleasant sadness' and his consequent Melvillean awareness of human fraternity in mortal woe. Then read the episode in the Tombs. Then read the epilogue. The juxtaposition must – should – create at least a sense of uneasiness in the critics who assert that the narrator never changes. There is, I submit, a palpable shift in Mel-ville's presentation of the narrator, and it is discernible at the crucial episode – almost exactly half way through the story – of the narrator's Sunday morning visit to his office. Up to that moment Melville has the narrator disclose only those self-reve-latory ironies and pseudo-sympathies that destroy the lawyer's assumed image. He is indeed the bad guy. But for the remaining half of the story Melville has the narrator vacillate between continued self-exposing hypocrisy and puzzled concern and pain, with the power of the sympathetic passages – the Tombs, the epilogue – gaining ascendency over the others. The nature of the narrator's consciousness be-gins to change. Does he still worry about being scandalized? Does he still try to explain Bartleby away? Is he still self-seeking and self-protective? Does he still fly into a rage? Does he still try to evade Bartleby? Of course. That is the truth. It is nothing but the truth. But it is not the whole truth. In the first half of the story there are no expressions of pain (astonishment, outrage, anger, and bewilderment, yes, but not the pain of his own deepest self's contact with Bartleby) or of confusion deeper than those of the law office proprieties. The last half of the story is full of them, including among them such awarenesses as the fact that 'I might give alms to his body; but his body did not pain him; it was his soul that suffered, and his soul I could not reach.' It is the narrator, after all, who becomes aware of Bartleby as 'alone, absolutely alone in the universe. A bit of wreck in the mid-Atlantic.' Con-tinuing to act the hypocritical burgher, nevertheless, the narrator now has his con-sciousness focused on the knowledge that he has to wrench himself, almost in tears, 'from him whom I had so longed to be rid of.' Nowhere in the first half is there a physico-psychic jolt of current running between the narrator and Bartleby as there is in the death scene in the Tombs. And in the context of the Tombs the grub-man, fittingly named Mr Cutlets in the original *Putnam's* version, makes even the lawyer's attempt to cheer Bartleby by pointing to grass and sky less a matter of blind smugness than one of pathetic failure. (Food as a pervasive motif in 'Bartleby' should be the subject of a short critical essay, for the story is filled with instances of food and feeding. The negative relationship of oral gratification to total separation is a psychological rendition of the central question of nourishment and sustenance for human hope, for the ability of the human spirit to bear consciousness and pain and still live and remain human.) The narrator's reply to the grub-man, 'with kings and counselors,' draws the clear and distinct distance in insight, sympathy, and pain between the lawyer and the grub-man. At the beginning the lawyer was to Bartleby as the grub-man now is to the lawyer. One can refuse to recognize a meaningful change in the lawyer only by refusing to recognize that the second half of the story does prepare for an undeniable difference between the lawyer and the grub-man. Were there no change there could be no difference between the lawyer and the grub-man, for Mr Cutlets is but a meaty, mindless, and relatively moneyless version of what the lawyer was at the beginning. Mr Cutlets is an official grub inhabiting the same world of grubby morality that the lawyer's walled-in office does, and he can no more supply sustenance for Bartleby than can the lifeless bust of Cicero in the lawyer's office – the Cicero, no doubt, of *De officiis*. Yet, at the end of the story the difference between the grub-man and the narrator is a qualitative difference, not a mere difference in manner and education, but a difference in insight and sympathy, which is exactly what is denied by an unmixed view of the narrator. Even before the midpoint of the tale the narrator is not unmixed in his given qualities. Consider the following passage:

> He lives, then, on ginger-nuts, thought I; never eats a dinner, properly speaking; he must be a vegetarian, then; but no; he never eats even vegetables, he eats nothing but ginger-nuts. My mind then ran on in reveries concerning the probable effects upon the human constitution of living entirely on ginger-nuts. Ginger-nuts are so called, because they contain ginger as one of their peculiar constituents, and the final flavoring one. Now, what was ginger? A hot, spicy thing. Was Bartleby hot and spicy? Not at all. Ginger, then, had no effect upon Bartleby. Probably he preferred it should have none.

This passage can be and has been fitted into ideologies that polemicize against the narrator. Yet all such critical ingenuity always misses one humble, simple, tonal, surface fact: the passage is mildly funny. The narrator has a sense of humour. The presentation of the clerks discloses an observer with a sense of humour that makes his paternalistic relationship to their vagaries not totally and solely a matter of selfish exploitation. Scattered throughout the tale on either side of the midpoint are small instances of humour which create the expectation that this same smug narrator might yet be a man with enough sensibilities to recognize a connection with Bartleby. As that metaphysical wanderer-narrator, Ishmael, from the very beginning is hintingly given qualities which will enable him to see the Ahab he admiringly repudiates as an extended aspect of his own human identity, so too that prudentially selfish lawyer-narrator from the very beginning is hintingly given qualities which will enable him to see that the Bartleby he will compassionately leave is inextricably interrelated with his own human identity. Surely there is a tonal difference not only between the narrator and the grub-man but also between the lawyer and all the other inhabitants and landlords and lawyers who do not for a moment see Bartleby as anything but a nuisance to be got rid of. The difference between the lawyer and the successors to his chambers is scanted or ignored by critics who fix the narrator as a single moral quantity, and for the same reasons that make them miss the intermittent humour of the tale.[18]

But, as I say, the tonal aspect of change in the lawyer cannot be argued: either you hear it or you do not. Rather, I would open a question which seems to me quite pertinent. Why has there been so much commentary on 'Bartleby'? Why so much varied and fascinated response beyond the agreement about the preliminary characterization of the lawyer and of Bartleby as his opponent? Clearly one answer must be that there is something about the tale that creates Melvillean nuance; *something* about this story must offer ambiguity and multiplicities of meaning. But what is the effect of a rigid definition of the lawyer as unmixed villain? The effect is to remove ambiguity, multiplicity, and subtlety by reducing the story to a simple tale of good versus evil (defined by whatever Gestalt). Problems of meaning remain in the superimposition of Gestalts upon the story and in conflicts between Gestalts – lots of room for explicators still – but moral ambiguity, moral evaluation is removed as a problem. And is not that problem precisely the central one that remains to puzzle the reader and itch in his mind? Remove shiftings of moral evaluations, and all that is left is the working out of equivalents to hang around the lawyer and Bartleby – which is what, I think, accounts for so much critical cleverness and narrowness in much of the criticism of 'Bartleby.' To see the lawyer as a fixed value is to remove him as a source of that itch that engages the reader in the first place and that the spate of criticism undeniably announces. And to remove the narrator as a source is to be quite tricky indeed, not only because the narrator is the only source of information we have about Bartleby but also because the narrator is the only continuing source of response to Bartleby. To fix the narrator is to place the burden for *all* the creation of multiple meaning in the story on Bartleby alone. Yet, why do all readers come away from the story with the impression that in the narrator they have met a person – whether they scorn him or not – and that in Bartleby they have met – what? – a quality? And embodied in a repetitious cadaver, at that?

There is in this question a serious matter that must be met, but which is all but unmentioned in 'Bartleby' criticism, and that is the matter of types of characterization. It is neither accidental nor insignificant that all critics confront the story by characterizing the narrator in social, political, religious, and economic, as well as moral, terms, and by characterizing Bartleby in typal or mythic terms. Furthermore, all readers come away from the story with the sense that it is weird. The sense of weirdness is a result of the same factor that accounts for the ways in which critics characterize the lawyer and Bartleby. That is, the lawyer and Bartleby are characters from two distinctly different modes of fiction. The narrator comes from a recognizable world and can be measured in terms of that world: he is the kind of character who inhabits the province of realistic fiction. Bartleby, however, in every way inhabits a world other than the narrator's. He comes from the province of allegorical fiction, or romantic fiction, or both. The narrator is a human character; Bartleby is a metaphor. The narrator is sociologically explicable; Bartleby is no more sociologically explicable than is Ahab. The vehicle for the realistic character is verisimilitude; the lawyer, like his clerks, is given human, peculiar characteristics by which he is recognized, and the verisimilitude of characterizing human peculiarities is the vehicle for individuation, regardless of purpose – sentiment, rebellion, reportage – in realistic fiction. The narrator and his clerks come from the fiction of a writer like Dickens. But the vehicle for the allegorical character is typalism. Bartleby is given metaphoric weightings by which he is recognized, mysterious qualities independent of verisimilitude or realistic statistication. He comes from the fiction of a writer like Bunyan turned into Kafka – the emblematic quality of characterization remains, but all the rubrics have been erased from the labels for which the character is beast of burden. The science-fiction and gothic impingement of alien worlds gives 'Bartleby' its weirdness. One does not expect the preternatural or the preternaturalistic to be accommodated into simultaneous existence with the realistic or the naturalistic. It is the calm intrusion of one world into another that gives 'Bartleby' its Kafkan tones and makes it seem so very modern in its techniques and surfaces. In terms of action within the recognizable or naturalistic or Dickensian world the realistic character has dynamic dimensions: his fate and his character may both change along with his insights and experiences. But the inhabitant of the typal world is fixed. In speech, action, and possibility Bartleby *as character* is as rigidly fixed as a corpse. In the problem of moral evaluation, when the question is, what should the character do? Bartleby offers the narrator no world in which to do anything. He offers only the possibility of becoming like Bartleby, which is to say the possibility of leaving altogether the world of reality as it is defined for characterization within the demands of realistic fiction. The very nature of the differences in fictive worlds, fictive methods, and fictive characterization suggests that if either of the characters may undergo change, it is the lawyer, not Bartleby. I submit that in relation to Bartleby, it is the narrator who is not the fixed value. Nor, I should add, does this suggestion make a freak of 'Bartleby the Scrivener' within the canon of Melville's works. The mixing of characters from different worlds of fictive mode is a constant Melvillean technique and always accounts for the element of weirdness in his fiction. For instance, is not the magnificently created sense of displacement, discontinuity of worlds, and disproportion in the confrontations between Ahab and Starbuck attributable to the fact that they are confrontations between a raging myth and a man from Nantucket, Massachusetts? And Melville's typal characters are disconnected from the humanity of verisimilitude and the world of its realities. What is Ahab's past? A hint from Elijah. And as for Bartleby, there is only an uncertain rumour about the Dead Letters Office. Consistently and pervasively Melville's typal characters are not of woman born, have no dimensions taken from realistic fiction's world of verisimilitude. They are characters without a past and without social measurements.[19]

In fact, what do we know of Bartleby? Only what the lawyer tells us, and he warns us from the very beginning that Bartleby does not inhabit the same dimensions as other scriveners, about whom he could write some amusing and sentimental vignettes. 'While of other law-copyists I might write the complete life, of Bartleby nothing of that sort can be done. I believe that no materials exist for a full and satisfactory biography of this man ... Bartleby was one of those beings of whom nothing is ascertainable, except from the original sources, and in his case, those are very small. What my own astonished eyes saw of Bartleby, *that* is all I know of him, except, indeed, one vague report, which will appear in the sequel.' The appropriate question to ask, since Melville obviously knew he would furnish no sudden world of verisimilitude out of Bartleby's past, is why Melville chose to add the 'sequel' about the Dead Letter Office; and in order to answer that question it becomes necessary to ask what it is we know of Bartleby without the epilogue.

Here again, the body of criticism gives us a solid agreement: Bartleby is the *isolato* who has come to the nadir of pallid despair in which all things are equal ('I am not particular') and all things are pointless ('I prefer not to'). The ordinary world that demands reasonableness is seen by Bartleby to be a dead end of meaninglessness that mocks all attempts to copy a non-existent law and order ('At present I prefer not to be a little reasonable'). There is at least this much preliminary bedrock of agreement. The criticism divides on the identification and evaluation of Bartleby. To some he is entirely heroic; to some he is mixed in his qualities. As is to be expected, those critics who see the lawyer as all villainous tend to see Bartleby as all good; those critics who see the lawyer as a changing quality tend to see unchanging Bartleby as a quality demanding a mixed response. If we are to be thrown on Bartleby as the sole source of ambiguity and multiplicity, we find that the criticism provides ample evidence that we cannot settle on a fixed response to him. Readers who conclude that Bartleby is the type of the hero, the rebel of whatever – art, nihilism, Christian morality, political honesty, metaphysical awareness – never satisfactorily handle those hard stumbling-blocks of facts which are the specifics whereby Bartleby is shown to us.

Would we have him stand as a life-principle, a rebellion against claustrophobic immurement in the dehumanizing world of the respectable lawyer? Would we have him the representative of true Christianity, true art, or the true revolution in his nay-saying to the mechanical world of law-copyists? To do so goes beyond the basic recognition that Bartleby prefers not to participate in any activity whatsoever; to do so assigns meanings to him that are not verifiable in the actual facts of the story. Because Melville is so heavily involved in metaphysical ideas, because Melville makes mirrors, the temptation is great to assign meanings out of the Gestalt of the critic, but to do that is to reduce criticism to a game of filling in the blanks: the lawyer equals ————; Bartleby equals ————. But when we look at the specific details through which Bartleby is in fact presented, it becomes a bit difficult to turn our impression of a pallid, sick, corpse-like, motionless, silent fixed being into the life-principle or the humanity-principle or the rebel-principle or the reality-principle or an active body of moral principles. What are the specific terms that actually present Bartleby? In this long short story the catalogue surprisingly is not so long that the salient facts cannot be listed conveniently; and when the concrete instances are precisely isolated, they become quite instructive in the revelation of what is repeated.

Bartleby's movements are most often accompanied by the word 'gliding,' and his voice is most often described as 'mild.' He is 'pallidly neat, pitiably respectable, incurably forlorn'; 'he wrote on silently, palely, mechanically'; his face is 'leanly composed; his gray eye dimly calm'; he has absolutely no 'agitation, uneasiness, anger, or impertinence,' nor is there 'anything ordinarily human about him'; his corner is called a 'hermitage' (four times); he is 'gentle' or totally silent; he appears 'like a very ghost'; he is 'a pale young scrivener'; he is characterized by 'his steadiness, his freedom from all dissipation, his incessant industry (except when [in a] ... standing revery ...), his great stillness, his unalterableness of demeanor'; his is a 'lean visage'; he is an 'apparition'; he has a 'cadaverously gentlemanly nonchalance'; he is 'eminently decorous'; he will not be seen in dishabille and would not 'by any singular occupation violate the proprieties' of Sunday; although he has very few belongings, he owns a blacking box and brush to keep his shoes shined; although he does not care for money (he does not touch the conscience money twice given him by the narrator), he frugally saves his salary and keeps it knotted in a handkerchief 'bank' hidden in the recesses of his desk; he has no interest in or apparent need for food or drink; he has a 'pale form' that appears as though 'laid out, among uncaring strangers, in its shivering winding-sheet'; he is 'thin and pale' with an air of 'pallid haughtiness'; his tones are 'mildly cadaverous'; he 'would prefer to be left alone here'; 'he seemed alone, absolutely alone in the universe [like] ... a bit of wreck in the mid-Atlantic'; his triumph over the narrator is a 'cadaverous triumph'; he becomes both totally silent and totally motionless; he 'silently acquiesced' in 'his pale, unmoving way'; and he is 'prone to a pallid hopelessness.'

It will not do to object that these are only the narrator's vision of Bartleby, for everything we know about Bartleby is given through the narrator's vision, regardless of the meanings we would affix to Bartleby. Melville could have chosen to give us, through the narrator, other kinds of details for constant repetition, but he did not. What he did choose to give was a repetition of details that result in two major categories of impression. One is that of a silent, motionless, emaciated, pale, cadaverous negativism and withdrawal, a suggestion of the implacable stubbornness of a corpse, of death itself. The other is that of a mechanically industrious, mild, and seemly respectability. Just as the details that present the narrator begin to change at that crucial Sunday morning mid-point of the story, so they change for Bartleby, too. On the Tuesday following that Sunday Bartleby announces, 'I have given up copying' and abandons his industry altogether. From that moment the details of presentation begin to emphasize the characteristics of silence, motionlessness, and death much more than those of respectability. In short, just as the narrator's responses begin to be mixed with anguish and sympathy, Bartleby's characteristics begin to be associated with total withdrawal and extinction.

It is also important to note that from the mid-point on, the lawyer's strange sense of private connection with Bartleby also intensifies. 'I never feel so private as when I know you are here,' he says, thinking of Bartleby. The lawyer discovers that it is Bartleby who mysteriously has the unaccounted-for key to his private chambers. The lawyer has to tear himself away from the Bartleby he had longed to be rid of. And, finally, when the lawyer touches the hand of Bartleby's foetally curled corpse, 'a tingling ran up my arm and down my spine to my feet.' Melville has the lawyer supply ample hints that Bartleby has an essential, interior, and intimate connection with him. When one considers that up to the mid-point the lawyer was smugly, snugly, and actively respectable and that Bartleby was pallidly, forlornly, and mechanically respectable, there is an opening for speculation about Bartleby as an inversion, or at least a version, of the narrator. And after the mid-point the more the narrator becomes agonizingly aware of his connection with Bartleby, yet fails to give up his way of life, the more Bartleby repudiates him ('I know you, and I want nothing to say to you'), and retreats into suicide by refusing any of the food of this world. It is as though the lawyer came to learn that in seeing the repressed and negativistic Bartleby he saw himself, the logical, or at least spiritual extension of his very life which offers neither nourishment nor hope for everything within us that is buttoned up beneath the surfaces of conventional acquiescence to forms and values. It is just this possibility that leads some critics to contend that the narrator is changeless, unredeemed, and unredeemable: he does not, after all, give up his life when confronted with the apparition of Bartleby. But when religious or political meanings are affixed to Bartleby, the nagging questions fail to disappear. If Bartleby is the narrator's conscience or the spirit of true Christianity, why should he tend more towards death, isolation, withdrawal, and silence than towards strength, activity, and expression, as the narrator becomes increasingly tortured by the pain of sympathy? If Bartleby is the spirit of rebellion against the culture that is, why should he droop, fail, and withdraw just as the narrator becomes aware in anguish of a strange kind of justice in Bartleby's existence – just as the narrator finds he *cannot* rationalize Bartleby away with charges of vagrancy or any other charges?

I am convinced that the explications that tend towards a one-to-one identification of Bartleby and the critic's political or religious Gestalt fail and will continue to fail to satisfy the logic, the psycho-logical demands, that the story sets up. On the level of metaphysical points of view, there is, at least, a general basic agreement in the critical canon. As the narrator, at least at first, represents the materialistic world of hypocritical and blind bourgeois selfishness, Bartleby is the woebegone representative of a view of existence that denies all the shallow rationality and expectations of predictability, purpose, law, and meaning that the comfortably mindless and selfish commercial world self-justifyingly assumes to be the nature of the universe: God's in his heaven and all's right with the world. On this level there is general agreement that the lawyer, at least at the beginning, and Bartleby are the conflicting and obverse sides of human vision and human experience. If one is a vision of orthodox optimism and institutionalized belonging, the other is a vision of existential absurdity, the vision of the outcast stranger. This vision reduces to absurd meaninglessness all the activities of the lawyer's institutionalized world. On the level of metaphysical vision the psychological expectations are satisfied: as there are no alternatives in the institutionalized world for Bartleby's vision and no point in any kind of action on his part, pallid and silent withdrawal follows.

But when we parallel the level of metaphysical vision with the tempting levels of politics, the psycho-logics are not satisfied. On this level the narrator is the capitalist boss who exploits those who work for him, denying them full human existence and identity; Bartleby is the nay-sayer who refuses to copy the law-and-order of the narrator's world any longer. But on this level the story must remain psychologically frustrating, especially because there is certainly enough material that 'fits.' One might expect the fury of an Ahab or the activity of a Joe Hill or even the unaware, protesting dissoluteness of the *Lumpenproletariat*, but hardly the ghost of a motionless cadaver. The fictive mode from which Bartleby characterologically comes is not that which satisfies in any way the demands of realistic fiction. On this level 'Bartleby' criticism becomes confused about the difference between the victim and the victim-rebel. Even if Bartleby were to be seen as victim only, what the story would then need would be something like a Hurstwood, or a Clyde Griffiths, but what we have is – Bartleby. And, on the political level, the story certainly does not psychologically support the view of Bartleby as rebel-hero if the type of pure victim is to be abandoned.

The same is true of the view of Bartleby as hero-artist. One might think of Joyce's silence, exile, and cunning as fitting Bartleby, but the 'fit' squeezes a bit with the cunning, and it does not take too much thinking before one runs into equally tight fits with the differences between Joyce's – or even Stephen Dedalus's – silence and exile and Bartleby's. Again, if Bartleby is to be 'the artist,' he is victim rather than victim-hero-rebel, closer to Kafka's hunger artist than to Dedalus. And, even at that, unlike the hunger artist Bartleby has no art of his own (he is himself either a mail-clerk or a copyist) that is sacrificed: abstemiousness is certainly not treated in Melville's story as it is in Kafka's. All that one can say is that Bartleby finds no food for his sustenance or values worth copying in the established world – and we are back to the one area of agreement, which is on the level of metaphysical vision, and which cannot really be specified in a one-to-one relationship to 'the artist.'

And if the ideologies of Christianity replace those of politics or artistic identity as the something further that is to parallel the level of metaphysical vision, psychological expectations run into further difficulty in the basic question of why Bartleby should choose suicide just as he has begun to make some meaningful impact upon the lawyer. What the specifics of the story and the inflexibly unrelenting characterology of Bartleby suggest in tandem with the strengths and weaknesses of critical commentary is either that there is no really useful particular level with which to parallel the level of metaphysical vision, or that if there is, the fruitful directions are to be found in the psycho-logics rather than the political logic or Christian logic of the critic's Gestalt. What remains, I suggest, for 'Bartleby' criticism that will not be merely another repetition of what has already been said too often is not a one-to-one connection between Bartleby and a clinical category of psychopathology, but an exploration of psychological theory concerning various aspects of the self, theory that will provide a parallel to the metaphysical connections between the lawyer and Bartleby as somehow interrelated beings.

The matter of the epilogue bears strongly upon my view of approaches to 'Bartleby.' For those who see no change in the narrator the epilogue is unsatisfactory because it creates too sympathetic a perspective for the narrator to possess; or, alternatively, the epilogue becomes one more irony in which Melville creates a merely sentimental perspective with which to establish the narrator's shallowness. In fact, the epilogue does sound like any number of sentimental pieces in the gift-book and periodical literature of the nineteenth century. But even if one were to isolate a 'Dead Letters Office' tradition in sentimental literature, the basic question would still remain: how does Melville use it? The fact of the tradition is much less important than its function within this tale, especially when one is cognizant of the fact that in *Pierre*, written only a little more than a year before the writing of 'Bartleby,' Melville had used various elements of the popular sentimental literary tradition for very unpopular and unsentimental reasons. Let us consider the epilogue for a

moment from the point of view of the writer rather than from the desire for interpretation.

What were Melville's necessities by the time he came to the epilogue? He had
promised the epilogue at the very beginning of the story, when he obviously had
the entire tale clearly in mind. One thing is certain: by the end of the tale Melville
has not 'explained' Bartleby. He had planned, from the very beginning of the first
instalment, not to say what happened to Bartleby to make him that way. But what
could he say to answer this question? What events could he invent which would be
horrible enough? And suppose he invented something truly hideous enough so
that the character of Bartleby himself were not simply maudlin. In that event, the
details of the destruction of all hope, all meaning, and all purpose – all life
itself – would demand the writing of another story, something like the day-to-day
to day-to-day incremental buildup of the horrors of an Auschwitz, or some other
hell. But that was not the story Melville had in mind, and the story he told was the
story he wanted to tell. All he could do was suggest, and merely suggest at that, a
vision of some sort that would hint at universal possibilities of dead hopes, closed
lives, pointless endeavours, and missed connections. Moreover, he had to avoid a
hint so lurid that it would shift the emotional emphasis, dragging the weight of the
story and the reader's attention from all that had preceded the epilogue to the
epilogue itself. Consciously or not, Melville was evidently aware that a hint that
really tried to account for Bartleby's life would defeat the very purpose it was there
for: to prevent a shift of the reader's engagement to a demand for seeing *more*.
The mild, brief universal so lightly hinted about the affairs of mortal men, the
Dead Letters Office, says, in effect, 'there is no more.' That is, the uncertain
rumour about the Dead Letter Office at once universalizes Bartleby and keeps the
focus exactly where Melville wants it – on the effect of Bartleby's condition, not on
the cause of it.

Bartleby as a victim of the established world also comes to seem a victim of
existence itself, and this, I think, is at the centre of what I take to be Melville's
purpose – a speculation not about stoicism but about victimization. In much of his
fiction he is anguished by victimization, compassionate with it, fascinated by it, and
yet he also finds that in inexplicable ways the victim acquiesces in his victimization
and intensifies the process. It is to ask the question, 'What else could Bartleby do?'
Neither the universe nor the established world of the lawyer allowed him any alternatives. He could only assume his victimization and accept the death that is the
consequence of it in his uncompromisingly honest view of a world empty of real
alternatives – and thereby expose the nature of the world. But if the lawyer is to be
attacked as the dehumanized organization man, is not Bartleby presented as dehumanized both explicitly and implicitly throughout the story, saying to the life around
him, 'I prefer not to live it'?

My contention is that if one is willing to accept the facts of the story's characterization rather than attempt to fit those facts into an ideology, one has to conclude
that Melville found not only heartbreak and terror in human victimization but also
something mysteriously acquiescent and repelling about the dehumanized victim.
The human possibilities for inhumanity construct rationalizations for the perverse
desire to barbarize the victim precisely because of his passive victimization: the
smug narrator burns to be rebelled against in order to justify his own sense of
separation from the victim: the bastard is getting what he deserves. I suggest that
Melville's psychological insights are too keen, when he puts them in the lawyer's
mind that crucial Sunday morning, to dismiss them as merely more instances of the
lawyer's selfishness – especially since those insights occur, as they do, in the context
of the true melancholy that the narrator, deeply shaken for the first time in his life,
experiences for the first time in his life. 'My first emotions,' he says, 'had been those
of pure melancholy and sincerest pity; but just in proportion as the forlornness of
Bartleby *grew and grew in my imagination*, did that same melancholy merge into
fear, that pity into repulsion. *So true it is, and so terrible, too*, that up to a certain point
the thought or sight of misery enlists our best affections; but, in special cases, beyond
that point it does not. They err who would assert that invariably this is owing to the
inherent selfishness of the human heart. It rather proceeds from a certain hopelessness
of remedying excessive and organic ill' [italics added]. The lawyer's naked glimpse of
Bartleby is as though one could imagine the anachronistic possibility of the good,
Christian, prudent, American businessman doing a thriving, profitable business with
the Nazis and suddenly becoming soul-shakingly aware of the death-camps at Auschwitz. The lawyer's speech is partly self-defensive. But it also expresses the horror that
goes beyond a defence of one's self in shallow selfishness and becomes a fearful revulsion that includes the victim – take it away, make it not be. Yet what could the victim
do but be? Either he must *be*, in the face of the observer's desperate desire for him to
go away, not to be, or he himself must also prefer not to be. The first choice can only
increase the observer's shock and horror; the second can only increase the observer's
guilt and remorse because of his own psychological complicity in the victim's death.
The more Bartleby preferred not to, the more the lawyer wished him to vacate the
premises. The intimate, interior oneness of Bartleby and lawyer must be contemplated
in the intricate and complex context of victimization.

But once a consideration is admitted into evidence, it cannot be used by the prose-
cution only. If we ask the question, but what else could he do? we must be willing to
apply it to the lawyer as well. In the longest and most intelligent attack on the narrator
and defence of Bartleby as hero, Kingsley Widmer (see note 3) concludes that the
'narrator never ... changes his view and way of life.' It is a charge that subsumes within
it the many narrower, less thoughtful, and less suggestive attacks on the lawyer and
defences of Bartleby. But in terms of Bartleby as the only alternative to the lawyer,

what, indeed, could the lawyer do? To apply equal sanctions to Bartleby and narrator is to create no contest. As metaphor Bartleby simply is not subject to the kinds of reality that are inevitable for the lawyer, who is derived from realistic characterology. Arguing from his own political and philosophical Gestalt, Widmer asserts that because culture is the product of the inhuman lawyer's world and serves only to civilize that world's enormities, against which Bartleby rebels, it is a sign of the dehumanizing failure of meliorism. As the lawyer's culture is a lie in human terms, culture up to the total revolution of Bartleby is to be repudiated. Bartleby's naysaying unto death is the truly revolutionary response. In sum, not only is the present to be put to death as a sacrifice to a metaphor of the liberated future, but so is the past as well. (Is it not fitting that Bartleby, who is heroic to Widmer, and who has no emulative present, is a man with no past?) But to me there is a familiar Melvillism in the fact that, being totally committed to his vision and thus isolating himself from all connections with the shallow lee-shore present, Bartleby in his monomania leads not to full life in the future but pallidly to death. It is clear to me that if Melville does not condone the culture of *is*, neither does he advocate a destruction of *was*. Not, at least, the multiple Melville, the mirror-maker, that we know in the totality of his works. One cannot make the corpselike Bartleby a sign of life without wrenching that cadaver out of Melville's presentation of him and into the polemics of one's own Gestalt.

Widmer's charge is extra-literary, for, like all strong art, 'Bartleby the Scrivener' leads strong readers beyond the literary fact itself, and Widmer is justified in stepping beyond. In my disagreement with his view I wish simply to meet him on his own grounds. True, within the story itself, one can find instances to rebut the charge against the narrator. One instance that is always either slighted or virtually ignored in attacks on the narrator is the moment in which he does offer to open his life to Bartleby, to support him, to stay with him, and to assume responsibility for him: '"Bartleby," said I, in the kindest tone I could assume under such exciting circumstances, "will you go home with me now – not to my office, but my dwelling – and remain there till we can conclude upon some convenient arrangement for you at our leisure? Come, let us start now, right away."' At this point it is more than clear that were Bartleby to accompany the narrator, he would never leave for 'some convenient arrangement' elsewhere. The narrator offers no less than a lifelong 'arrangement.' And he does not offer gradualism either; the delays, assumptions, and illusions are gone: 'Come, let us start now, right away.' But even with this evidence those who wish to simplify the story into a totalistic choice of Bartleby-hero versus narrator-villain can argue that the lawyer wishes only to get Bartleby out of the public building and into his private home – as though the connection between public and private, outer and inner, were not the essence of the connection in victimization between the lawyer and Bartleby in the first place.

So we return to the question, what else could the narrator do? What life could the narrator change to, other than Bartleby's? And again Melville gives us no alternatives other than the lawyer and Bartleby. With this inescapable given, then, let us abandon the evidences within the story for a moment and step outside it with Widmer to the arguments beyond. Widmer identifies the true essence of humanity as nihilism, 'that simply recurrent human reality – the vital desire to angrily negate [sic] things as they are' (Widmer, p 128). It is significant that Widmer feels it necessary to intrude that word 'angrily,' for it provides the human and psychologically necessary dimension that the characterologically typal Bartleby most patently lacks. But, given Widmer's premise, the story 'reveals the confession of a decent, prudent, rational "liberal" who finds in his chambers of consciousness the incomprehensible, the perverse, irrational demon of denial, and of his own denied humanity' (Widmer, p 119). 'The attempt to wryly force [sic] benevolent American rationalism to an awareness of our forlorn and walled-in humanity provides the larger purpose of the tale' (Widmer, p 120). But if we must assume that the spirit of denial is deeply human, must we assume, then, that it is the only deep or true humanity, much less the total essence of humanity, as Widmer assumes? Is not the need for self-deception as human as the desire for denial? Is not the conscious as *real* as the unconscious? Is not the invention of predictable meaning as human as the nihilistic response to the revelation of cosmic absurdity? By what fiats may critics *assume*, like that man of assumptions, the lawyer, total categories of the really human and the falsely human in human behaviour and in human history and in human perception? What is true is that we wish to identify as human what affirms life rather than what denies it, what enlarges personality rather than what claustrophobically walls it in. It is also true that as a repressive principle the narrator in the first half of the tale is dehumanizing. But can the denials of Bartleby really be held up as a model of what affirms life and enlarges personality? For Widmer Bartleby becomes 'a small wan Ahab' who 'defiantly butts all ... blind walls' (Widmer, pp 106–7). Thus Bartleby becomes an 'abstract personification of the attorney's own humanity' (Widmer, p 107), as though, again, the principle of defiance were the totality subsumed under the category 'human.' Will, preference, in and of itself, and not rationality – certainly not rationality – becomes the true human characteristic. The true morality, therefore, is the demonic, not the common morality. 'The scrivener provides the human completion, the rage [and here again, significantly, is Widmer's response to the demands of psycho-logic and he invents for Bartleby a characteristic of which Bartleby is, in fact, completely devoid] to the restraint, the covert rebellion to the conviction that "the easiest way of life is the best," the assertion of *human* preferences against depersonalized assumptions, and the melancholy pessimism to balance the bland optimism' (Widmer, pp 112–13, italics added). For Widmer anything less than Bartleby's willingness to go to death in his denials of the present points away from the true morality on the other side of the nihilistic revolution and is merely meliorism. Again, there is nothing the narrator can do short of becoming Bartleby. But the good world on the other side of Bartleby's pallid and unvarying negations comes from Widmer's Gestalt, not from Melville's story. For not only is Bartleby no small, wan Ahab, he is the complementary opposite of Ahab, and offers none of the Ahabian rage that Widmer consequently has to supply for him. More-over, the imputation to Melville of millennial views of history is most strange in the context of invoking Ahab's spirit. For surely if Melville saw anything in that con-text, it was Ahab's murderous miscalculations about the possibilities of experience. If our context is Melville's rather than Widmer's Gestalt, what we have is not the total rebel ushering in the ultimate revolution, but the endless, indeterminate con-tinuations of history, as repetitive and as illuminating of human limitation as the great shroud of the sea that rolls on as it did five thousand years ago. The totalistic critical view makes demands and meanings that entirely subvert and are deaf to the despairing tone of the tale as well as to its indeterminateness.

It is precisely at the point of turning everyone into Bartleby, which for Widmer would be the salvation of the revolution accomplished, that Melville draws back – the same Melville who looks askance at romantic and nihilistic versions of history and the human essence; the same Melville who says that if oysters and champagne are the foods of the body, get you your oysters and champagne; the same Melville who warmly sees the inescapable necessity of the lee shore for all that is kindly to our mortalities even as he urges Bulkington to keep the open independence of his soul's sea from the lee shore's lawyer-like slavish and shallow copy-assumptions; the same Melville who would repudiate the mast-head visions in order to ameliorate the ship's course with the first hint of the hitching tiller; the same Melville who has Ishmael learn that man must eventually learn to lower or at least shift his conceit of attainable felicity. He is, to the point, the same Melville who leaves the stage to the lawyer, not to Bartleby. Because he is the Melville who is so gnarledly aware that the only operable human actuality is the despised and limited *now* trapped between absolutes of infinity and eternity, he draws back from the absolutist prescriptions of totalistic literary criticism that would have the world go even unto death for salva-tion in the future. He will not annihilate the limited human existence within mortal history, the source of realistic fiction, for the triumph of the absolute quality of typalism, even when heroic. Much less does he do so for idea, the bloodless univer-sal, the pallid metaphor. In 'Bartleby' the problems of fictive characterization *are* the problems of metaphysics and psychology. If Edwards on the will and Priestly on necessity, if Locke and Paley are not justifications of necessity that Melville accepts, the deathlessness of the white whale and the deathfulness of Bartleby are. I take it that the real agony of the story comes from Melville's seeing that man must smash the surfaces of respectable and established vision to become fully human, but that if, in doing so, truth turn out to be the frozen absurd or the new vision become the monomania of totalistic defiance, man is plunged into even more deadly and deathly dehumanization. Both Bartleby and the lawyer are victims of human limitation; both suffer dehumanizations, and 'Bartleby' is indeed a speculation about the process of victimization. The cosmic truth kills. The comfortable lies blind us and destroy our hearts that should be enlarged by woe. Both the defiant vision and the lee shore are needed, both are inescapable, and to wake from the world of one into the world of the other is mortal despair, overpowering, stinging melancholy. It is this impingement of worlds that is Melville's constant technique in mingling the characters of different fictive modes to suggest his view of the dilemma of men.

Ah, Bartleby! Ah, humanity!

Perhaps it is a deep knowledge that one possible corollary of the total revolution is generational suicide – *that* as a possibility at least as much as the good world that is supposed to lie beyond the revolution of total negation – that continues to make the masses, who desire nothing so much as a secured present, the despair of the total revolutionaries. I do not mean for a moment that Melville endorses the status quo he presents in the narrator's world. I do mean that through his vision of Bartleby the narrator is awakened to the perception of vulnerable nakedness and woe that makes us all monkey-rope brothers. Paradoxically it is 'revolutionary' Bartleby, not the narrator, who is the one-dimensional man.

When I called 'Bartleby' a speculation, I meant just that. To see it as a polemic rather than as a query is to substitute the Gestalt of the critic for the Gestalt of the story. To reduce the narrator to a fixed moral quantity is to deny the extent to which the story continues to nag and itch after you have read all the criticism that affixes weightings, labels, answers, to what Melville created as lasting question marks. To insist upon ideological equivalents for the details of the story is to lose the suppleness and openness of the story, which is, I think, why critiques of the story always seem to be so much more rigid than the tale itself. To fix an ideology upon this tale is to substitute a desire for a satisfying *quod erat demonstrandum* in place of the continuing perturbation left by the tale, and which is a mark of its particular art. The substitution of polemical answers for Melville's questions is merely to discover the face in the mirror[20] – it is, finally, to substitute the lesser imagination behind fixed quantities for the greater imagination behind the tale. The paradox, as I see it, is that the critics who dismiss the narrator as merely smug and bad in his narrow solipsism are guilty of exactly the same sin of which they indict him.

I suggest that as a speculation about human victimization 'Bartleby the Scrivener' is a despairing recognition that neither the lee-shore life nor the truth-piercing total vision that repudiates it provides adequate sustenance for our hungry humanity.

Yet, a glimpse of the victim's woe can become the woe that is wisdom, and, given that, a man is on his way to becoming human even in his only present world, for that world will never be the same to him again. Perhaps that is the birth of revolution. (I suspect, in my memory of his works, that Melville would say, 'No, no – that *is* the unending revolution.') When I say, then, that we can declare a blessed moratorium on saying certain kinds of things about Bartleby and the narrator, I do not mean that we can declare a moratorium on speculations that continue to explore the story both within and beyond itself. All readers provide that 'beyond' out of their own times and visions and will continue to know the headache of trying to explore the story in that beyond. On errands of contemplation art speeds to – contemplation, and leaves us – ah, Melville! ah readers! – with our own dead letters offices. And with kings and counsellors.

GAY WILSON ALLEN

Walt Whitman and Stoicism

The popular conception of Walt Whitman is that he might have been a disciple of Epicurus, but hardly of Zeno. In 1856 a critic in the *New York Daily Times* asked: 'What Centaur have we here, half-man, half-beast, neighing defiance to all the world?'[1] Such a creature does not resemble a stoic, or even an Epicurean, if the term is properly understood. Although in some lines of *Leaves of Grass* the poet may sound like a neighing centaur, in the larger context of his total writings he was an ethical didacticist, with a high regard for *virtue* in the stoic sense – especially in the sense expounded by Epictetus and Marcus Aurelius, two of his lifelong favourite authors.[2]

In naming the great authors who had influenced him Whitman nearly always included Epictetus, sometimes Marcus Aurelius, and occasionally Seneca.[3] In reminiscing to Horace Traubel, in 1886, he said, 'All the great teachers – Epictetus, Plato, Aurelius – seem ... to rest their faith on the ethical laws,'[4] as Whitman did himself. On another occasion he said:

> Epictetus is the one of all my old cronies who has lasted to this day ... He ... is a universe in himself. He sets me free in a flood of light – of life, of vista ... [He was a youthful favourite] ... I think even at sixteen. I do not remember when I first read the book. It was far, far back ... One day or other I found an Epictetus [in a second-hand bookstore of Brooklyn or New York] – I know it was at that period: found an Epictetus. It was like being born again.[5]

A year before his death, on 7 May 1891, Whitman made this statement to a reporter for the *Boston Transcript*:

> I guess I have a good deal of the feeling of Epictetus and Stoicism – or *tried to have* [italics supplied] – But I am clear that I allow and probably teach some things Stoicism would

frown upon and discard – Let Plato's steeds prance and curvet – but the master's grip and eyes and brain must retain the ultimate power, or all things are lost.[6]

The same year Whitman made a similar statement in a letter to his English friend, J.W. Wallace, who had written about hearing a lecture on stoicism. Whitman wrote that the stoics 'are specially needed in a rich & luxurious, and even scientific age.'[7] But he said that he was aware of differences between his teachings and those of stoicism. There is no doubt, therefore, that Whitman tried on his own terms to be a stoic, though he realized that neither Epictetus nor Marcus Aurelius would have claimed him as a follower.

When Whitman first read Epictetus,[8] he probably read only the 'Manual' or *Encheiridion*; in fact, he never mentioned the 'Discourses.' When he first read Marcus Aurelius is less certain, though it was probably also during his 'teens. It is certain that he encountered some stoic ideas even earlier in a popular interpretation of Epicureanism by Frances Wright [D'Arusmont], whom he worshipped at twelve.[9] This work, entitled *A Few Days in Athens*, and published in 1822, pretends to be a translation of a Greek manuscript discovered in Herculaneum.[10] Whitman read it while he was a printer's apprentice. He told Traubel it was 'daily food to me: I kept it about me for years.'[11] Significantly, the Epicureanism presented by Frances Wright, who was born in Scotland, was somewhat eclectic, with accretions from the empiricism of John Locke, the epistemological scepticism of David Hume, and the 'Common Sense' philosophy of Scotland.

A Few Days in Athens dramatizes the experiences of a young man named Theon, a disciple of Zeno the Stoic, in the third century BC. Though Miss Wright lets Zeno speak only briefly, what he says and Epicurus's allusions to him indicate the basic stoic ideas: right reason, which governs the universe, is the model of human existence; though fate determines events, its operation is fundamentally rational; virtue is inherent in the laws of nature and is essential in human relations, both with men and nature; human conduct should emulate the grandeur and calm of cosmic order, accepting events with a tranquil mind and avoiding the excesses which cause men to feel anxious or fearful; human happiness is the product of life according to nature; right action characterizes a wise man, the stoic ideal of excellence; duty is one of the highest virtues.

In third-century Athens three schools of philosophy attempted to find human solutions to the monumental outside dangers and the chaotic strife within the city-state. Stoicism taught men to bear their suffering with courage, rational conduct, and without complaint; Pyrrhonism to question everything and doubt the reliability of the senses; Epicureanism to withdraw in contemplation from the disorder of the world.[12]

To return to *A Few Days in Athens*: after listening to Timocrates denounce the 'garden of Epicurus,' Theon leaves the portico of Zeno exclaiming: 'Ye Gods! and will ye suffer your names to be thus blasphemed? How do ye not strike with thunder the actor and teacher of such enormities?' (FDA, p 7). But presently in his fuming reverie he meets an impressive sage, robed in white, with the voice of a divinity, who apologizes for breaking the young man's meditation. He assumes that Theon is from the 'groves of the academy' [a follower of Plato], but learns that he is 'from the portico' [the *Stoa*, or painted colonnade, from which the stoics got their name]: 'Ah! I had not thought Zeno could send forth such a dreamer. You are in a good school,' he continued, observing that the youth was confused by his remark, 'a school of real virtue; and, if I read faces well, as I think I do, I see a pupil that will not disgrace its doctrines.' (FDA, p 9).

Theon is impressed, but confesses that he is discouraged: 'I have looked upon Zeno with admiration and despair.' The stranger suggests: 'Learn rather to look with love. He who but admires virtue, yields her but half her due. She asks to be approached, to be embraced – not with fear, but with confidence – not with awe, but with rapture' (FDA, p 10). He thinks that Theon is qualified to attain virtue; all he needs is confidence. Thousands never discover 'the seeds of excellence in them.' While all men may not become philosophers or poets, 'all men may be virtuous.'

Theon's father, a scholar himself, had wanted his son to attend all the schools, and he had tried to do so. Once he had nearly become a Pythagorean, before choosing the portico of Zeno. The stranger says that he should explore other philosophies and then discriminate for himself. A few turns in 'the garden of Epicurus' might be good for him. 'What!' Theon exclaims. 'To hear the laws of virtue confounded and denied? To hear vice exculpated, advocated, panegyrized? Impiety and atheism professed and inculcated? – To witness the nocturnal orgies of vice and debauchery?' (FDA, p 13).

These views of Epicurus, the stranger says, are false. Then he reveals that *he* is Epicurus. After Theon's astonishment subsides, his curiosity is aroused. Zeno has told him that, 'You [Epicurus] own no other law, no other principles of action, than pleasure.' This is correct, Epicurus says, but he does not, as Zeno accuses, 'teach men to laugh at virtue, and to riot in luxury and vice' (FDA, p 26). In subsequent discussions Theon learns that Epicurus does indeed lead his followers on 'the path to virtue,' but 'Thorns are not in it, nor is it difficult or steep,' as the stoics insist (FDA, p 28). 'Zeno hath his eye on man; I – mine on men; none but philosophers can be stoics; Epicureans all may be' (FDA, p 29). All schools teach virtue, and 'is it not happiness? and is not happiness virtue?'

- The stoics deny that pain is an evil, but Epicurus holds it to be 'the greatest of all evils.' To deny it is an evil is like 'Elean's denial of motion: that must exist to man which exists to his senses ... I feel myself virtuous because my soul is at rest: With evil passions I should be disturbed and uneasy; with uncontrolled appetites I should be disordered in body as well as mind – for this reason, and this reason only, I avoid both' (FDA, p 30). Temporary pleasure that results in pain later is not a virtue. Fame, vanity, and ambition, for example, are not bad in themselves, but may lead to pain later. The desire for distinction may be fortunate in the head of a genius, in the heart of a sage, and in a situation convenient for its development and gratification (FDA, p 42). 'The perfection of wisdom, and the end of true philosophy, is to proportion our wants to our possessions, our ambitions to our capacities' (FDA, p 43).

As Theon is leaving the house of Epicurus, he meets his friend Cleanthes, who denounces him for having been in a mansion of vice and folly, and thereby disloyal to Zeno. Theon tries to explain that he has not deserted Zeno, and that Epicurus has been misunderstood and maligned, to which Cleanthes replies: 'Rouse, rouse up your energies! Oh! be firm to Zeno, and to Virtue! I tell you not – Zeno tells you not, that virtue is found in pleasure's repose. Resistance, energy, watchfulness, patience, and endurance – these ... must be your habit, ere you can reach the perfection of your nature. The ascent is steep, is long, and arduous' (FDA, p 51).

As Cleanthes works himself into a frenzy – unbecoming to a stoic – Zeno enters. The description of his appearance could have served as a model for Whitman's many descriptions of himself – certainly for his ideal of a poet-prophet:

> ... he stood by the head and shoulders above the crowd: his breast, broad and manly; his limbs, cast in strength and symmetry; his gait, erect, calm, and dignified; his features, large, grand and regular, seemed sculptured by the chisel for a colossal divinity: the forehead, broad and serene, was marked with the even lines of wisdom and age; but no harsh wrinkles nor playing muscles disturbed the repose of his cheeks ... Wisdom undisturbable, fortitude unshakable, self-respect, self-possession, and self-knowledge perfected, were in his face, his carriage, and his tread.   (FDA, p 53)

Zeno excuses Cleanthes' agitation as weakness of his body, not of his mind. And when Theon asks permission to reply to Cleanthes, Zeno grants it because 'in teaching austerity, [I] do not teach ingratitude' (FDA, p 59). Having learned candour from Zeno, Theon testifies that the stoics do not have a monopoly on virtue, and that those who accuse Epicurus of sensuality and wickedness slander him. Epicurus himself arrives in time to hear this plea for tolerance, and his physical appearance provides a symbolical contrast to the majestic severity to Zeno:

> The face was a serene mirror of a serene mind; its expression spoke like music to the soul. Zeno's was not more calm and unruffled; but here was no severity, no authority, no

reserve, no unapproachable majesty, no repelling superiority; all was benevolence, mildness, openness and soothing encouragement. To see, was to love; and to hear was to trust. (FDA, p 61)

Theon, says Epicurus, 'had lost in the Garden [during his one visit] no virtues, if a few prejudices.' His words and manner of speaking so impress Zeno that he says: 'I feared you yesterday, but I fear you doubly to-day. Your doctrines are in themselves enticing, but coming from such lips, I fear they are irresistible' (FDA, p 62). Greece, he regretfully admits, is rapidly succumbing to Persian luxury and effeminacy, as a result of the Peloponnesian War and the Macedonian conquest. 'Our youth, dandled in the lap of indulgence, shall turn with sickened ears from the severe moral of Zeno, and greedily suck in the honiyed [sic] philosophy of Epicurus ... our degenerated country shall worship you, and expire at your feet' (FDA, pp 63–4).

Zeno, sternly uncompromising and unbending, sees man 'as he should be,' Epicurus says, but he himself sees him 'as he is,' with all his weakness and errors. Yet Epicurus would lead men to happiness not by encouraging their self-indulgence, but by helping them to gain self-control – a goal similar to Zeno's, though the method is vastly different. 'Let us quiet our passions, not by gratifying, but subduing them; let us conquer our weariness, not by rest, but by exertion.' Epicurus, unlike Zeno, does not seek to suppress sensibility, but to turn it to good. As a consequence, 'when the sublime motives of Zeno shall cease to affect an enervated generation, the gentle persuasions of Epicurus shall be heard and obeyed' (FDA, p 67). This will cause the stoics to slander, misinterpret, and attempt to disgrace Epicurus. How many times in later life Walt Whitman might have said the same thing about his enemies!

There is also a striking parallel between Epicurus's attitude towards knowledge and Whitman's. 'Knowledge,' says the master, 'is the best riches that man can possess.' But he often mistakenly thinks 'knowledge one with erudition, and shutting himself up in his closet, he cons all the lore of antiquity; he fathoms the sciences, heaps up in his memory all the sayings of the dead.' But 'learning is not wisdom, nor will books give understanding' (FDA, p 85). While preparing his first edition of *Leaves of Grass*, Whitman spent many hours in the Astor Library in New York City, attended lectures on astronomy, read books on science, religion, and history.[13] But he did not confuse information thus gained with wisdom, or believe that books give understanding. (See, for example, 'When I Heard the Learn'd Astronomer.')

Chapter 10 of *A Few Days in Athens* contains the epitome of the philosophy of Epicurus, especially of ideas to be found later in Whitman's poetry. 'To be happy, we must be virtuous; and when we are virtuous we are happy.' But the advice to 'cast away our vanity and our pride' Whitman never took, making, instead, a virtue of both. However, the Epicurean philosophy of pleasure is implicit in many of

Whitman's poems, and especially those of the 1855 edition. 'Perfect pleasure,' says Epicurus, 'which is happiness, you will have attained when you have brought your bodies and souls into a state of satisfied tranquility' (FDA, p 89). The poet in 'Song of Myself' loafs and invites his soul, at ease 'observing a spear of summer grass' (SM, [sec. 1]); he is satisfied, and God sleeps beside him at night (SM, [sec. 3]).

Whitman also believed that 'prudence' is the 'mother of the virtues and the hand-maiden of wisdom' (FDA, p 89). He used the term in his 1855 Preface and wrote a poem for his 1856 Leaves called 'Poem of the Last Explanation of Prudence.' In The Solitary Singer I have summarized this idea as long-range prudential conduct, 'Epicurean in the true sense of the term: a sacrifice today may bring more lasting happiness tomorrow; or to paraphrase Whitman (and the New Testament), he who loses his life may gain eternal life; or a defeat may be a victory in disguise.'[14]

Prudence is also supported by temperance, which prevents disquiet to the soul and injury to the body; and 'fortitude shall strengthen you to bear those diseases which even temperance may not be efficient to prevent; those afflictions which fate may level at you; those persecutions which the folly or malice of man may invent. It shall fit you to bear all things, to conquer fear, and to meet death' (FDA, p 90).

Of all the Epicurean doctrines (with resemblances also to those of the stoics) that of death as natural, fortunate, and beautiful must have impressed Whitman most strongly. 'Philosophy cannot change the laws of Nature; but she may teach us to accommodate to them ... Nature levels us with death; but how mild is the death of Nature, with Philosophy to spread the pillow' (FDA, p 91).[15] Death is the gentle deliverancer, friend and never foe. It is fortunate to be 'laid to sleep while the sun of joy yet shines, before the storm of fate has broken our tranquility' (FDA, p 92). Epicurus (at least in Frances Wright's interpretation) anticipated both Wallace Stevens[16] and Whitman in this consolation: 'Should we value the lovely flower if it bloomed eternally, or the luscious fruit if it hung always on the bough?' (FDA, p 94). Therefore, men should bear with patience and fortitude the 'gentle termination, which it becomes us to meet with ready minds, neither regretting the past, nor anxious for the future' (FDA, p 95).

The theme of death in Leaves of Grass is too well known to need extensive citation, and a few examples should suffice. In 'Song of Myself' the poet says it is just as lucky to die as to be born – sections 7–8. In 'Out of the Cradle Endlessly Rocking' death is the 'low and delicious word' lisped by the sea, symbol of the cosmic ocean of life. In 'When Lilacs Last in the Dooryard Bloom'd' the poet chants an invocation to the 'dark mother always gliding near with soft feet':

Approach strong deliveress,
When it is so, when thou hast taken them I joyously sing the dead,
Lost in the loving floating ocean of thee,
Laved in the flood of thy bliss O death. (Sec. 14)

Whitman mentions neither Epictetus nor Marcus Aurelius often in his *Prose Works*, but he several times quotes or refers to them in ways that reveal his sustained interest. In *Specimen Days* (1882) he copies from his 'Common-Place Book': 'Preach not to others what they shall eat, but eat as becomes you, and be silent. – *Epictetus*.'[17] During his stay in Boston in 1860, while seeing the third edition of *Leaves of Grass* through the press, Whitman several times heard Father Taylor, the famous preacher to sailors. Reminiscing in *November Boughs* (1888), he remarks: 'One realized what grip there might have been in such words-of-mouth talk as that of Socrates and Epictetus' (PW, II, 550). And again in his essay on Elias Hicks he repeats the thought: 'Most of his discourses, like those of Epictetus and the ancient peripatetics, have left no record remaining – they were extempore' (PW, II, 640).

Epictetus, therefore – along with Elias Hicks, Father Taylor was heard too late – probably influenced Whitman to cultivate what some critics have called his 'oral style.'[18] Finally, in *Good-Bye My Fancy* (1891), in naming his favourite books, beginning with the Bible and Homer, he includes 'a very choice little Epictetus' (PW, II, 702). This was undoubtedly T.W. Rolleston's translation, called *The Teaching of Epictetus: Being the 'Encheiridion of Epictetus,' with Selections from the 'Dissertations' and 'Fragments.'* Rolleston, Whitman's ardent Irish admirer, sent him a privately printed copy in 1881, a few months before it was published by Kegan, Paul, and Trench in London.[19] Also in 1891 Whitman wrote his English friend, J.W. Wallace, after hearing that Wentworth Dixon had read a paper on stoicism: 'I guess I have a good deal of the feeling of Epictetus & stoicism – or have tried to have. They are especially needed in a rich & luxurious, & even scientific age. But I am clear that I include & allow & probably teach some things stoicism would frown upon and discard.'[20]

One reason for Whitman's often mentioning Epictetus to Traubel was the continuing pleasure Rolleston's gift gave him. He took a professional delight in the format, printing, and binding, and wanted to use it as a model for one of his own books. This personal notion has, of course, nothing to do with the words of Epictetus, except that his admiration for the author (and translator) enhanced his pride of ownership. Some of his specific references may sound rather banal, until one considers his own conduct. For example, Epictetus's advice to 'the youth who was bent upon seeing the Roman [sic] games – don't get heated, don't fret over results, accept the facts as they appear.'[21] This had been Whitman's ideal during all the years of hostility to his poems – though, being human, he did not always live up to it. Nevertheless, Epictetus no doubt deserves some credit for the serenity which many of Whitman's visitors in his own age commented upon.[22]

Assuming that it was only the *Encheiridion* which Whitman knew before Rolleston sent him his translation with its selections from the 'Dissertations' (some editors call them 'Discourses') and 'Fragments,' it may be interesting to run through the

'Manual' to see what passages seem most pertinent in the context of Whitman's life and career.

The *Encheiridion* begins with the stoic philosophy of 'things ... under our control.'[23] These include 'everything that is our own doing': conception (thinking), choice, desire, aversion, etc. Not under human control: 'our body, our property, reputation, office,' etc. Of course prudent conduct can increase the chances of having a healthy body, prevent loss of property or reputation, and help one obtain and hold office, if that is what he desires; yet chance controls these to a greater extent than does a man's *will* – or so Epictetus thought; and, of course, he lived in a very corrupt society in which a tyrant could take life with impunity. His attitude towards tyrants was: you can take my life, but you cannot control my mind. His stoic philosophy was: in the things that really count to me, no one can harm me except myself (E, II, 483). Naturally, Whitman's position was not so extreme or so absolute – though Emerson's was. Yet Whitman's stance amidst the vicissitudes of life was also stoic:

> My dinner, dress, associates, looks, business, compliments, dues,
> The real or fancied indifference of some man or woman I love,
> The sickness of one of my folks – or of myself .... [24] or ill-doing .... or loss or lack of
>   money .... or depressions or exaltations,
> But they are not the Me myself. (SM, sec. 4)

Or again:

> I exist as I am, that is enough,
> If no other in the world be aware I sit content,
> And if each and all be aware I sit content. (SM, sec. 20)

Sometimes Whitman makes use of Epictetus's key terms, such as 'interior' and 'exterior,'[25] as in 'A Song of Joys' (1860):

> O while I live to be the ruler of life, not a slave,
> To meet life as a powerful conqueror,
> No fumes, no ennui, no more complaints or scornful criticisms,
> To these proud laws of the air, the water and the ground, proving my interior soul
>   impregnable,
> And nothing exterior shall ever take command of me. (Lines 134–8)

('Complaints' and 'laws' are also familiar stoic terms.)

Whitman's desire to be at all times natural, and to do nothing in violation of the operations of nature, could have come from any number of sources; nevertheless, he and Epictetus have in common many attitudes, especially keeping one's 'moral purpose in harmony with nature' (E, II, 487). Of course Epictetus wanted to remove every desire for anything not under his control in order to prevent disappointment or pain, whereas Whitman scorned everything unnatural (or artificial) and was confident that he was nature's darling because of the purity of his 'moral purpose in harmony with nature.'

When Whitman was a young man, he felt himself to be as healthy as an Apollo, yet when debility came as his 'fate,' he was not lacking in stoic fortitude. Perhaps he had absorbed Epictetus's teaching:

> Disease is an impediment to the body, but not to the moral purpose, unless that consents.
> Lameness is an impediment to the leg, but not to the moral purpose. And say this to
> yourself at each thing that befalls you; for you will find the thing to be an impediment
> to something else, but not to yourself.   (E, II, 491)

In a note written in his old age, Whitman wrote: 'Nature seem'd to use me a long while – myself all well, able, strong and happy – to portray power, freedom, health. But after a while she seems to fancy, may-be I can see and understand it all better by being deprived of most of these' (PW, II, 708).

Whitman was especially fond of Epictetus's saying that 'What is good for thee, O Nature, is good for me!' (Traubel, I, 423). Once he enlarged this to: 'What is good enough for the universe is good enough for me!' (Traubel, I, 149). And on another occasion, after quoting the first of these sentences, he added: 'indeed, I am sure that whatever death is it is all right' (Traubel, II, 397). Possibly Whitman took Epictetus's 'readiness to yield' at a banquet (E, II, 495) in a narrower sense than the stoic intended, but he liked the advice on eating so well that he preserved this sentence in his Common-Place Book: 'Preach not to others what they should eat, but eat as becomes you, and be silent' (PW, I, 271; see also E, II, 529 – slight change in wording).

Whitman believed that fate (or whatever controls human destiny – he was as vague as were the stoics about what that controlling force might be) had assigned him a role in life. Epictetus said:

> Remember that you are an actor in a play, the character of which is determined by the
> Playwright: If He wishes the play to be short, it is short; if long, it is long; if He wishes
> you to play the part of a beggar, remember to act even this rôle adroitly; and so if your
> rôle be that of a cripple, an official, or a layman. For this is your business, to play
> admirably the rôle assigned you; but the selection of that rôle is Another's.   (E, II, 497)

In 1888, in 'A Backward Glance O'er Travel'd Roads,' Whitman admitted frankly that from a 'business point of view "Leaves of Grass" has been worse than a failure,' and that the public still 'shows mark'd anger and contempt more than anything else.' But, 'I had my choice when I commenc'd. I bid neither for soft eulogies, big money returns, nor the approbation of existing schools and conventions' (PW, II, 712–13). True, in the heady summer of 1856, after receiving Emerson's famous 'greeting' letter,[26] Whitman did seem to have such ambitions. But his subsequent career of a poet-forced-to-be-his-own-publisher bears out this claim. Change 'philosophy' to 'poetry' and it can be said that he took the advice of Epictetus when he taught:

> If you yearn for philosophy, prepare at once to be met with ridicule, to have many people jeer at you, and say, 'Here he is again, turned philosopher all of a sudden,' and 'Where do you suppose he got that high brow?' But ... hold fast to the things which to you seem best, as a man who has been assigned by God to this post; and remember that if you abide by the same principles, those who formerly used to laugh at you will later come to admire you. ... (E, II, 499)

Whitman always knew that he would get the last laugh, in life or in death. And his attitude towards money[27] was Epictetian also: 'If I can get money and at the same time keep myself self-respecting, and faithful, and high-minded, show me the way and I will get it' (E, II, 501). To Whitman money was not in itself an evil, but the method of getting it could be. Nor would he compromise himself to buy praise (E, II, 505).

Though the influence of Epictetus seems to have begun in Whitman's youth, it was renewed around 1860 (note 'A Song of Joys') and again at the end of the decade. The best evidence of the latter is a crude version of a poem which Whitman copied into a notebook dated 1868–70. It is headed 'EPICTETUS/(Description of a Wise Man),' and reads:

> He reproves nobody –
> Praises nobody
> Blames nobody
> *Nor ever speaks of himself*
> If anyone praises him, in his own mind he condemns the flatterer
> If any one reproves (? or insults) him he looks with care that it does not irritate him.
> All his desires depend on things within his power.
> He transfers all his aversions to those things which nature commends us to avoid.
> His appetites are always moderate.
> He is indifferent whether he be thought foolish or [ignorant] wise.
> He observes himself with the nicety of an enemy or spy, and looks on his own wishes as
> betrayers.[28]

This tentative composition is followed by an extract-paraphrase (so Whitman says) from Heine's Diary, though it sounds like the wise man Epictetus, and was evidently the poet's own personal ambition on the night of 25 November 1868 (his date):

> to live a *more Serene Calm philosophic Life – reticent, far more reticent* – yet cheerful, with pleased spirit and far less of the gusty, pleased manner – the capricious – the puerile – No more attempts at smart sayings, or scornful criticisms, or harsh comments on persons or actions, on private or public affairs.[29]

In 1868 Whitman was going through an emotional and moral crisis,[30] which continued (or recurred) into 1870. On 15 July 1870 he was in 'pursuit' of someone or something coded as '164,' now believed to have been his young friend Peter Doyle. On this date he resolved to give up his incessant and enormous 'perturbations.' In an additional note he calls it 'feverish, fluctuating.' He could have borrowed the term *perturbation* from a lecture on astronomy he had heard or read (meaning 'disturbance in the regular motion of a celestial body produced by an outside force'),[31] but Sholom Kahn points out that the word 'occurs often in discussions of the Stoic ideal.'[32] It is interesting, too, that the famous description of himself in 'Song of Myself' (sec. 24) as 'Disorderly fleshy and sensual' reads, in the 1867 edition, 'Turbulent ...'

A further reason for attributing Whitman's desire of avoiding 'perturbations' to the influence of stoicism rather than astronomical lore is seen in an 1860 poem expressing the ideal of imperturbability:

> Me imperturbe.
> Me standing at ease in Nature,
> Master of all, or mistress of all – aplomb in the midst of irrational things,
> Imbued as they – passive, receptive, silent as they,
> Finding my occupation, poverty, notoriety, foibles, crimes, less important than I thought;
> Me private, or public, or menial, or solitary – all these subordinate (I am eternally equal with the best – I am not subordinate;)
> Me toward the Mexican Sea, or in the Mannahatta, or the Tennessee, or far north, or inland,
> A river-man, or a man of the woods, or of any farm-life of These States, or of the coast, or the lakes, or Kanada,
> Me wherever my life is to be lived, O it is self-balanced for contingencies,
> It confronts night, storms, hunger, ridicule, accidents, rebuffs, as the trees and animals do. –[33]

Though the poem was written, seemingly, in an effort to overcome the poet's tendencies away from stoic poise and self-control (most acute around 1859–60 and again at the end of the decade, as revealed above), it indicates a rediscovery (or turning back to) Epictetus and/or Marcus Aurelius.

The sustained influence of stoicism can also be seen in Whitman's theological attitudes, from the first edition to the last of his poems. Scholars have suggested various sources for his religion,[34] but it is noteworthy that he said very little specifically about theories of God, and even scorned those who did:

> And I call to mankind, Be not curious about God,
> For I who am curious about each am not curious about God,
> No array of terms can say how much I am at peace with God and about death.
> (SM, sec. 48)

In spite of Whitman's insistence on his belief in immortality, his faith was tainted by a strain of stoic agnosticism. In one of his final poems, 'Good-Bye My Fancy!' (1891), he says, 'I'm going away. I know not where.' But he was sure of the 'commonplace,' such as Epictetus believed in, too, as in Whitman's 1891 poem 'The Commonplace':

> The commonplace I sing;
> How cheap is health! how cheap nobility!
> Abstinence, no falsehood, no gluttony, lust;
> The open air I sing, freedom, toleration,
> (Take here the mainest lesson – less from books – less from the schools,)
> The common day and night – the common earth and waters,
> Your farm – your work, trade, occupation,
> The democratic wisdom underneath, like the solid ground for all.

In some of these words there are connotations more Whitmanian than Epictetian, yet basically he and the Greek stoic found the same moral and personal values in the 'solid ground' common to all men.

Whether Whitman discovered Marcus Aurelius at the same time he bought his first copy of Epictetus in the second-hand book store about 1825 is not known. His surviving personal copy of *The Thoughts of the Emperor M. Aurelius Antonius*, translated by George Long, was published in Boston in 1864.[35] But his frequent association of the two names in his reminiscences to Traubel suggests that he first read a translation earlier than Long's. Kahn finds echoes of Marcus Aurelius in the 1855 Preface.[36] And a case can be made for parallels and probable influence in his preparatory notebooks.[37]

It is often difficult to separate the ideas and moral sentiments of Marcus Aurelius from his Greek master, for, as Charles Reginald Haines says, 'Epictetus the Phyrigian slave was his true spiritual father, but we do not find in the Emperor the somewhat rigid didacticism and spiritual dogmatism of his predecessor. Marcus is more humble and not so confident. The hardness and arrogance of Stoicism are softened in him by an infusion of Platonism and other philosophies.'[38] In many ways the *Meditations* of Marcus, intended only for himself, seem closer (at least to this writer) in spirit to Whitman's ideas than the moral instruction in the *Encheiridion*, especially concerning the soul, the relations of nature and the supernatural, and on death.

Marcus believes that nature, God, and the universe are identical. 'Cease not to think of the Universe as one living Being,' he writes (M, book IV, 40), 'possessed of a single Substance and a single Soul.' The Substance, however, is 'broken up into countless bodies individually characterized' (M, XII, 30). 'There is one Intelligent Soul, though it seem to be divided.' He thus differentiates Substance (matter?) and Soul (spirit), yet both to him are so integrated in nature (the cosmos) that he thinks of them as essentially the same, or as two sides of one coin. 'Through the universal Substance as through a rushing torrent all bodies pass on their way, united with the Whole in nature and activity, as our members are with one another' (M, VII, 19).

In one of Whitman's pre-*Leaves of Grass* notebooks we find similar ideas:

> The soul or spirit transmits itself into all matter – into rocks, and can live the life of a rock – into the sea, and can feel itself the sea – into the oak, or other tree – into an animal, and feel itself a horse, a fish, or bird – into the earth – into the motions of the suns and stars –[39]

Marcus often calls the Soul the 'Seminal Reason of the Universe, which is scattered alike into the atoms' (M, VI, 24). Whitman, in his early notebook remarks:

> The effusion or corporation of the soul is always under the beautiful laws of physiology –
> I guess the soul itself can never be anything but great and pure and immortal; but it makes itself visible only through matter – a perfect head, and bowels and bones to match is the easy gate through which it comes from its embowered garden, and pleasantly appears to the sight of the world. –[40]

Marcus Aurelius was not so sure of 'immortality' as was Whitman; only of the permanence of the universal Substance and Intelligent Reason. He usually precedes his speculation with 'if' or 'either':

> For either there is a scattering of the elements out of which I have been built up, or a transmutation of the solid into the earthy and of the spiritual into the serial; so that these

too are taken back into the Reason of the Universe, whether cycle by cycle it be consumed with fire or renew itself by everlasting permutations.   (M, X, 7)

Marcus wondered: 'If souls outlive their bodies, how does the air contain them from times beyond ken?' (M, IV, 21). He suspected that eventually they also decayed, like matter. He asked also: 'How does the earth contain the bodies of those who have been buried in it for such endless ages?' For the latter nature operates by dissolution, transference, and diffusion. Whitman expresses a similar idea in 'This Compost' (1856). He wonders why the ground itself does not sicken from all the decaying flesh it has absorbed from time immemorial. How does the earth grow 'such sweet things out of such corruptions.' Yet,

> It turns harmless and stainless on its axis, with such endless successions of diseased
>   corpses,
> It distills such exquisite winds out of such fetor,
> It renews with such unwitting looks its prodigal, annual sumptuous crops,
> It gives such divine materials to men, and accepts such leavings from them at last.

The exuberant poet of 'Song of Myself' cheerfully declares of his own inevitable death:

> I bequeath myself to the dirt to grow from the grass I love,
> If you want me again look for me under your boot-soles.   (Sec. 52)

There is, to be sure, some difference between the stoic resolution 'To wait with a good grace for the end, whether it be extinction or translation' (M, V, 33) and Whitman's faith in the latter. Marcus was never sure whether death was dispersion or extinction of the soul: 'Either dispersion if atoms; or, if a single Whole, either extinction or a change of state' (M, VII, 32). But he believed firmly that 'fluxes and changes perpetually renew the world' (M, VI, 15), so that in the long run he and Whitman share almost the same idea. Whitman frequently chants of progressions, cycles, and even transmigration:

> The souls moving along . . . . are they invisible while the least atom of the stones is
>   visible?   (SM, sec. 8)

In section 49 of 'Song of Myself' he calls death 'the accoucheur,' giving 'relief and escape' from the physical life.

> And as to you corpse I think you are good manure, but that does not offend me,
> I smell the white roses sweetscented and growing,

I reach to the leafy lips . . . . I reach to the polished breasts of melons,
And as to you life, I reckon you are the leavings of many deaths,
No doubt I have died myself ten thousand times before.

In spite of the similarities, however, Whitman has two modifications of the
'eternal return' that differ somewhat from Marcus Aurelius's. For Marcus the
survival of the atoms in transmuted form is more like the principle of the conser-
vation of energy, with extinction, apparently, of all consciousness. Whitman's pro-
gressive 'return' has been strongly influenced by nineteenth-century theories of
evolution, geological discoveries of how the earth developed, and something like
Hindu transmigration (popular with some of the American transcendentalists).
Whitman is confident, too, of some kind of personal survival of ego, psyche, or
individual soul, which does not disperse into the universe in a manner that obliter-
ates 'identity':

My embryo has never been torpid . . . . nothing could overlay it,
For it the nebula cohered to an orb . . . . the long slow strata piled to rest it on . . . . vast
    vegetables gave it sustenance,
Monstrous sauroids transported it in their mouths and deposited it with care.
(SM, sec. 44)

Greek and Roman science had not progressed so far that Marcus could visualize the
progress in these evolutionary images. But they rather extend his philosophy than
contradict it, and his cyclic theory of nature's method was not altogether different
from Whitman's description of the cosmic process:

There is no stoppage, and never can be stoppage;
If I and you and the worlds and all beneath or upon their surfaces, and all the palpable
    life, were this moment reduced back to a pallid float, it would not avail in the long run,
We should surely bring up again where we now stand,
And as surely go as much farther, and then farther and farther.   (SM, sec. 45)

Another trait that Whitman shared with Marcus Aurelius was *love* of nature and
the universe. Though the stoic ideal, and especially Epictetus's, was not to be too
fond of anything in life in order to be able to bear disappointment and not dread
death, Marcus thought that the parts of nature were in love with each other, and he
shared the emotion: '*The earth is in love with showers and the majestic sky is in love.
And the Universe is in love with making whatever has to be. To the Universe then I
say: Together with thee I will be in love. Is it not a way we have of speaking, to say,
This or that loves to be so?*' (M, X, 21).

Whitman's so-called 'mysticism' is mainly a kind of cosmic joy, in which he plays the role of *lover* of all Creation. A fine example is the prodigal love for the earth felt by the 'I'[41] of 'Song of Myself' (section 21):

> I am he that walks with the tender and growing night;
> I call to the earth and sea half-held by the night.
> ...
> Smile O voluptuous coolbreathed earth!
> ...
> Smile, for your lover comes!
> Prodigal! you have given me love .... therefore I to you give love!
> O unspeakable passionate love!

There is no utterance so sensuous as this in Marcus Aurelius's *Meditations*, though he was far more sensuous, compassionate, and sensitive than Epictetus. Compassion was deficient in Epictetus, entirely alien to Seneca, but Marcus could say: 'For that which proceeds from the Gods is worthy of reverence in that it is excellent; and that which proceeds from men, of love, in that they are akin, and, at times and in a manner, of compassion' (M, II, 13).

Marcus Aurelius might well have given Whitman the motif for his 1855 poem 'To Think of Time':

> Take a bird's-eye-view of the world, its endless gatherings and endless ceremonials, voyagings manifold in storm and calm, and the vicissitudes of things coming into being, participating in being, ceasing to be. Reflect too on the life lived long ago by other men, and the life that shall be lived after thee, and is now being lived in barbarous countries; and how many have never even heard thy name, and how many [who have] will very soon forget it, and how many who now perhaps acclaim, will soon blame thee, and that neither memory nor fame nor anything else whatever is worth reckoning.   (M, IX, 30)

In 'To Think of Time' Whitman takes a 'bird's-eye-view' of life past, present, and future with reference to a single human identity:

> To think of time .... to think through the retrospection,
> To think of today .. and the ages continued henceforward.
> Have you guessed you yourself would not continue? Have you dreaded those earth-beetles?
> Have you feared the future would be nothing to you?   (Sec. 1)

This is almost a paraphrase of the passage from Marcus quoted above, except that Whitman develops the pathos of mortality:

> To think that the rivers will come to flow, and the snow fall, and fruits ripen . . and act
> upon others as upon us now . . . . yet not act upon us;
> To think of all these wonders of city and country . . and others taking great interest in
> them . . and we taking small interest in them.   (Sec. 3)

Both the pathos and irony are perhaps implied in Marcus Aurelius's statement, though his conclusion that the transcience of human experiences makes nothing 'worth reckoning' is not Whitman's conclusion. Rather

> It is not to diffuse you that you were born of your mother and father – it is to identify you,
> It is not that you should be undecided, but that you should be decided;
> Something long preparing and formless is arrived and formed in you,
> You are henceforth secure, whatever comes or goes.
>
> The threads that were spun are gathered . . . . the weft crosses the warp . . . . the pattern
> is systematic.   (Sec. 7)

Thus Whitman conquers the fear of death (or tries to), finally, not with stoic indifference, but with faith in the purpose of death:

> If otherwise, all things came but to ashes of [or?] dung;
> If maggots and rats ended us, then suspicion and treachery and death.
>
> Do you suspect death? If I were to suspect death I should die now,
> Do you think I could walk pleasantly and well-suited toward annihilation?   (Sec. 8)

Instead of annihilation, Whitman sees immortality in nature everywhere. Everything, he asserts again as in his early notebook, 'has an eternal soul' – the trees, the weeds of the sea, the animals:

> I swear I think there is nothing but immortality!
> That the exquisite scheme is for it, and the nebulous float is for it, and the cohering is
> for it,
> And all preparation is for it . . and identity is for it . . and life and death are for
> it.   (Sec. 9)

Yet is this actually more than Marcus Aurelius's indestructible atoms, which are forever changing into new combinations? Whitman's examples do not prove more than transmutations and endless cycles of death, decay, germination, and rebirth in the 'exquisite scheme.' He believed that the vast 'preparation' was for something beyond this, though he was never able to define what it was. This leaves him, perhaps, a stoic in spite of himself, but he was not reconciled to stoicism. He said he tried, but it did not satisfy him. In fact, it might be said that his underlying motive in writing *Leaves of Grass* – a psychological and philosophical *leit motif* – was to overcome the haunting idea that the end of his life would be annihilation.

MUNRO BEATTIE

Henry James: 'The Voice of Stoicism'

We know before we look that it will be vain to seek out in his novels and tales a direct statement of Henry James's 'pilosophy of life.' 'How can you say,' he once chided Hugh Walpole, 'I do anything so foul and abject as to "state"?'[1] Of all literary artists James adhered most faithfully to the modes of indirection and implication. For the explicit, then, we must turn to his other writings, especially to his letters and notebooks; now and again in their pages we come as close as we are ever likely to come to a direct utterance of his guiding principles.

Among James's numerous correspondents the closest and most constant, outside the members of his family, seems to have been Charles Eliot Norton's sister, Grace. Their friendship endured from his earliest residence in Cambridge, at the outset of his twenties, until the end of his life. Although ten years his elder, she outlived him by ten years, and preserved one hundred and sixty of his letters to her. From time to time, in grief or despondency, Miss Norton turned to Henry James – and, on occasion, to his brother William – for solace. For her comfort James in several letters besought her to act upon his own code for coping with the miseries of existence – 'that personal philosophy, of whatever nature it may be, which is our refuge in the last resort.'[2] For his philosophy James had a specific name: 'I am determined,' he wrote to Grace Norton in 1883, 'not to speak to you except with the voice of stoicism.'[3]

He urged upon her the stoic strategy of sheer endurance: 'Don't think, don't feel, any more than you can help, don't conclude or decide – don't do anything but *wait*. Everything will pass ... I insist upon the necessity of a sort of mechanical condensation – so that however fast the horse may run away there will, when he pulls up, be a somewhat agitated but perfectly identical G.N. left in the saddle.'[4]

Twenty-five years later, James drew on the same philosophy to fortify Edith Wharton in a time of domestic distress: 'Only sit tight yourself *and go through the movements of life* ... Live it all through, every inch of it – out of it something valuable will come – but live it ever so quietly; and – *je maintiens mon dire* – waitingly!'[5] When again Mrs Wharton was facing the future with despair, James gave her the same kind of counsel, advice of the most salutary sort though not the easiest to act upon: 'Sit loose and live in the day – don't borrow trouble, and remember that nothing happens as we forecast it.'[6] Yet another instance of his attitude to adversity may be drawn from a letter to Mrs Clara Benedict on the death of her sister, James's friend Constance Fenimore Woolson: 'Meanwhile, only live, and think of living, from hour to hour, and day to day; it is perfect wisdom and it takes us through troubles that no other way can take us through.'[7]

The tone of these letters, and of others in a similar vein, demands implicit belief in the hard-won authenticity of James's personal philosophy. It came out of his own engagements with adversity. Invalidism plagued him throughout his life, particularly during the period of the Civil War, following the injury to his back incurred in 1861, and in the closing decade of his life. How much of his youthful disability was what is called psychosomatic, how much hypochondriac, is too large a theme for the present, and not sufficiently relevant.[8] To James himself it was suffering and restraint, which had to be overcome in the interests of full consciousness and the unfolding of his career. More oppressive than pain and physical fatigue, more pervasive and more recurrent, were the torments of his nervous system. He partook of the James family's proneness to hypersensitiveness and melancholia. There is no record of his plunging so deeply into terror as his father in his experience of 'vastation' or his brother in the grip of a vision of sheer evil begotten by melancholia ('the worst kind of melancholy ... which takes the form of panic fear') and centred on memories of a patient observed during a visit to an asylum; nor was he ever, as far as record remains, so overwhelmed as was his sister, Alice, by the tides of neurasthenia.[9] Akin, however, to episodes such as all three recorded was his recollection of a twilit sense of doom in 1869 at the commencement of his first sojourn in London. Homesickness generated the mood, and a paralysing dread of the great city ominously crouched all round him outside his lodgings in Half Moon Street. It was only with an effort of will and the therapy of composition that he restored his equilibrium.[10]

Melancholy, indeed, marked him for her own. His career, it is true, was not frustrated in its beginnings, as William's was, by prostration, depression, and irresoluteness; he emerged earlier and more easily into the clear air of achievement. Others in his life were driven to tragic conclusions, whose ends he marked with particular insight: Clover Adams, for instance, who 'succumbed to hereditary melancholia,' or Constance Fenimore Woolson, victim at last of 'her habitual depression ... chronic melancholy ... liability to suffering.'[11] Nevertheless, the 'knottiness of existence,'[12] which for these two, and others, could be resolved only by suicide, was a bane also to Henry James. Fits of depression marked every stage of his life, culminating in the breakdown which was sequel to the commercial failure of the New York edition of his works.[13]

To several of James's acquaintances his customary gravity of demeanour intimated a sombre view of life. Max Beerbohm, an especially keen and affectionate observer, noted of James that he 'never smiles – rather appalled by life – cloistral.' In conversation Beerbohm recalled that 'Henry James took a tragic view of everyone, throwing up his hands and closing his eyes to shut out the awful vision.'[14] These characteristic gestures, remembered by others who knew James, carry a hint of the histrionic. There seems to have been in James's behaviour, especially when the gathering was congenial and the atmosphere conducive, a marked strain of the performer, the tragic comedian. Even at times perhaps there was a descent to the melancholy buffoon, as in Somerset Maugham's sardonic account of James's trepidation in face of the terrors of the Boston tramway system. 'American streetcars,' he warned Maugham, were 'of a savagery, an inhumanity, a ruthlessness beyond any conception.'[15] Histrionic phrasing and emphasis abound in the letters and the reported conversations of the later phase, the Lamb House – Carlyle Mansions phase of James's life. Who but Henry James would have referred to Christmas as 'this fell anniversary' or announced to his nephew his imminent arrival, in 1905, in the United States in these mock-cowardly terms: 'I can't tell you how I thank you for offering me your manly breast to hurl myself upon in the event of my alighting on the New York dock, four or five weeks hence, in abject and craven terror'?[16] Again and again, in speech or in a letter, he sketches a simple situation in terms redolent of nightmare and portentous with symbols. 'I wander about these great empty streets of Boston,' he confided to Maugham, 'and I never see a soul. I could not be more alone in the Sahara.'[17] What to the casual or unsympathetic spectator appeared ludicrous, mere fussiness and fidgetiness in James's manners and mannerisms, was expressive of a deep-seated trepidation and unremitting vacillation, combined with a paralysing compulsion to consider every alternative, every qualification, offered by even the most mundane of circumstances. It sprang, ultimately, from a sense of the general complexity of life at its best and dreadfulness at its worst. 'Strange and terrible is life,' he declared to Arthur Benson, and, on another occasion, in an unforgettable phrase: 'But I have the imagination of disaster – and see life indeed as ferocious and sinister.'[18] The letters to A.C. Benson belong, it is to be remembered, to a period when James was feeling old and often miserable; moreover some quality of Benson's nature perhaps inspired James, always as a letter-writer acutely conscious of his reader, to a more than usually melodramatic turn of phrase. Even to the privacy of his notebook, however, he could cry out in one of the most resonant passages in modern letters: 'Why does my pen not drop from my hand on approaching the infinite pity and tragedy of all the past? It does, poor helpless pen, with what it meets of the ineffable, what it meets of the cold Medusa-face of life, of all the life *lived*, on every side. *Basta, basta!*'[19]

Yet, for all this, the picture we have received of James among his many friends and acquaintances, on innumerable social and sociable occasions, is not of a man stricken by doom and riddled with gloom. On the contrary, a remarkable robustness of body and mind is transmitted through, for example, such a montage of memories as Simon Nowell-Smith's compilation, *The Legend of the Master* (1948). Most of the examples of James's remarkable prowess as a conversationalist, a monologuist, display good nature and good sense – buoyancy, benignity, shrewdness; above all, humour ranging from the ironic to the roguish and even slightly ribald, couched in language of an almost Micawberian orotundity. Some few listeners grew bored and exasperated as he slowly and experimentally constructed his astonishing periods, but to most hearers they brought long-remembered delight. What man of letters or artist of his times joyed in a wider or fonder circle of friends? To how many did he vouchsafe a glimpse of the ultimate loneliness, the sense of dread that was never obliterated? What was it but discipline, the discipline of the stoic?

'Life,' he wrote to Edith Wharton in 1908, 'is terrible, tragic, perverse and abysmal – besides, *patientons*.'[20] The creed is here pronounced in the voice of the sixty-four-year-old James, but it must have been lived by all his life. Endurance under adversity – cheerful endurance – marked every stage. It was what led his mother to compare him, while he was in his thirtieth year, with William, his brother: 'If, dear Harry, you could only have imparted to him a few grains of your own blessed hopefulness, he would have been well long ago.'[21] William, in his turn, quite capable at times of severely censuring his brother and his works, could write all the same of the 'angelic humility' with which Henry received such criticism. To Alice, his sister, he figured as 'Henry the patient.' 'I have given him endless care and anxiety but notwithstanding this and the fantastic nature of my troubles I have never seen an impatient look upon his face or heard an unsympathetic or misunderstanding sound cross his lips.'[22]

'I have seen him ill,' wrote A.C. Benson, 'fatigued, melancholy, but never either dreary or listless ... '"One has to be *equal* to things," I can hear him say.'[23]

This was the discipline of love and friendship. More vital still was the discipline of art. How highly Henry James esteemed mastery and control as an artist is conveyed by many of his writings, by *The Tragic Muse*, for instance, or *Roderick Hudson*, or his numerous stories of painters and writers. For his own career the discipline of art bore several meanings: diligence, integrity, flexibility, unremitting self-criticism and revision, the fascination of the difficult ('it being really, at bottom, only difficulty that interests me'[24]). Discipline signified also the surmounting of disabilities that might keep the artist from the proper execution of his art: illness, despondency, loss, apprehensiveness. He was capable, that is, of applying to his own case the cure he prescribed for Grace Norton and Edith Wharton. Overcome the anguish by living it through to its ultimate pang. Rout it by going through the motions of life.

We can observe this process at work, on a small scale, in that letter written to his mother out of the homesickness and dread that gripped him during his first hours as a lodger in Half Moon Street in 1869. The letter displays line by line the very process of exorcism. First he gives way utterly to the devastating mood. Then he works his way out, concluding: 'But I have scribbled enough. Cancel, dearest mother, all the maudlinity of the beginning of my letter; the fit is over; the ghost is laid; Richard's himself again. I assure you, I shall do very well.'[25]

What is still more significant and more relevant is his application of the same remedy to certain crises in his career as a writer. Confronting these and surmounting them, he achieved something greater than equilibrium, a sort of transcendence of anxiety or discouragement. Practical everyday stoicism, the mechanics of survival – my much-disciplined patience'[26] – rose on these occasions to the height of creative stoicism. Out of disaster came new resolve, new accomplishment. Sheer plod sufficed for survival. From the major crises he drew elation, re-invigoration as an artist, re-orientation as a theorist. Such an instance is documented in the notebook entry for 22 October 1891, written while he still felt bowed down in spirit by the 'déboires and distresses consequent on the production of The American by Edward Compton.' Nonetheless, he puts down his confidence in theatrical success in the future, and continues in this strain:

> Meanwhile the soothing, the healing, the sacred and salutary refuge from all these
> vulgarities and pains is simply to lose myself in this quiet, this blessed and uninvaded
> workroom in the inestimable effort and refreshment of art, in resolute and beneficent pro-
> duction ... To keep at it – to strive toward the perfect, the ripe, the only best; to go on, by
> one's own clear light, with patience, courage, and continuity, to live with the high vision
> and effort, to justify one's self – and oh, so greatly! – all in time: this and this alone can be
> my only lesson from *anything* ... The consolation, the dignity, the joy of life are that
> discouragements and lapses, depressions and darknesses come to one only as one stands
> *without* – I mean without the luminous paradise of art. As soon as I really re-enter
> it – cross the loved threshold – stand in the high chamber, and the gardens divine – the
> whole realm widens out again before me and around me – the air of life fills my lungs –
> the light of achievement flushes over all the place, and I believe, I see, I *do*.[27]

The entry for the following day makes clear that the mood of 'indolence ... vagueness ... nervousness' was not to be short-lived, and makes equally clear that James knew how to find a way out of despair. The years that followed upon these entries were among the most productive of his career.

Another, and more devastating, engagement with disaster was the catastrophic première of *Guy Domville* on the evening of 5 January 1895. Here was disaster in every way: the shutting-down of hope for fame and fortune as a dramatist; the wastage of time and energy; the nightmare confrontation with an audience a sizable part of which loudly proclaimed their contempt for his exquisite theatrical confection. 'There followed an abominable quarter of an hour,' he wrote to his brother four days later, 'during which all the forces of civilization in the house waged a battle of the most gallant, prolonged and sustained applause with the hoots and jeers and catcalls of the roughs ... It was a cheering scene, as you may imagine, for a nervous, sensitive, exhausted author to face – and you must spare my going over again the horrid hour, or those of disappointment and depression that have followed it; from which last, however, I am rapidly and resolutely, thank God, emerging.'[28]

To this horrifying experience the sequel was an act of heroism, personal and artistic. The letters and notebook entries which speak of the period of recuperation testify magnificently to James's prodigious resilience and fortitude, his capacity to turn disaster to triumph. The notebook entry for 14 February 1895 mounts to a veritable ecstasy of mastery regained. Again, as in the letter to his mother, he can be seen to be in the act of cheering himself up by the process itself of considering the catastrophe. On this occasion, however, as in the entries of October 1891, the notebook records an outcome that is more than a mere salvaging operation. It is redemptive and creative. James discovers in the exertions of his dramatic years a clue to richer achievement in his true *métier*:

> Has a *part* of all this wasted passion and squandered time (of the last 5 years) been simply the precious lesson, taught me in that roundabout and devious, that cruelly expensive, way, *of the singular value for a narrative plan too* of the ... divine principle of the Scenario? If that *has* been one side of the moral of the whole unspeakable, the whole tragic experience, I almost bless the pangs and the pains and the miseries of it ... IF, I say, I have crept round through long apparent barrenness, through suffering and sadness intolerable, to that rare perception – why my infinite little loss is converted into an almost infinite little gain ... But how much of the precious there may be in it I can only tell by trying.[29]

On that same day, 14 February, James returned in his notebook to two themes which, as his powers recovered and increased, would within a decade yield fulfilment in two of his masterworks, *The Wings of the Dove* and *The Golden Bowl*. He had, indeed, risen to the consummation that had shone out for him on 23 January, a mere eighteen days after the evening of fiasco in the theatre:

> I take up my *own* old pen again – the pen of all my old unforgettable efforts and sacred struggles. To myself – today – I need say no more. Large and full and high the future still opens. It is now indeed that I may do the work of my life. And I will ... I have only to *face* my problems.[30]

Such episodes vividly exemplify the stoicism which James preached and practised. Its first phase is given over to bare survival, the holding of one's position
against the onslaughts of illness, depression, calamity. 'Sorrow comes in great
waves ... but it rolls over us, and though it may almost smother us it leaves us on the
spot and we know that if it is strong we are stronger, inasmuch as it passes and we
remain.'[31] So he wrote to Grace Norton in 1883 and, twenty-three years later, in a
letter to W.E. Norris, he adheres faithfully to the same principle: 'The prize (of long
activity and sweet survival) is with those whose hardness is greater than other
hardnesses.'[32]

In its second and more splendid phase it seems to have made use of adversity as a
spur to creativity. Suffering became the alembic by which consciousness was made
more intense. Here was a moral and psychological procedure that served James well
throughout his long life as a man and as an artist. Even late in his life, when his
physical and mental system was most exposed to pain and despondency, he could
draw rueful gratification from the privilege of existence. As late as 21 March 1914 he
could respond optimistically to the pessimism of Henry Adams, to the 'melancholy
outpouring' with which Adams acknowledged his receiving *Notes of a Son and
Brother*. That they are both 'lone survivors,' James concedes, and that their past
lives appear as though at the bottom of an abyss. 'Of course ... there's no use talking' – here James is probably echoing Adams's letter – 'unless one particularly
wants to.' The point for James, and the point of his autobiographical writings, is, as
he reminds Adams, that 'one *can*, strange to say, still want to – or at least can
behave as if one did.' And so he continues, in a veritable ironic flourish of triumph:

> I still find my consciousness interesting – under *cultivation* of the interest. Cultivate it
> *with* me, dear Henry – that's what I hoped to make you do – to cultivate yours for all that
> it has in common with mine. *Why* mine yields an interest I don't know that I can tell you,
> but I don't challenge or quarrel with it – I encourage it with a ghastly grin. You see I still,
> in the presence of life (or of what you deny to be such) have reactions – as many as
> possible – and the book I sent you is a proof of them. It's, I suppose, because I am that
> queer monster, the artist, an obstinate finality, an inexhaustible sensibility. Hence the
> reactions – appearances, memories, many things, go on playing upon it with consequences
> that I note and 'enjoy' (grim word!) noting. It all takes doing – and I *do*. I believe I
> shall do yet again – it is still an act of life.[33]

The 'ghastly grin' of the old stoic celebrates, however ruefully, the artist's power of
extracting precious substance from every kind of experience.

This letter of 1914, when James was nearly seventy-two, marks the culmination
of a lifelong practice of his own variant of stoicism. With stoicism as a formulated

system James was acquainted from early manhood. He contributed to the April 1866 issue of the *North American Review* a review of *The Works of Epictetus* by Thomas Wentworth Higginson. In this early essay James decides that the writings of 'the great Stoic moralist' have limited but undeniable relevance for modern readers, as 'a theory of conduct,' a practical guide to living and acting, a rule of life, 'as far removed as possible from metaphysics.' 'We say,' the twenty-two-year-old Henry James wrote of stoicism, 'System of morals, because it is in effect nothing of a philosophy ... Virtue consists in a state of moral satisfaction with those things which reason tells us are in our power, and in a sublime independence of those things which are not in our power.' James continued:

> It is easy to understand the efficacy of such a doctrine as this in the age of Nero and Domitian, before Christianity had had time to suggest that virtue is not necessarily a servitude, and that the true condition of happiness is freedom ... Stoicism, then, is essentially unphilosophic. It simplifies human troubles by ignoring half of them. It is a wilful blindness, a constant begging of the question. It fosters apathy and paralyzes the sensibilities ... if the majority of mankind become Stoics, it is certain that social immobility would ensue as the result of so general an assumption of passivity.[34]

The character of the author Epictetus James found admirable – 'he must have been a wholesome spectacle in that diseased age' – but he rejects the doctrine of stoicism as Epictetus advocated it. 'Let us take Epictetus as we take all things in these critical days, eclectically.' It is evident that the kind of workaday stoicism that James urged upon his distressed friends and applied to his own woes was far from doctrinaire; even more, that the creative kind of response to adversity testified to by his notebooks and letters far transcended the submissiveness and narrowness of the classical formulation. In his novels and tales, moreover, the stoic element in his view of life found another kind of expression.

> The great question as to a poet or novelist is, How does he feel about life? what, in the last analysis, is his philosophy? When vigorous writers have reached maturity we are at liberty to look in their works for some expression of a total view of the world they have been so actively observing. This is the most interesting thing their works offer us.[35]

In such unqualified terms James declared his position in an essay of 1874 on the novels and stories of Turgenev. From this position he chides in turn Dickens, Balzac, Gautier, and Charles de Bernard. 'A novelist soon has need of a little philosophy,' he maintains in the course of his censorious comments on *Our Mutual Friend*.[36] In Balzac, the novelist whom on the whole he considered 'The Master of Us All,' he deplored the same sort of defect as he discerned in Dickens:

[Balzac] had no natural sense of morality, and this we cannot help thinking a serious fault in a novelist. Be the morality false or true, the writer's deference to it greets us as a kind of essential perfume. We find such a perfume in Shakespeare; we find it, in spite of his so-called cynicism, in Thackeray; we find it, potently, in George Eliot, in George Sand, in Turgénieff. They care for moral questions; they are haunted by a moral ideal. This southern slope of the mind, as we may call it, was very barren in Balzac.[37]

No novelist was ever more persistently aware of the peculiar relationship between philosophy and fiction than was Henry James. Overt exposition of doctrine must always be, in his theory of the novel, pernicious. A vital passage in his essay 'The Art of Fiction' is given over to a repudiation of Walter Besant's criteria for the novel; none is more vigorously rejected than 'a conscious moral purpose.'[38] Open didacticism figured to James as a breach of the aesthetic contract between the work of literature and the reader's imagination. At the same time, where is there to be found a novelist so 'moral' as James? Implied discriminations greet us in every paragraph, every line, but always within the fictional context, as reflections or utterances by the characters, or as incitements in the narrative to the reader's judgment. 'The southern slope of the mind' is luxuriant in James and the seedbed of some of his most memorable effects. 'The deepest quality of a work of art will always be,' James maintained in 'The Art of Fiction,' 'the quality of the mind of the producer.'[39]

We cannot be surprised, then, that James's characters should partake of his sense of life and provide enactments of his kind of response to its demands. They are all, in varying degrees, creatures of concern, functioning within the dialectic of consciousness and conscience. To themselves their moral natures are defined with acute precision. Situations demand choice and choice begets consequences, which are foreseeable and, almost always, painful. Adaptation to pain or self-denial illustrates character and evaluates decisions. Stoicism – adjustment to moral necessity – may include a range of responses, from the numbness of barely holding on to the power of transforming deprivation into magnanimity. Of all James's characters, at any rate of the major ones, it can be said that they manage to maintain their dignity. They are strong enough to make the decision, to accept the situation, that integrity seems to impose upon them, and they have the grace to walk away from the scene unbowed and unflustered. Stoicism, in James's fictive world, is a manifestation of style.

Such is the style in which Lambert Strether sticks by his decision to return to America – though perhaps not to Woollett, Massachusetts – at the close of *The Ambassadors*, rejecting the sanctuary offered him by Maria Gostrey, and fully aware of the value of what he rejects, as well as the consolations of whatever kind that Madame de Vionnet would be prepared to provide. '"But all the same I must go ... To be right ... That, you see, is my only logic. Not, out of the whole affair, to have got anything for myself."' To the point, indeed, is Miss Gostrey's rejoinder: '"It isn't so much your *being* 'right' – it's your horrible sharp eye for what makes you so.'' [40] When the choice is made with so much grace, such deference to the claims of one's moral nature, 'renunciation' seems an inept word and 'stoicism' inadequate. Strether's practice of that rule of life will begin with his return to the United States. Another instance, less clear cut, is that of Fleda Vetch in *The Spoils of Poynton*. This is a novel that many readers find exasperating; Fleda strikes them as a victim of moral hysteria rather than an exponent of rational decency. It is a good test of a reader's devotion to James. To him Fleda was a compositional triumph. Both in his notebook entries while he was working on *The Spoils of Poynton* and in the preface written for the New York edition, he exults over having created so consummate an example of the 'free spirit': 'the free spirit, always much tormented, and by no means always triumphant, is heroic, ironic, pathetic or whatever, and, as exemplified in the record of Fleda Vetch, for instance, "successful," only through having remained free.' [41] Free, yes, to make a choice, but bound by her moral nature to choose the way of stoicism. Fleda is of the same Jamesian breed as Strether. 'She was one of those who could pick themselves up' (SP, p 105). She knows to the last spasm of pain what she is doing. She misses out on even the Maltese Cross, retaining as sole souvenir and emblem of her repudiated 'romance' with Owen Gereth the 'small pin-cushion, costing sixpence, in which the letter F was marked out with pins' (SP, p 64), but she has maintained her own moral logic and preserved her dignity. Nor is her course of action entirely devoid of beauty. This quality James confers in the tone and imagery with which he describes Fleda as sensing the old maid aunt's presence at Ricks – ' "the impression somehow of something dreamed and missed, something reduced, relinquished, resigned: the poetry, as it were, of something sensibly *gone* ... a great accepted pain –" ' (SP, p 249). Isabel Archer, in *The Portrait of a Lady*, who seems to herself and for a while to the reader, to be a free spirit, is manoeuvred by circumstances and her own temperament into a situation within which at last she has even less space to operate than Fleda Vetch. Her final decision, to speed down the straight and narrow path from Caspar Goodwood's inordinate embrace to her husband's house in Rome, has been described as ambiguous, but it seems scarcely to be doubted that Isabel Archer returns to do her duty, to watch over her stepdaughter Pansy, to resume a life almost flagrantly stoical.

As James perceived in his youthful reading of Epictetus, stoicism tends to be a 'philosophy' of servitude, submission, and shrinkage. Examples abound of characters who diminish their desires to fit their circumstances. There comes to mind the ultimate image of *Washington Square*, of Catherine Sloper sentencing herself, with stoic resoluteness, to emotional life-imprisonment; the image of Mrs Brash, eponymous character of 'The Beldonald Holbein,' who has, it strikes the observer-narrator, 'known how to be ugly – it was the only thing she had learnt save, if possible, how not to mind it'; [42] the image of Juliana Bordereau in *The Aspern Papers* who, having had an abundance of life in her earlier years, can summon the fortitude for accepting the terms of her final phase: '"I've sat here many a day and have had enough of arbours in my time. But I'm not afraid to wait till I'm called."'[43] Ralph Touchett, too, contrives to acknowledge his limitations with grace: 'A secret hoard of indifference ... came to his aid and helped to reconcile him to sacrifice ... His serenity was but the array of wild flowers niched in his ruin.'[44] In the central irony of *The Portrait of a Lady* Ralph's single move towards enlarging his prison condemns Isabel.

The interaction of destinies must be effected more discreetly. Several of James's shorter pieces written between 1900 and 1910 are versions of the same situation, of a man and a woman who join forces for mutual solace and support as they confront the question of what can still be salvaged from 'the ugliness, the grossness, the stupidity, the cruelty'[45] of life. This is a pattern into which Lambert Strether and Maria Gostrey are not to be permitted to subside. John Marcher and May Bartrum of 'The Beast in the Jungle' represent, on the other hand, the annihilation of hope by false stoicism: the egotism of the man who 'marches' through life, his sensibilities stifled by self-regard, negates the woman's capacity for silent endurance and understanding. 'The Bench of Desolation' interestingly reverses the pattern. The woman takes the initiative and intervenes in the man's destiny. Kate Cookham successfully sues Herbert Dodd for breach of promise; ten years later she re-enters his life proffering the money the courts had awarded her with the profits on it she has built up over the years – years which have ground him down to total destitution and loneliness, ten years of bitterness and squalid struggle for him and his wife. Kate Cookham did it all for him, to compel him to an effort he would never, unspurred, have been capable of. Now, as then, all she desires is to take care of him. His life has been ruined, his personality shrivelled – whereas she has been made finer by her years of thrift and labour – but as the story beautifully closes they are united in a tremulous pact against the miseries of the remaining years. At last, 'she was,' in the story's final sentence, 'beside him on the bench of desolation.'[46] Somewhat more buoyant is the union against adversity of the plucky young pair of journalists in 'The Papers' or of the failed novelist, Mrs Harvey, and Stuart Snaith, the failed painter, of 'Broken Wings.' Out of their common failure they can rise, together, not merely to resignation but to a common revival of hope and energy:

> 'If we're beaten!' she then continued. 'Let us at least be beaten together!' He took her
> in his arms; she let herself go, and he held her long and close for the compact. But when
> they had recovered themselves enough to handle their agreement more responsibly, the
> words in which they confirmed it broke in sweetness as well as sadness from both
> together: 'And now to work!'[47]

On several of the fine-grained middle-aged celibates of James's final period is imposed a peculiarly harrowing test of endurance: the horrors of the modern metropolis. 'The Jolly Corner' (1908), 'Crapy Cornelia' (1909), and 'A Round of Visits' (1910) derive images and obsessions from James's revisitation of his natal city early in the century, observations and sensations of the sort so graphically recorded in *The American Scene* (1907). The protagonists of these stories seem to have grown out of James's own experience and reactions; indeed, in a letter to Henrietta Reubell, who had admired and understood 'Crapy Cornelia,' he made the identification explicit; 'You are not Cornelia, but I am much White-Mason, and I shall again sit by your fire.'[48] For White-Mason, as for Spencer Brydon in 'The Jolly Corner,' an alternative to the atrocities of the new New York is to accept sanctuary by the fireside of a perceptive and sensitive woman, who knew him when he was young and who is content to comfort and companion him as he grows older. In her serene and sedate little haven, furnished with a few good pieces from the old, discriminating New York world, silver, photographs, and an ambience of ciga-rette-smoke and security, they can wait out together the rest of their lives. Not so felicitously provided for, Mark Monteith in 'A Round of Visits,' presumably James's last story in this vein, is obliged to achieve moral equilibrium for himself and by himself:

> The miracle indeed soon grew clearer: Providence had, on some obscure system, chosen this very ridiculous hour to save him from the cultivation of the sin of selfishness, the obsession of egotism, and was breaking him to its will by constantly directing his attention to the claims of others.[49]

These small-scale pictures of life from James's late years, some of them among his finest things, are centred on the defeated and aging who have come to terms with their condition. The same period produced two masterpieces – *The Golden Bowl* and *The Wings of the Dove* – in which the altruism of youth is dedicated to preserv-ing what is of value in the present and making possible a better future. Maggie Verver of *The Golden Bowl* is the busiest little stoic of all James's characters. In her silent and solitary campaign to correct her domestic situation without disturbing its equilibrium – 'all this high decorum would hang by a hair'[50] – Maggie, the Princess, adopts stoicism as a strategy. Once she has divined that her husband and her father's wife are adulterously allied, she resolves to forgo the egotism of passionate resent-ment – 'the blind resentment,' her friend and confidante, Fanny Assingham, calls it, 'with which, in her place, ninety-nine women out of a hundred would act' (p 125). But Maggie does not act, does not utter a word of complaint: 'she hadn't com-plained, not by the quaver of a syllable ... she would be hanged – she conversed with herself in strong language – if she had been from beginning to end anything but pliable and mild' (p 44). She exploits her talent for hypocrisy (p 142), she accepts the ignominy of the scapegoat (p 234), she submits to Charlotte's public embrace (pp 251–2), she lies as frequently as circumstances demand. She is impressed, Fanny Assingham is impressed, even the reader is impressed, by how much Maggie can endure. She proclaims the limits in a famous exchange: 'I can bear anything.'

'Oh, "bear"'!' Mrs Assingham fluted.
'For love,' said the Princess.
Fanny hesitated. 'Of your father?'
'For love,' Maggie repeated.
It kept her friend watching. 'Of your husband?'
'For love,' Maggie said again.   (Pp 115–16)

Maggie's motives are mixed, her course of action is devious, her ultimate victory ambiguous, a mingling of bliss and dismay. Readers divide sharply in their responses to *The Golden Bowl*. Of a clearer and purer quality, it may be, is the suppression of egotism in Milly Theale of *The Wings of the Dove*. 'She showed nothing but her beauty and her strength,'[51] says Merton Densher of their last meeting after she has learned that their relationship means less than she has taken it for. Milly has ardently desired to live, to love, and to be loved. Her immense inner strength, reconfirmed by her musings in Regent's Park, in one of James's most powerful scenes (pp 248–54), gathers to its utmost in her reception of Lord Mark's blighting news. 'He dealt her his blow,' marvels Mrs Stringham, 'and she took it without a sign' (p 285). Even in her anguish Milly masters her passion. 'She doesn't *want* to die ... She lies there stiffening herself and clinging to it all. So I thank God ... that she's so quiet ... She's more than quiet. She's grim' (p 274). But out of her desolation Milly, magnificently, confers upon Densher and Kate a kind of benediction – a magnanimous and munificent gift, timed for arrival, after her death, on Christmas Eve, which should make their marriage possible. 'I used,' says Kate at the end, 'to call her, in my stupidity – for want of anything better – a dove. Well, she stretched out her wings, and it was to *that* they reached. They cover us.' And Densher concurs. 'They cover us' (p 404). Kate's image suggests an irony that Milly certainly never intended. But her strength and beauty have, in the working out of the situation, transformed the relationship between Densher and Kate – 'We shall never be again as we were' (p 405) – the strength and beauty of transcendent stoicism.

RICHARD ALLAN DAVISON

A Reading of
Frank Norris's *The Pit*[1]

Although I have discovered no direct evidence that Frank Norris read Marcus Aurelius or the stoic philosophers, much that is urged in their philosophy is evident in many of Norris's writings, particularly in his last novel, *The Pit*. When describing the Roman emperor's stoic philosophy, one finds oneself using words and phrases such as 'duty,' 'patience,' 'obligation,' 'courage,' 'fortitude,' 'practical goodness,' and 'divine reason.' Norris extols all these virtues in his writings, placing them in a more clearly Christian context. When his characters violate these rules of conduct, they are out of the rhythm of an ordered universe and suffer accordingly. The only characters that seem to survive or die with dignity are those who have learned the lessons preached by the stoic Marcus Aurelius and his Christian predecessor St Paul.[2] These characters function in the context of a moral reality. Furthermore, attunement to this moral order is ameliorative.

Even in what has often been called one of Norris's most naturalistic works, 'The Puppets and the Puppy,'[3] the central character announces: 'And each time I am re-melted and re-cast I become a finer soldier – larger, firmer on my base, more life-like. Thus the race is improved. Immortality is but the betterment of the race.' Although in 'Lauth'[4] the hero's death is hardly stoical, Norris talks of a 'mysterious impulse [that] drives us to seek paths that lead upward.' Vandover's weakness, in *Vandover and the Brute* (1914), is the antithesis of stoicism and he is destroyed without gaining enlightenment.[5] In *Blix* (1899) Condy Rivers learns self-discipline and honesty from Travis Bessimer, Norris's spokeswoman. Fortitude, duty, and determination are crucial to Ward Bennett of *A Man's Woman* (1900), but it is another spokeswoman for Norris, Lloyd Searight, whose speech on heroism, courage, patience, and endurance prompts Bennett to overcome his guilt at not reaching the Pole on his first expedition. It is the stoical strain in Lloyd that convinces her new husband to undertake another expedition that threatens years of separation. Her enlightened sense of noble duty and sacrifice transcends Bennett's pure determination that earlier allowed 'no light of reason in his actions.'[6] All three major characters in *McTeague* (1899) violate the major principles of stoicism. They are all destroyed. Magnus Derrick of *The Octopus* (1901) reaches his lowest ebb when he violates stoic principles. Shelgrim's sophistic 'Blame conditions, not men' (II, 285) would seem to excuse his irresponsible actions as well as Derrick's. The central core of the novel, however, is better reflected in Vanamee's admonitions that 'Good never dies' and in his vision of a moral reality, a framework of reason in the universe. It is Annixter's belated acceptance of a philosophy embracing the virtues of love and goodness that makes his death so poignant, so nearly tragic.[7]

While St Paul is quoted extensively and used centrally in *The Octopus*, overt references to religion in *The Pit* are not as evident, often confined to Curtis Jadwin's adherence to D.L. Moody's Sunday school morality. But religion in the sense of a transcendental moral law is every bit as evident, albeit muted, in Norris's last novel. Both novels reveal the dangers of sophistry. Both Shelgrim and Jadwin rationalize and excuse their abuses of power, their toying with the laws of nature. Norris nowhere condones Jadwin's attempt to corner the wheat market any more than he condones the manipulations of Magnus Derrick or Shelgrim. Page Dearborn (functioning as a lesser Vanamee) is a barometer reflecting the moral impulses in *The Pit*. Through her (and eventually through Laura Dearborn) Norris points to a muted optimism that smacks of humanistic stoicism, made mutedly optimistic by Pauline Christianity, and affirms the principle of moral order in the universe. The dramatic exploration of his characters's involvement in this universe is handled with a clear sense of structure and artistic control.

In a letter to Isaac Marcosson, Norris demonstrates the awareness of a purpose, if one not always followed. It contains his only extant comments on the structure of *The Pit*:

> The story is told through Laura Dearborn. She occupies the center of the stage all the time, and I shall try to interest the reader more in the problems of her character and career than in any other human element in the book. The two main themes, consequently, are the story of Jadwin's corner of the May wheat and the story of his wife's 'affair' with Corthell. I shall try to show that all these are American issues, modern, typical and important. The 'big scenes' will be the scene between Laura and Corthell in her apartment the evening that Jadwin fails to appear, and the scene on the floor of the Chicago Board of Trade when the Jadwin corner breaks.[8]

Norris, then, planned to make Laura's character development the central element in the novel. However, although he did succeed in interesting the reader more in Laura than 'in any other human element in the book,'[9] the fascination of the giddy price fluctuations of the wheat in the huge monolithic Board of Trade Building threatens to overshadow all else. It is Jadwin's attempt to corner the nation's wheat and the wheat's inevitable cornering of him that are the most dynamic elements in a novel that draws its very title[10] from the scene of his most enthralling battles. It is the scene of Jadwin's crushing defeat in the Pit that is the bigger of the two 'big scenes.' And, although Jadwin's character lacks the depth and complexity of Laura's in Norris's portrayal, his character is both the more magnetic and the more sympathetic. In fact, Jadwin, as memorable as Silas Lapham or Frank Cowperwood, is potentially one of the great figures in American literature. Why does he fall short? How important to the limitations of Jadwin's characterization is the effect of Norris's major emphasis on Laura?

An examination of the aesthetic unity of *The Pit* reveals Norris's growing awareness of the potential tragedy involved in lack of communication among individuals and the problems that transpire when one is out of tune with the tenets of stoicism and the moral forces of the universe.

By narrowing his canvas to one city in one locale of America, Norris again follows his dicta in 'An American School of Fiction.'[11] In fact most of the action, with the exception of the first scene, occurs in two buldings – the Chicago Board of Trade and the Jadwin mansion. Having spent his childhood in Chicago and months of research on the market there, Norris once more drew upon personal experiences[12] to flesh out a skeleton plot. However autobiographical and locally American much of the action may be, his probings of the human condition in an affluent society have enough universal implications to make *The Pit* a worthy successor to *The Octopus*. It is a sturdy middle link in what was to be a world-spanning wheat trilogy.[13]

Perhaps because of this happy blend of universals with particulars, Norris achieved his deepest penetration into the psychology of his characters in *The Pit*. Jadwin is a more sympathetic character to us than is Magnus Derrick, and Laura becomes more alive than Hilma Tree. Even the other, minor, characters are more complex than their counterparts in *The Octopus*. Just as the entire novel is dichotomized into two major conflicting centres of interest from the initial counterpoint of business and art in chapter 1, so there is a contrast in each of the main characters.

The Pit contains considerable evaluation of various fields of art. Much of this commentary Norris puts into the mouth of the aesthete, Sheldon Corthell, but it becomes apparent that, even though Corthell demonstrates a refined taste for art, his pontifications are pretentious. If his snobbishness, delicately trimmed beard, and preference for cigarettes over cigars do not suggest that he is as overbalanced on the artistic side[14] as Jadwin is overbalanced in his commercial drive to corner the wheat, then Landry Court's astute criticism and the artist's own almost psuedo-Le Contean[15] speeches on aesthetics should. Through Landry's comments Norris reveals in Corthell's otherwise appealing character a falseness that is reminiscent of the bohemian dilettantes Norris lambastes in his critical writings, and of such ignoble types as Mrs Cedargist's leeching 'artistic' protégés in *The Octopus*.[16]

Corthell does point out some palatable artistic truths, such as the superiority of Liszt's 'Mephisto Waltz' over the 'Anvil Chorus.' However, his lengthy disquisition on the categories of art and the passion of musical creativity (dramatically interrupted by Jadwin's announcement of his 'killing' on the market) seems too precious for Norris to be offering in earnest. Corthell, having just demonstrated his musical abilities on the organ in the Jadwin library, speaks to an enraptured audience of one – Laura:

> 'Of all the arts, music, to my notion, is the most intimate. At the other end of the scale you have architecture, which is an expression of and appeal to the common multitude, a whole people, the mass. Fiction and painting, and even poetry, are affairs of the classes, reaching the groups of the educated. But music – ah, that is different, it is one soul speaking to another soul. The composer meant it for you and himself. No one else has anything to do with it. Because his soul was heavy and broken with grief, or bursting with passion, or tortured with doubt, or searching for some unnamed ideal, he has come to you – you of all the people in the world – with his message, and he tells you of his yearnings and his sadness, knowing that you will sympathize, knowing that your soul has, like his, been acquainted with grief, or with gladness; and in the music his soul speaks to yours, beats with it, blends with it, yes, is even, spiritually, married to it.'
>
> And as he spoke the electrics all over the gallery flashed out in a sudden blaze, and Curtis Jadwin entered the room, crying out:
>
> 'Are you here, Laura? By George, my girl, we pulled it off, and I've cleaned up five – hundred – thousand – dollars.'[17]   (IX, 240–1)

In this scene Norris is deftly undercutting both the pseudo-romantic, unrealistic verbal claptrap of an aesthete trying to impress a sensitive, but critically naive, young woman with his fine sensibility, and the hard-headed, rather boorish, tunnel-visioned concern of a market speculator who has momentarily shut out all else from his life but business. At the same time Norris's dramatic, rather comical juxtaposition of the two most extreme points of view in the novel suggests a need for some communication between these disparate worlds, each with its own peculiar weaknesses and strengths.

Norris here, as in *The Octopus*, is attempting to demonstrate the efficacy of the surging power in the continuum of nature on man, and the dynamics of love on human relationships. Only for this novel his camera shifts from the railroad agents and wheatfields of California to the stockbrokers and the Pit of the Chicago Board of Trade; from characters whose stage is ten thousand broad acres of prairie to those whose dramas are enacted in the tight enclosure of city rooms. Instead of depicting the maturation of several characters, he focuses on one. I do not agree with Charles Kaplan's statement: '*The Pit* could, with equal (or greater) appropriateness have been called *The Rise of Curtis Jadwin*.'[18] For it is Jadwin's lack of growth that leads to his destruction. His only spiritual movement is away from his wife and their early marital happiness. The greatest manifestation of change is seen in his mental and physical deterioration. The morality in his Sunday school projects and his abhorrence of gambling are easily brushed aside by the temptations of the Pit. Unlike Silas Lapham, Jadwin hardly takes the time to rationalize his inconsistencies; at no time does he make a choice against his speculative impulse for moral or ethical betterment. *The Rise of Laura Dearborn Jadwin* would be a far more appropriate title than Kaplan's.

Not enough has been said about the effect of the experience of love and suffering on Laura's maturation – a maturation that Norris develops from the slow-paced early pages of exposition to the stirring pages of the climax.

The structure of *The Pit*, embodying and reinforcing Norris's most mature observations, is more complex than most critics have noted.[19] Reinforcing the broader structural elements are more subtle strands and threads that give the novel a greater toughness. The business-art dichotomy that permeates the entire work warrants closer examination. Critics have mentioned Corthell as artist and Jadwin as businessman, between whom Laura is torn, but they have neglected the structurally important antitheses in each one of the other characters, many of whom bridge this gap between the uncompromising business world and the world of art so often associated with Laura's romantic reveries. Most of the major and minor characters alike are mirrors or sounding-boards for either Laura or Jadwin.

Page Dearborn, impressionable, serious, naive about her own life through much of the novel, demonstrates a growing, penetrating influence on her older sister's character. She serves as a kind of philosophical instructress. Relatively unimportant in her own right, she is one of many strong links between the love plot and the business plot. It is Page who first attempts to draw her sister's attention towards the business world (IX, 6). It is Page who continually hammers at Laura's proud, selfish exterior, sees the blindness in Laura's attempt to live up to the affected *hauteur* of her 'grand manner' (IX, 11). Page rapidly outgrows her own morbid attachment to the deceptive allurement of romantic novels and offers her older sister practical advice about human relationships. This advice is crucial to Laura's maturing love for Jadwin. Yet, human and fallible, Page also retains much of the naivety of inexperienced youth. Although she strives to understand Landry's business affairs, by the time of their marriage she has achieved only a general awareness of the complex workings of the market. It is Norris's allowance of her semi-comprehension that makes Page such a perfect witness to the 'Jadwin failure' from the gallery overlooking the Pit. Much of the scene, climaxing in Jadwin's Bull charge into the Pit, after which he is jeered at by the victorious Bears and led dumbly off the floor by Landry, is viewed through Page's eyes. Page brings to Laura the report of a great man whom some cheered on appearance, but who seemed to have suffered a severe defeat. She admonishes Laura to take a greater interest in Jadwin's affairs. Only later do these words make their impression. But it is largely because of Page's constant demand for practical goodness and adherence to moral obligations that Laura shifts her intellectual allegiance and emotional sympathy to her husband when he appears in the doorway, haggard and exhausted, obliterating her impulsive decision to run away with Sheldon Corthell.

Landry Court, clerk in 'the great brokerage firm of Gretry, Converse and Co.,' erstwhile suitor of Laura, later husband of Page, is also an effective link between the two major plots. It is Landry who buys and sells Jadwin's wheat from the first scene in the Pit to the very last. His admiration for Jadwin as a financial genius and magnetic father-figure carries over from the Pit into the love plot. Jadwin's personality has affected Landry so deeply that he harbours no jealousy when the older man wins Laura, even though Page is a soothing consolation prize. Landry's praise of Jadwin and his refusal to desert him during the devastating moments of the crash succeed in underlining the more sympathetic qualities of the financier as well as his own sense of loyalty. Landry embodies the qualities that Norris admired in many of his bright fraternity brothers at Berkeley. Successful in business, receptive to culture, Landry, in his marriage to Page, represents a merging of two worlds that are so long to remain apart in the Jadwin-Laura marriage. Landry and Page's marriage prefigures the subsequent harmony of the Jadwins's.

But Landry, too, is a mixture of contradictions, only some of which are resolved. He is also a dual personality.[20] He is little Landry Court, the callow suitor of Laura, who forgets appointments and makes social *faux pas*. In the Pit he is Landry Court the businessman, a fighter with a level head, fortitude, and a keen financial sense. In the same dual manner Norris draws the other characters, all of whom participate in or comment upon the main action.

Cressler is the calm, steady, kindly feeder of pigeons who admonishes Jadwin of the evils of speculation; he is also a reckless speculator. Mrs Cressler is a good friend of Jadwin and quick to praise his virtues to Laura; she is also a gossip. Crookes is a double-dealing, cold-blooded tycoon who can give tribute to a better man even if he thinks the man a partial fool. The closest candidate for villain in the novel, Crookes, does not embody the evil, the nearly motiveless malignancy, of S. Behrman of *The Octopus*. Like all those struggling in the Pit, Crookes is concerned with his private fortune. Although he lacks the propensity for joy and excitement of battle that is Jadwin's chief reason for fanatical involvement in the Pit, Crookes does have a respect for the wheat that Jadwin does not learn until he has experienced what is his first and final defeat. Crookes acknowledges a force in the universe that is more powerful than he. Unlike Behrman, he will not allow himself to be crushed by the wheat. He knows that Jadwin's failure is due to no lack of greatness or genius, but to the overwhelming power of millions of bushels of wheat, pouring from thousands of farms all over the world in a torrent that sweeps out of its path all who attempt to block it in its rush to the sea and the open mouths of Europe and Asia. Crookes also knows that Jadwin's failure is partly due to the rebellion of other speculators. With all this insight Crookes embraces many of the opportunistic attitudes of a Behrman or a Shelgrim, unmixed with either the magnetism of one or the stature of the other. Norris dared not make Crookes too powerful because he did not want a human to be Jadwin's main adversary, but rather Jadwin's own pride and wilful humanity. He wanted the wheat, both material and symbolic, to be Jadwin's nemesis.

Even Hargus, the bankrupt, half-crazed old man who once had a corner on the market, has his complexities. Obviously he is an ever-present reminder of the foolhardiness of excessive speculation and he foreshadows Jadwin's imminent defeat. He is in the background of all Jadwin's victories. Just before his first big speculative venture with Gretry, Jadwin notices the tattered old man 'mumbling a sandwich' and does not recognize him. When Gretry assures him it is Hargus, the revelation turns Jadwin cold: 'I don't want to think of it, Sam!' (IX, 78). It is fitting that the old man later refuses to lend Jadwin the very money that Jadwin has given to him with compulsive magnanimity. At the price of his sanity Hargus has learned a cruel lesson about speculation that Jadwin cannot learn second-hand. The old man still has a tinge of the gambling urge; he may still beg another for a market 'tip' and try to make a living as an 'eighth grabber,' but Jadwin's gift of 'about' half a million dollars will accumulate its 4 per cent interest. Hargus's niece will be provided for. Thus Hargus guards his niece's future while Jadwin recklessly sacrifices his own wife's spiritual and material comfort. It is only pride that prevents Jadwin from also sacrificing Laura's small personal fortune.[21] Gretry represents the happiest combination of these extremes of reckless Bull speculation and conservative Bear patience and self-control. His brokerage house does not collapse as Jadwin's did.

Finally, Sheldon Corthell also embraces conflicting qualities. He is both the calm, cool, aloof, prejudiced critic of art and the passionate would-be lover of Laura. Although Corthell courageously removes himself to Europe after Laura's first rejection, his restraint fails him before her final rebuff.

Norris neatly divides the novel into ten chapters with a brief conclusion whose iterative function is similar to that of the conclusion of *The Octopus*. There is a three-year break, almost exactly in the middle, between chapters 5 and 6. Kaplan's insistence that Laura's story (which dominates the first five chapters) slips into the background as Jadwin's business career takes the spotlight is only partially valid. Laura's deepest complexities are explored in the second half of the novel. Although much of the space is taken up with Jadwin's turbulent affairs, Laura remains equally conspicuous. Fascinating in its own right, the business plot serves primarily both to counterpoint and to complicate the love plot. Norris uses the wheat as a catalyst for his examination of the nature of human love and connubial happiness seen against the backdrop of an ordered universe. The parallels that exist between the Jadwins and Norris's own eventually divorced parents suggest a possible explanation for his preoccupation with marital problems. *The Pit*, however, transcends a compulsive attempt to expiate the divorce of the elder Mr and Mrs Norris. Norris's use of the workings of the market along with some details from Joseph Leiter's life (on which he based Jadwin's cornering of the wheat)[22] further suggests that he was a creative artist, and not merely a writer of thinly veiled autobiography.

The first chapter is largely one of exposition. Necessary background material is presented; all the major characters appear; and the major and minor comparisons and contrasts are set up. Norris uses the opening device of the opera party brilliantly to draw most of the important characters together and to test their various reactions to the opera (art), the market (business), and each other. The tension of the vigil before the late arrival of the Cresslers combines with the violent action of the opera to create a mood of anticipation and turmoil. Norris's calculated mixture of art, business, and courtship in the chapter's less than forty pages is excellent. All the vital elements that Norris explores in the rest of the novel are present in the first chapter. Most of them foreshadow the action to come.

Laura enters with 'the coiffure of a heroine of romance, doomed to dark crises' (IX, 2).[23] The icy cold weather of the Chicago streets struggling to upset the warmth of the theatre lobby in which the inexperienced Laura waits suggests her own future turmoil. The closeness of wealth and poverty is suggested by the icy wind's battering of both the rich disembarking from their plush carriages, and the less fortunate people on the pavement. The sun shines very rarely in this novel. Most of the drama is enacted in an atmosphere of gray or rainy skies.

From the outset Page is 'more metropolitan' than Laura. She is more knowledgeable regarding both the worlds of art and of business. Overhearing the men in the lobby talking of the Helmick failure, she tries to share her concern with her older sister: 'But Laura, preoccupied with looking for the Cresslers, hardly listened' (IX, 6). When the Cresslers arrive with Landry Court and Sheldon Corthell, the reader learns of Cressler's near ruin as the result of his corner of the wheat years before. 'Never since then had he speculated ... Speculation he abhorred as the small pox, believing it to be impossible to corner grain by any means under any circumstances' (IX, 14). Norris summarizes Cressler's argument against any attempt at a corner – the moral implications of which Cressler is to elaborate on to Jadwin in chapter 7:

'It can't be done: first, for the reason that there is a great harvest of wheat somewhere in the world for every month in the year; and, second, because the smart man who runs the corner has every other smart man in the world against him. And, besides, it's wrong; the world's food should not be at the mercy of the Chicago wheat pit. (IX, 14)

Jadwin hedonistically closes his eyes to both the practical and moral stands throughout his speculating career.

To this discussion of business Norris again contrasts the equally specialized world of the artist, Sheldon Corthell, creator of stained-glass windows and purveyor of dilettantish criticism. His several marriage proposals to Laura have been rejected partly because of her 'vague ambitions to be a great actress of Shakespearian rôles' (IX, 15). Once seated in the Cresslers's box Laura becomes spellbound by the music and enveloped in self-centred daydreams.[24] But both the opera and her reveries are broken into by more whispered comments about the Helmick failure. Laura is offended. 'Why could not men leave their business outside? Why must the jar of commerce spoil all the harmony of this moment?' (IX, 20). She is later to ask this same question of Jadwin, with more poignant intensity. During the intermission Corthell renews his declaration of love and Laura, in her flirtatious immaturity, succumbs to the flattery of being loved. Page, disturbed by her sister's 'grand manner,' registers silent disapproval. Throughout the last act Laura's active mind is busy comparing the virtues of these two contrasting men. Already she favours Jadwin who, unlike Corthell, has made her feel 'that she had a head as well as a heart' (IX, 31). In a rare flash of insight about her future husband's love of the excitement of the business world, Laura understands his bemused attitude towards opera: 'How small and petty it must all seem to him!' (IX, 31).

On her way home Laura muses over the events of the evening. As her thoughts again reveal a selfish immaturity and a desperate need to be loved, the carriage passes the business district, lighted up because of the Helmick failure. Now the opera is seen in another context. She realizes that while this terrible struggle of the business world continued, 'she and all those others had sat there in that atmosphere of flowers and perfume, listening to music' (IX, 36).

Through a flashback in chapter 2 Norris further reveals a toughness in Laura in her earlier defiance of New England prudery and its attempts to retain a stranglehold on American culture. Laura's desire to be a great tragedienne could not be realized in Barrington, Massachusetts. But her reaction to a group of lady deaconesses, who called on her because she had travelled to Boston alone to the theatre, gives the reader a glimpse of her spirit. The committee 'came to themselves in the street ... dazed and bewildered ... stunned by the violence of an outbreak of long-repressed emotion and long-restrained anger, that like an actual physical force had swept them out of the house' (IX, 40–1). Such a display of passion lends credibility to her short-lived decision to run away with Corthell after experiencing frustration of a far greater intensity.

Chapter 3 focuses on Jadwin and the world of business. It is the only chapter that does not include Laura directly. Aside from the brief conculsion, it is also the shortest chapter. The entire action centres on one day in the wheat Pit. The struggle that Laura tends to romanticize is shown in a very realistic light. As Jadwin walks to Gretrey's brokerage office in the Board of Trade Building, he reflects on the tremendous, uncontrollable power of the wheat Pit and experiences a flash of insight. '"There's something in what Charlie [Cressler] says,"' he mutters to himself. '"Corner this stuff – my God!"' (IX, 75). The scene shifts to Landry who awaits his orders for the day's trading. Norris's details allow the reader to visualize the setting for all the action that centres on the Pit, especially the action of the final act.

Chapter 4 opens on a rehearsal of Jadwin's benefit play for his mission children. During the evening all three suitors press their courtships, the unfortunate Landry making the mistake of kissing Laura goodnight. For the first time Laura is aware of the seriousness of her flirtations, but her extreme reaction is as impulsively immature as was her frivolous encouragement. Hurt pride prompts her three letters of discouragement. Each recipient reacts in character.

During a rehearsal break Cressler launches off on an elaboration of his earlier diatribe against speculation. Once more the immorality of the practice is attacked as Laura and Jadwin listen:

> 'If we send the price of wheat down too far, the farmer suffers, the fellow who raises it; if we send it up too far, the poor man in Europe suffers, the fellow who eats it ... The only way to do so that neither the American farmer nor the European peasant suffers, is to keep wheat at an average, legitimate value. The moment you inflate or depress that, somebody suffers right away. And that is just what these gamblers are doing all the time, booming it up or booming it down. Think of it, the food of hundreds and hundreds of thousands of people just at the mercy of a few men down there on the Board of Trade.'
> (IX, 121–2)

Since Jadwin does not grasp the contradictions in his own dual morality, Cressler continues, this time with a direct warning of the danger to the speculator. He predicts what is to happen to himself and Jadwin:

> 'I tell you the fascination of this Pit gambling is something no one who hasn't experienced it can have the faintest conception of. I believe it's worse than liquor, worse than morphine. Once you get into it, it grips you and draws you and draws you, and the nearer you get to the end the easier it seems to win, till all of a sudden, ah! there's the whirlpool ... "J.," keep away from it, my boy.' (IX, 123)

Jadwin good-humouredly puts his fingers on Cressler's breast as if to turn off a switch. Most of the group join in the laughter. But 'Laura's smile was perfunctory and her eyes were grave' (IX, 123). Immediately before Laura's announcement of her engagement to Jadwin, Cressler mentions that '"Curtis has been speculating again ... He and Gretry are thick as thieves these days ... Always seems to win ... since his deal in May wheat he's been getting into it more and more"' (IX, 149).

Laura's feelings remain selfish and immature. Mrs Cressler asks if she loves Jadwin. Laura says she doesn't know:

> 'Yes, I – I suppose I must love him, or – as you say – I wouldn't have promised to marry him. He does everything, every little thing I say ... I think I love him ... sometimes. And then sometimes I think I don't ... I thought when love came it was to be – oh, up-lifting, something glorious like Juliet's love ... something that would shake me all to pieces!' (IX, 152–3)

The matronly Mrs Cressler assures her that '"that's what you read about in trashy novels ... or the kind you see at the matinées"' (IX, 153).

A week later Laura breaks into one of Page's morbid moods to tell her the news of her engagement. Under her younger sister's questioning she states her haughty philosophy of love:

> 'A man ought to love a woman more than she loves him. It ought to be enough for him if she lets him give her everything she wants in the world. He ought to serve her like the old knights – give up his whole life to satisfy some whim of hers; and it's her part if she likes, to be cold and distant. That's my idea of love.' (IX, 159)

She adapts Mrs Cressler's words in attributing the shocked Page's view of love to trashy novels and frivolous matinées. And Laura is only half teasing when she tells her equally astounded Aunt Wess that she 'would marry a ragamuffin if he gave me all these things – gave them to me because he loved me' (IX, 162).

Until she is alone immediately after the wedding ceremony Laura evidences little apparent deep emotion towards Jadwin.

> Then suddenly Laura, reckless of her wedding finery, forgetful of trivialities, crossed the room and knelt down at the side of the bed. Her head in her folded arms, she prayed, – prayed in the little unstudied words of her childhood, prayed that God would take care of her and make her a good girl; prayed that she might be happy; prayed to God to help her in the new life, and that she should be a good and loyal wife. (IX, 177)

She feels an arm laid on her firmly, evenly, and looks up 'for the first time – direct into her husband's eyes' (IX, 177). There is a moment of complete understanding between them: 'No woman, not her dearest friend; not even Page had ever seemed so close to her as did her husband now' (IX, 178). Suddenly she draws his face down to hers and kisses him many times, asking his forgiveness for her earlier coldness, and expresses a love that had in fact been growing, a love she had not realized until that unique moment of intimacy between husband and wife. It is a love that transcends business or art; a love that keeps the marriage going after all seems to be lost. It is the same love that in *The Octopus* transformed Annixter and brought Vanamee out of his nadir to know the fullness of joy.

This crucial ingredient of love Warren French leaves out of his interpretation. I cannot agree with his statement regarding Laura's marriage: 'despite her fantastic egotism, things proceed smoothly for three years.'[25] Ignoring this last scene, French skips from Laura's most selfish definition of a one-way love to a period three years after the marriage. He ignores her more mature unselfish declaration of love, just as he ignores a vital scene Laura recollects three years later in chapter 6. She recalls the night on their honeymoon when her deepest love was realized:

> That night was final. The marriage ceremony, even that moment in her room, when her husband had taken her in his arms and she had felt the first stirring of love in her heart ... had been ... a whirl, a blur. She had not been able to find herself. Her affection for her husband came and went capriciously ... Then, all at once, she seemed to awake. Not the ceremony at St. James' Church, but that awakening had been her marriage ... she belonged to him indissolubly, forever and forever, and the surrender was a glory. Laura in that moment knew that love, the supreme triumph of a woman's life, was less a victory than a capitulation.
>
> Since then her happiness had been perfect. (IX, 194)

Certainly her love has not yet reached the depth of maturity apparent at the end of the novel, but the Laura of the second half of the novel is not the shallow, selfish egotist suggested by French. Laura has not attained complete self-awareness. She is still uninterested in Jadwin's business life; but she clings to this love through all his speculative madness. Jadwin's monomania tests a far more mature person than the little flirt of the first three chapters who took selfish delight in the attentions of several suitors. But her maturity does not come easily; nor is it complete by the end of the novel.

For the first three years of their marriage the Bears have been 'strong, unassailable'; the price of wheat has sagged to seventy-two cents a bushel. 'All over the world the farmers saw season after season after season of good crops.' But the low price of wheat 'kept the farmers poor' (IX, 179).

> Jadwin, inevitably, had been again drawn into the troubled waters of the Pit. Always, as from the very first, a Bear, he had once more raided the market, and had once more

been successful. Two months after this raid he and Gretry planned still another coup,
a deal of greater magnitude than any they had previously hazarded. (IX, 180)

Even Laura 'who knew very little of her husband's affairs' – to which he seldom
alluded – 'sees by the papers the near failure of the deal.' By now Jadwin 'no longer
needed Gretry's urging to spur him. He had developed into a strategist ... delighting
in the shock of battle, never more jovial, more daring than when under the stress of
the most merciless attack' (IX, 180–1). Jadwin senses a change in the market that
winter. He announces dramatically to Gretry that he is about done with the Bear
game and that he is going to buy.

Norris attempts what James managed in *The Portrait of a Lady* in showing the
change marriage had wrought in Isabel Archer.

The three years that had just passed had been the most important years of Laura Jadwin's
life. Since her marriage she had grown intellectually and morally with amazing rapi-
dity ... She was no longer the same half-formed, impulsive girl who had found a delight
in the addresses of her three lovers ... Love had entered her world. (IX, 192–3)

James is more successful because he dramatizes Isabel's new 'tragic awareness';
Norris mainly announces that Laura has grown. The Laura presented above had
breadth; she is yet to acquire an even deeper understanding of herself and Jadwin
through their mutual suffering. She is still innocent of the intensity of his fanatical
attraction to the Pit. Norris describes these first three years as idyllic. But their
happiness is largely untested. Norris does not mean to imply that marriage has
wrought a miraculous change in Laura. Even before Jadwin becomes enveloped in
his speculation the servants experience Laura's 'grand manner' and much prefer
Jadwin to their condescending mistress. She notices their genuine affection for Jadwin and is disturbed by it, realizing some of her own shortcomings. But Norris
establishes the couple's growing love through cozy after-dinner scenes where they
'shut themselves in the library,' and Laura reads to her husband. Significantly,
Jadwin is partial to Howells: 'Lapham he loved as a brother' (IX, 205). He does not
follow Lapham in the latter's ultimate refusal to separate morality from the expediency of business. 'Continually Jadwin grew richer ... He was a Bear always, and on
those rare occasions when he referred to his ventures in Laura's hearing, it was
invariably to say that prices were going down' (IX, 206). Then secretly he '"turned
Bull," with the suddenness of a strategist' (IX, 206).

Chapter 7 opens with Laura's first spoken objections to her husband's speculation. She accuses him of neglecting her for business, claiming that speculation has
changed him, and complains of her growing loneliness. Through Jadwin's rational-
ized plea for understanding Norris makes a penetrating comment on the lifestyle of
the contemporary rich:

'What are we fellows, who have made our money, to do? I've got to be busy ... And I
don't believe in lounging around clubs, or playing ... horses, or murdering game birds, or
running some poor, helpless fox to death. Speculating seems to be about the only game,
or the only business that's left open to me – that appears to be legitimate. I know I've
gone too far into it, and I promise you I'll quit. But it's fine fun.'   (IX, 221)

Jadwin remains impervious to Laura's plea for humanity in her restatement of Cressler's moral argument against manipulating the price of food.

It is in an anxious state of mind that Laura encounters Corthell. Dining alone with
him she 'remembered that in the old days, before she had met Jadwin, her mind and
conversation, for undiscoverable reasons, had never been nimbler, quicker, nor
more effective than when in the company of the artist' (IX, 231). Business keeps
Jadwin away from home and throws them together. Corthell inspires Laura with
lively conversation sprinkled with gentle criticisms of her taste in art and music. In
the art gallery he plays for her Beethoven and Liszt instead of Verdi. Slowly she
again becomes aware of the 'second' Laura Jadwin, the one that is not satisfied with
'the quiet life ... the duties of the housewife' and Mr Howells's novels (IX, 239–40).
At 'moments such as this she knew ...' a 'Laura Jadwin who might have been a great
actress, who had a "temperament," who was impulsive. This was the Laura of the
"grand manner," who played the rôle of the great lady' (IX, 239–40). Later Page
notices that 'Laura is terribly distressed' as Jadwin continues to spend virtually all of
his evenings at the office. Laura reads to an audience of one, herself, when she isn't
entertaining Corthell.

In chapter 8 the action speeds up as both plots accelerate. Just as Jadwin becomes
increasingly preoccupied with the market, so Laura's growing loneliness throws her
closer to Corthell. Crookes, the most powerful Bear, persuades Cressler to join him
against the unknown Bull, but Cressler does not know he is to do battle with his best
friend. When he asks Jadwin if he is speculating, Jadwin lies, violating his code of
honesty, seeing himself 'stronger, bigger, shrewder than them all' (IX, 268). Laura's
silent reproaches prompt another rationalization of his actions – a rationalization
with strong echoes of Shelgrim's sophistic refusal to accept responsibility for circumstances:

'You think I am wilfully doing this! ... I corner the wheat! Great heavens, it is the wheat
that has cornered me. The corner made itself. I happened to stand between two sets of
circumstances, and they made me do what I've done. I couldn't get out of it now, with
all the good will in the world.   (IX, 270)

Chapter 9 describes the triumphant defeat of Crookes and displays Jadwin at the
height of his power and pride. But the same triumph that allows him to 'save'

Hargus ironically succeeds in killing Cressler. As Jadwin and Gretry look to the market struggle of the following day, Jadwin glories in his plan of revenge on Scannel, who had double-crossed Hargus years before. A charitable act this revenge is, but an act that represents Jadwin at his most prideful, a godlike judge of his fellow man, meting out rewards and punishments.[26]

With all Jadwin's heady success, Norris makes it clear that he has not won by himself. The confidence of the crowd of 'outsiders' is the key to his victory. It is their support that ultimately defeats Crookes. And it is when they lose confidence in Jadwin that he is in turn defeated. This is one of Norris's major observations in *The Pit*. It is more than an impersonal force of nature that topples Jadwin; it is also the combined wills of a mass of people. It is the same kind of mass will that can, if used in accord with the morally ordered universe for the public good (Norris suggests in *The Octopus*), combat the evil results of the tyranny of a man like Shelgrim. A powerful man can channel this energy for a time, but if he oversteps his abilities, he can be crushed. While Jadwin petulantly sweeps aside Gretry's objections to his plan to continue raising the wheat prices, in another flash of insight he articulates his own predicament: '"Corner wheat! It's the wheat that has cornered me. It's like holding a wolf by the ears, bad to hold on, but worse to let go"' (IX, 337).

The last formal chapter opens with Jadwin's shock and grief over the suicide of his best friend. Attempting to articulate an incoherent horror to Gretry, he blames himself for Cressler's death. But the pressures of business cause him to forget his grief very quickly as his 'luck' begins to change. Laura's own self-centredness and lack of sympathy through most of these final pages should not be ascribed to mere pettiness. The emotional strain during this period has brought her as close to the breaking-point as Jadwin. Since her traumatic discovery of Cressler's body she has released her feelings to no one. For 'three days – with the exception of an hour or two, on the evening after that horrible day of her visit to the Cresslers's house – she had seen nothing of her husband' (IX, 359).[27] Page sees laura as on the verge of hysteria.[28] Laura asks hereslf: 'Had the shock of that spectacle ... and the wearing suspense in which she had lived of late, so torn and disordered the delicate feminine nerves that a kind of hysteria animated and directed her impulses, her words, and actions?' (IX, 385). Rather than undercutting Laura's growth or stature, Norris is describing a very human psychological withdrawal resulting from a long period of mental strain compounded by a severe and sudden shock.

On the morning of Jadwin's defeat Landry rushes to Gretry's office for further orders and there he sees what Page is spared. A group has gathered: 'Jadwin stood there in the centre of the others, hatless, his face pale, his eyes congested with blood' (IX, 373). All try to reason with him, tell him that he can buy no more, that he has no more money. Insanely Jadwin declares his complete independence, reaching the state of complete self-isolation he has been moving toward for so many months:

'Get out of my way! ... Get out of my way! Do you hear? I'll play my hand alone from now on ... God curse you, Sam Gretry, for the man who failed me in a crisis.' And as he spoke Curtis Jadwin struck the broker full in the face. (IX, 374)

Jadwin rushes out into the Pit to buy: 'And then, under the stress and violence of the hour, something snapped in his brain ... Blind and insensate, Jadwin strove against the torrent of the Wheat. There in the middle of the Pit, surrounded and assaulted by herd after herd of wolves yelping for his destruction' (IX, 376). Then the battle's end occurs. The secretary of the Board of Trade appears on a little balcony opposite the visitors' gallery and announces that '"All trades with Gretry, Converse & Co. must be closed at once"' (IX, 378).

Carrying back from the gallery her impression of Jadwin's catastrophe, Page discovers Laura still waiting for him on this, her birthday. Laura has grown as monomaniacal about her own loneliness as Jadwin about his speculations: 'She seemed like one who had staked everything upon a hazard and, blind to all else, was keeping "her emotion back" with all her strength while she watched and waited for the issue' (IX, 381). Laura asks about Jadwin but waves aside Page's suggestion that he may have lost a lot of money: '"Oh, what do I care about wheat – about this wretched scrambling for money"' (IX, 383). Defending Landry, whom Laura belittles, Page again drives to the heart of her sister's self-absorption:

'If my husband had a battle to fight, do you think I'd mope and pine because he left me at home? No, I wouldn't. I'd help him buckle his sword on, and when he came back to me I wouldn't tell him how lonesome I'd been, but I'd take care of him ... and I'd help him.' (IX, 384)

But emotional pressures have driven Laura back into her childish dream world. She becomes lost in her semi-prophetic resolution that 'Life and death were little things. Love only existed; let her husband's career fail; what did it import so only love stood the strain and issued from the struggle triumphant?' (IX, 384–5). Momentarily Page's penetrating words come back provoking visions of 'a third [Laura Jadwin] that rose above and forgot the other two, that in some beautiful, mysterious way was identity ignoring self' (IX, 388). It is a realization that is vague and only very slowly will it result in change, evolution not revolution. The consummation was to be achieved in the coming years' (IX, 388). Now the enlightenment is quickly obscured by her wilfully childlike game: '"If you love me, you will come"' (IX, 389), she pouts. Pressures of Laura's nearly hysterical emotional state cause her to regress to the level of her self-pitying daydream during the introductory opera scene.

At eight o'clock it is Corthell who appears, not Jadwin. Her pent-up emotion is released in gratitude and infatuation for this man who 'remembered.' She gratefully receives his kisses like a love-starved child and agrees to go with him the next night, 'anywhere.' Immediately on his departure Jadwin appears. Her emotions unloosed by Corthell's gesture, Laura is now able to turn outward and share Jadwin's pain and demonstrate a more clearly Christian love. She realizes that theirs is a mutual need as they sit on the divan 'holding to each other, trembling and fearful, like children in the dark' (IX, 394).

The 'Conclusion' opens as the Jadwins leave the mansion that is empty of all but memories. Jadwin has recovered after 'a pretty bad siege' during which time Laura never left his bedside. Their relationship is deeper and more tender now. In exploring the marriage of the Jadwins Norris has commented on the trial period of all marriages, replacing the more usual bickering about household bills and cold eggs with the powerful disrupting forces of speculation and art. For the resulting misunderstanding and loneliness differ only in degree. The Jadwins have outridden the storm and are more mature because of it. Their marriage will survive largely because Laura wills it to. By throwing off her solipsistic shield she has shown herself the more responsible of the two. Jadwin repents, to be sure, but his failure, not any act of will, has put him into a repentant state. If Norris had allowed Jadwin a moral struggle and made his the choice that saved the marriage, the financier might have been a much greater creation. But this also would have made *The Pit* Jadwin's novel. Laura, contrary to Norris's plan, would have been relegated to an inferior position by contrast. Jadwin's speculative struggle serves as an insidious counterpoint to Laura's moral growth. Any more emphasis on Jadwin's character could have made *The Pit* a lopsided novel indeed.

As they await the hack that will take them west to a calmer, quieter life, the 'heavy rain' continues to fall as it has through most of the novel. Although nature seems to be an ultimately benevolent force in its nourishment of mankind, it does not directly involve itself with the more intricate problems of man's relationship to man. Certainly the rain engenders the new fertility in the midwest, a fertility which ultimately breaks the corner; but within this framework of inexorable forces the Curtis and Laura Jadwins of the world must solve their own spiritual problems.

A long letter, appropriately from Page, ties up many plot threads.[29] Although Page and Landry are not as great in stature as the Jadwins, she and Landry bring to their marriage reason plus mutual interests and a greater maturity than did the Jadwins. Their relationship, like that of Tom and Penelope in *The Rise of Silas Lapham*, becomes a kind of norm. Page's account of Landry's continued adoration of Jadwin is a touching tribute to a man who, only through failure, may begin to realize himself. Page reports that although eighteen brokers' houses failed in Chicago after Jadwin's crash, Gretry's did not. Jadwin did not sacrifice another friend. In a postscript she reports that a resigned Corthell will soon sail for Europe, closing that chapter in Laura's life.

The Jadwins leave for their new life in the west, a wiser couple. Laura will not admit even to herself that her husband was to blame for the many other failures he had precipitated, striving to convince herself by repeating 'over and over again' Jadwin's own rationalization. She believes that he has suffered enough. She chooses to accept his own explanation: '"The wheat cornered itself. I simply stood between two sets of circumstances. The wheat cornered me, not I the wheat"' (IX, 402). There is no longer reason for her to dwell upon his wilful acts that placed him between these circumstances; but we are left with the conviction that their new understanding, unlike the false optimism of the Theron Wares in Frederic's novel, will not tolerate a similar mistake.

Norris, then, has carefully plotted Jadwin's gradual entanglement in the webs of the Pit at the same time that he has traced Laura's more complex character development.[30] He allows the climaxes of both plots to break simultaneously with the major focus on Laura. It is she who rejects Corthell and saves her marriage when Jadwin's defeated countenance reawakens the fullness of her love and makes their mutual obligations clear. Through structured devices prominent in his previous novels Norris gives resonance to the twin climaxes.[31] His iterative, accumulative use of comparisons and contrasts, ironic juxtapositions, and dramatic counterpoint stresses the need for a philosophy of mature love and understanding achieved here only through sacrifices, suffering, and fortitude. Again Norris's control of analogical elements, incremental repetitions, parallelisms, and internal stitching provides a sinewy matrix for his stoical Christian philosophy. Norris's last novel may not realize the scope and near-greatness of *The Octopus*; but the character study and structure represent accomplishments that at times excel even those of his masterpiece.

ROGER B. SALOMON

The Mock-Heroics of Desire: Some Stoic Personae in the Work of William Carlos Williams

The air changes, creates and re-creates, like strength,
And to breathe is a fulfilling of desire,
A clearing, a detecting, a completing,
A largeness lived and not conceived, a space
That is an instant nature, brilliantly.   (Wallace Stevens, 'Chocorua to Its Neighbor')

There is nothing in literature but change and change is mockery.
(William Carlos Williams, *Kora in Hell*)

William Carlos Williams's description of Maxwell Bodenheim suggests a significant link between the stoic humanism of Cervantes and the characteristic stance of modern romanticism. Bodenheim, writes Williams in *Kora in Hell*,

> pretends to hate most people ... but that he really goes to this trouble I cannot imagine. He seems rather to me to have the virtues of self-absorption so fully developed that hate is made impossible. Due to this, also, he is an unbelievable physical stoic. I know of no one who lives so completely in his pretenses as Bogie does. Having formulated his world neither toothaches nor the misery to which his indolence reduces him can make head against the force of his imagination. Because of this he remains for me a heroic figure, which, after all, is quite apart from the stuff he writes and which only concerns him. He is an Isaiah of the butterflies.[1]

One significant aspect of this portrait is that it makes clear where romanticism has come out in modern times and, at the same time, indicates the complex attitude of major romantics like Williams and Stevens (as opposed, let us say, to minor figures like Bodenheim) towards what has happened. Bodenheim, in Williams's version, represents, in effect, the attenuation of romantic heroics and the necessary redefinition of the hero that has taken place in the light of this attenuation.

Joseph Riddel has noted that the direction of romanticism in the last hundred years has been from a sense of 'privileged consciousness' to 'dislocated self-consciousness.'[2] Like heroes before him, the romantic hero has increasingly been denied an environment commensurate with his will and vision, in this case a transcendental realm or dimension of power co-extensive with the imagination. To be sure, even at its point of highest expression in the nineteenth century, romanticism offered its heroes only a precarious identification of self and object – an identification tentative, in need of constant renewal, more involved with process than end, and already finding consummations largely in and through the artifice of art.[3] And, from the beginning, the sterile but tempting alternatives of solipsism and Platonism lurked as too easy alternatives to the full dynamics of the romantic vision.

With a later generation of romantics, however, the transcendental dimension has disappeared completely, and they are left with the continuing claim of the imagination as *the* source of value, but a claim now in active confrontation with material reality. This reality may remain something of a positive and attractive vehicle for the imaginative tracings of the self, or it may be more negatively felt as what Williams calls in *Paterson* 'a pustular scum, a decay, a choking / lifelessness.'[4] In any case, the concept of a noble self persists, but the locus of heroism necessarily shifts from the quality of ends to the quality of means, from results to effort. As Wallace Stevens puts it: 'the heroic effort to live expressed / As victory.'[5] Heroism becomes the pursuit of desire in the existential immediacy of a world which has only (at best) a casual relation to its fulfilment. Bodenheim in Williams's sketch achieves the status of stoic hero through the sheer rigour of self-absorption, a rigour whose power source is simply 'the force of his imagination.' Yet Williams's strong and sympathetic identification with Bodenheim is balanced by an equally persistent counter-rhythm of irony. Williams, at least, has the strong sense of the world and its claims that the other poet ignores. Bodenheim in Williams's splendid phrase is an 'Isaiah of the butterflies,' an authentic hero, perhaps, but only in a context so sharply limited as constantly to threaten (though it does not destroy) the very premises on which the heroic claims rest.

Alternatively, we might describe Bodenheim from Williams's point of view as a hero of authentic illusions, or what I prefer to call a 'mock-hero' in the intellectual and formal tradition of Cervantes. In a seminal essay on Cervantes, Américo Castro notes that

> Cervantes, a Christian and a stoic, relates to a Semitic tradition nine hundred years old; his art consisted of resolving the concept of life as an alternation of 'insides' and 'outsides' purely phenomenological (like a linear arabesque, without volume and open), with the Stoic-Judaic-Christian idea of man raising himself upon the rock of his will and upon the conscience of intimate freedom. Feeling 'one's own self' is achieved at the cost of the uninterrupted effort of sustaining one's self, without paying attention to circumstances.[6]

Self-realization, in other words, is an endlessly renewed *process* of being; the experience of Don Quixote and Sancho is a continual adventure, a pursuit of 'wonders,' open-ended, subject to a ceaseless rhythm of climax/anticlimax, fragmentary, vulnerable largely to exhaustion and death.

Castro goes on to point out that:

> According to the author of the *Quixote*, the reality of existence consists of being receptive to that impact of whatever can effect man from outside of him and continually transforming such impressions into visible processes of life. The illusion of a dream, the clinging to a belief – yearning in whatever form – introduce themselves into the existence of the one who dreams, creates or yearns, and thus what was an unarticulated externality of the process of living will become a real and effective content of life.[7]

Of course, even the Knight (not to mention Sancho!) has his occasional doubts; more significant is the elaborate and almost total context of doubt within which he operates to create his own authentic 'reality of existence.' The distinction between full heroic vision and Cervantean mock-heroic consists precisely in this dimension of doubt, a doubt in balance with commitment and its equal in intensity.[8] The mock-hero is, by and large, an ardent and receptive believer; his creator, both believer and doubter. From the perspective of Cervantes, what is introduced through complex narrative devices is not only commitment to self-realization as its own justification, but also strong doubt (if not denial) of the final efficacy or end of selfhood *beyond* itself. The Knight exists in a medium which at the same time offers him the possibility of imaginative transformations and mocks those transformations. The author, in turn, of a fiction of authentic illusions becomes his own Quixote. We are mockingly reminded of this by Jorge Luis Borges, whose eminent writer, critic, and editor, Pierre Menard, sets out to accomplish the 'astonishing' feat of composing the original *Quixote* 'word for word and line for line': 'There is no exercise of the intellect which is not, in the final analysis, useless ... There is nothing new in these nihilistic verifications; what is singular is the determination Menard derived from them. He decided to anticipate the vanity awaiting all man's efforts; he set himself to an undertaking which was exceedingly complex and, from the very beginning, futile.'[9]

In short, the paradoxes of later stoic humanism as explored by Cervantes find striking corroboration in the ambivalent commitments of the modern romantic sensibility, and both are echoed in Williams's portrait of Maxwell Bodenheim. Mock-heroic – as an attitude, a mode of characterization, indeed a form of narrative with its own stylistic determinants – expresses a rich, complex, and continuing tradition. It is to other mock-heroes of Williams that we must now turn for further explorations of this particular sensibility.

MINOR PERSONAE

Cervantean mock-heroic, it must be stressed, is a way of *preserving* the concept of nobility during a historical period which threatens otherwise to polarize into empty and obsolescent conventions and banal reality. In his well-known essay 'The Noble Rider and the Sound of Words' Wallace Stevens makes this essential point by comparing Verrocchio (for whom nobility 'was an affair of the noble style') and Cervantes, to the obvious advantage of the latter: 'With Cervantes, nobility was not a thing of the imagination. It was a part of reality, it was something that exists in life, something so true to us that it is in danger of ceasing to exist, if we isolate it, something in the mind of a precarious tenure.' Yet today, he goes on to note, 'we may derive so much satisfaction from the restoration of reality as to become wholly prejudiced against the imagination.' It is a question rather, Stevens says, of 'precise equilibrium.'[10]

For Williams, also, nobility involves a continuing and 'precarious' encounter between the imagination and reality, an encounter where claim and counter-claim are in complex and ineluctable balance – in some sort of 'equilibrium,' perhaps, but not in resolution. 'In front walks Don Quixote; Sancho follows' (*Imaginations*, pp 64, 291): Williams's reiterated statement suggests his self-conscious awareness of Cervantes and the crucial duality set up by the Spaniard, regardless of who walks 'in front.' Williams's stoicism – the strong capacity of his dramatic selves to 'bear' reality – comes, like that of Cervantes, squarely from the certain sufficiency of the mock-heroic compromise. The efficacy of the imagination, that is, for art and for self-realization within life, is not cancelled by its absurdity in other equally compelling contexts. In fact, the full acknowledgment of these contexts – or, more important, the creation of art forms which incorporate these contexts – protects the heroic claims by fully testing them at every vulnerable point by ironic counter-statement. Mock-heroic is a mirror art; heroic and absurd selves stand face to face. 'We look, we pretend great things to our glass – rubbing our chin,' writes Williams in *Kora in Hell*, adding: 'This is a profound comedian who grimaces deeds to slothful breasts' (*Imaginations*, p 78). Here both by image and tone the dramatic self incorporates mockery into its various 'profound' stances.

Williams's personae, of course, are quixotic not in their pursuit of abstract, obsolete ideals and social conventions, but, just the opposite, in their equally determined commitment to the new, the fresh, the improvisational, dissonant, and existential. He himself has noted the difference: 'There are no sagas – only trees now, animals, engines: there's that' (*Imaginations*, p 248). On rare occasions this commitment may result or may have resulted (such occasions are usually in the past) in true heroic consummation. Daniel Boone, for example, 'lived to enjoy ecstasy' by a 'descent to the ground of his desire' where the power so central to the romantic vision was fully released.[11] Or there is Williams's description of the life of the Aztecs, with its strong echoes of D.H. Lawrence's romanticism: 'Here it was [i.e., in their 'monstrous' stone and wood imagery] that the tribe's deep feeling for a reality that stems back into the permanence of remote origins had its firm hold. It was the earthward thrust of their logic; blood and earth; the realization of their primal and continuous identity with the ground itself, where everything is fixed in darkness' (IAG, p 33). To be sure, even on these occasions history has acted as ultimate mocker; the Aztecs are destroyed, and Boone keeps only one step ahead of the settlements. When Hilda Doolittle in an early letter accused Williams of 'flippancies' in his poetry, of mocking his own song, he replied in a line which I have used as appropriate epigraph to this entire essay: 'There is nothing in literature but change and change is mockery' (*Imaginations*, p 13). Time and history, in other words, are basically movement and, as such, inherently anticlimactic: new becomes old; stability and 'ends' are an illusion of the moment.

More often Williams stresses the element of anticlimax even in dealing with the experience of those historical figures whom he can conceive of as approaching consummation more closely than any contemporary persona. The process of time, indeed, involves not only the simple fact of change but a darker quality of 'emptiness' at the heart of things or, as Williams also describes it, 'the spirit of malice which underlies men's lives and against which nothing offers resistance' (IAG, p 27). Men may be 'possessed by beauty,' he says, but heroic commitment to imaginative vision can be celebrated only as its own adequate 'end' and in the full awareness that its empirical end is inevitably disastrous. Celebration, if possible at all, can take place only in a context of 'perennial disappointment.' Desire and the failure of desire are endemic to the experience of Williams's personae, a rhythm/counter-rhythm in an almost perfectly balanced and endless tension, as his epic invocation to Sir Walter Raleigh makes clear: 'Of the pursuit of beauty and the husk that remains, perversions and mistakes, while the true form escapes in the wind, sing O Muse' (IAG, p 59).

It is Columbus, however, who for Williams, as for Hart Crane, remains the touchstone of possibility, the figure seeking new forms and new freedom in a *Nuevo Mundo*, the persona closest to Williams's own heroic dream of himself. But even in the strong polemical context of *In the American Grain* Columbus's experience is described by Williams in terms of almost complete dislocation between dream and fact, pursuit and capture, conception and growth – a duality inherent in the deepest rhythms of life itself. According to Williams,

the Western land could not guard its seclusion longer; a predestined and bitter fruit existing, perversely, before the white flower of its birth, it was laid bare by the miraculous first voyage. For it is as the achievement of a flower, pure, white, waxlike and fragrant, that Columbus' infatuated course must be depicted, especially when compared with the acrid and poisonous apple which was later by him to be proved. (IAG, p 7)

The aesthetic ('pure, white, waxlike') flower of imaginative vision exists apart from the rank growth of reality in time. Columbus's passion is both noble and foolish ('infatuated') as he rigorously pursues his dream ('the illusive bright future') towards personal and social catastrophe; the greatest hero is the greatest illusionist. In *In the American Grain*, nevertheless, for many of the heroes of history the mock is muted, and they approach genuine tragic significance, where the heroic will simply encounter its final limits in the overriding predestined plans of the gods. As I have noted in another essay, the mode of Cervantean mock-heroic is almost invariably tragi-comic (the exact mixture of elements varying from work to work), expressing at the same time much of the irreconcilability of tragic idealism and much of the sense of absurdity that comes from strong social and philosophical awareness of the ridiculousness involved in the pursuit of any fixed idea or plan.[12]

Elsewhere in Williams's work the comic dimension is clearer and the mock harsher. In *The Great American Novel* De Soto is obviously viewed as a Don Quixote wandering in weird costume over the plains of La Mancha: 'The Spanish stand still. What an ass a man will make of himself in a strange country! In armor De Soto wandering haphazard over Alabama. The Seminoles for guides. Buried him in the Mississippi ... The cat-fish ate it [his body]' (*Imaginations*, p 192). Or there is the great historic pratfall of Aaron Burr, both described and imitated in the dying fall of the narrative voice: 'What chit of a girl could have appreciated you, my darling boy, as I do. A man of your personality, so fresh in wit, so brimming with vigor and new ideas. Aaron my dear, dear boy, life has not yet begun. All is new and untouched in the world waiting ... for you to pluck it ... For you everything is possible. Bing! and Hamilton lies dead' (*Imaginations*, p 191). Not surprisingly, in the earlier book Columbus is seen as someone whose sound business sense quickly mitigates his visionary excesses: 'For a moment Columbus stood as if spell-bound by the fact of this new country. Soon however he regained his self-possession and with Alonzo Pinzón ordered the trunks of trifles to be opened which, being opened, the Indians drew near in wonder and began to try to communicate with these gods' (*Imaginations*, p 185). As an actual adventurer, with his 'trunks of trifles,' Columbus is, in effect, a harsh parody of his own dream, in life a pretend god with fake wonders.

The Great American Novel is, of course, the *new* American novel, and its difference of tone from *In the American Grain* reflects Williams's sense of the particularly pressing contingencies within which the contemporary explorer of new forms acts and has his being. In the full context of his own existential drama the Williams persona is more sharply aware of the possible ironies involved in seeking out models (even new models who are models of the spirit of the new) from the American past. The very *act* of modelling deepens his sense of parody, his awareness not only of the self-parody involved in the actions of his historical figures (as they 'imitated' their own dreams), but, most important, of himself as second-hand imitator of an imitation or perhaps as someone who can only *desire* to imitate. Williams shares with many of his contemporaries a sense of historical 'lateness' or diminution. Progress is out of the question – dismissed by the narrator as 'damn foolishness ... a thieves game' (*Imaginations*, p 165). He attempts to substitute a theory of 'involution' for that of 'evolution': 'We struggle to comprehend an obscure evolution ... when the compensatory involution so plainly marked escapes our notice.' Invoking the great historical names, he goes on to propose writing 'the natural history of involution,' but this proposition itself trails off in mockery as he describes the 'return' of great heroes:

> Borne on the foamy crest of involution, like Venus on her wave, stript as she but of all consequence – since it is the return. See they return! From savages in quest of a bear we are come upon rifles, cannon. From Chaldeans solving the stars we have fallen into the bellies of the telescopes. From great runners we have evolved into speeches sent over a wire.
>   But our spirits, our spirits have prospered! Boom, boom.
> Oh, yes, our spirits have grown –   (*Imaginations*, p 215)

Involution might suggest that time, if not consequentially redemptive, offers at least a cycle of continuing human spiritual possibility. In fact, its invocation by the narrator is simply an aspect of the mock-heroics of desire. Elsewhere he wonders 'if it were too late to be Eric' (*Imaginations*, p 182). The season of *The Great American Novel*, moreover, is autumnal, and spring is no longer a matter of founded hope but of unfounded desire, even of nostalgia: 'Yet sometimes it seems that it [spring] would still be possible. And this is romance: to believe that which is unbelievable. This is faith: to desire that which is never to be obtained, to ride like a swallow on the wind – apparently for the pleasure of flight' (*Imaginations*, pp 179–80).

The narrator's faith, it should be noted, exists in contexts of mockery more fundamental even than the disappointments of history in its past and present possibility. His measurement of potential as a 'new' writer in a 'new' world with a 'new' American language leads him to a consideration of language itself, the particular medium of the writer, but, in larger terms, the medium through which all human beings encounter and formalize their relationship with reality. In this case, as with the meditations on history, the form of *The Great American Novel* remains the very expression of its subject: desire is affirmed concretely through the continuing willed commitment to expression of a self-conscious monologist whose dual perspectives express endlessly in complex antiphony both the will and the limits of will. His 'romantic' commitment to the swallow's flight, for example, which I have just quoted above, is immediately followed by an empirical examination of the metaphor, then by an actual test of its immediate relevance to himself. He notes first that 'the swallow's bill is constructed in such a way that in flying with his mouth open tiny insects that enter are ensnared in hair-like gills so that he is fed.' Obviously for the swallow the medium of air, while it may give pleasure, is also practically sustaining; the self survives on its actual encounters with objects. The human parallel, as the narrator describes it, is more purely solipsistic and more incomplete. His medium is simply imagination and its formalization in words. He thinks: 'Here are a pretty pair of legs in blue stockings, feed. Yet without the thought of a possible achievement.' He imagines an encounter with the girl: 'there is one word you must hear' from his own lips. Yet he does not keep his appointment and is left 'thinking, thinking of the words he will make, new words to be written on white paper but never to be spoken by the lips to pass into her ear' (*Imaginations*, p 180).

At best he is left with words, which he calls elsewhere his 'poetic sweet-heart' and occasionally mocks harshly: 'Ugh. Poetic sweetheart. My dear Miss Word let me hold your w. I love you. Of all the girls in school you alone are the one –' (*Imaginations*, p 166). In his mock-heroic encounter with language the monologist is, of course, reflecting one of the great philosophical themes of this century: the disassociation of language from any necessary or effective relation with reality. The Austrian Fritz Mauthner argued as early as 1901 that 'language is only a convention, like a rule of a game: the more participants, the more compelling it will be. However, it is neither going to grasp nor to alter the real world.'[13] For twentieth-century writers as diverse as Joyce, Borges, Nabokov, Stevens, and Williams himself (to mention only a few prominent names), the most fundamental mock-heroic commitment is the artist's commitment to language itself. The narrator-monologist of *The Great American Novel* is obsessed with the problem: 'I am a writer and will never be anything else. In which case it is impossible to find the word. But to have a novel one must progress with the words. The words must become real, they must take the place of wife and sweetheart ... Am I a word? Words, words, words –' (*Imaginations*, p 166). He realizes he is imitating Joyce – and mocks not only his own imitation but Joyce himself, an 'epicurean of romance,' someone mistaking his art for 'Rosinante' (*Imaginations*, pp 168–9). The hero of new words, in fact, is as ironically limited by the very process of change as the earlier explorers of new worlds: 'Words are not permanent ... words progress into the ground ... Now I am not what I was when the word was forming to say what I am' (*Imaginations*, p 158). Word-making, in short, is an exercise that never gets beyond itself: 'If I make a word I shall make myself into a word' (*Imaginations*, p 160).

Irony, nevertheless, however categorical, only establishes the context of belief. It does not reduce the narrator's commitment to believing, but simply turns him into a pretender. 'Hans Anderson didn't believe,' he notes at one point, 'he had to pretend to believe' (*Imaginations*, p 160). 'Deeply religious' (as he describes himself), this mock or pretend Columbus, in the face of almost total doubt, resolutely pledges himself again and again to the quest – or at least the *process* or *game* of questing, since the absolute end of the quest remains concealed or is determined by purely arbitrary means: 'Somehow a word must be found ... A novel must progress toward a word. Any word that – Any word. There is an idea' (*Imaginations*, p 165). Williams suggests (and struggles in *The Great American Novel* to achieve) what Joyce the year before in *Ulysses* had so convincingly demonstrated: that the 'new' novel, like its protagonists, would be a parody of traditional forms, that a concept of life as parody was itself the meaning of the new forms.

Heroics must exist, in short, solely in the quality of means used to no discernible end – in life *style*, so to speak – desire courageously pursued but intensifying only into self-realization. This is Williams's stoic model, the star, for example, invoked in the early poem 'El Hombre':

It's a strange courage
you give me ancient star:

Shine alone in the sunrise
toward which you lend no part![14]

Or there is his elegy to D.H. Lawrence, whose 'unfading desire' is betrayed by the abortive hopes of the seasonal cycle, Lawrence 'worn with a fury of sad labour / to create summer from / spring's decay' (SP, pp 96–8). The persona of the early experimental prose is himself a figure of 'unfading desire' who engages in an endless quest for a sustaining theory of art and the imagination. This quest, however, is largely self-reflexive, a reiterated 'activation' of the mind whose only results are the released and manifest energy of self-assertion, in Williams's terms, the 'dance' or 'design' of self-assertion. As the form and actual title of *Kora in Hell: Improvisations* make clear, the self can engage only in discrete 'improvisations': '*the sad truth is that since the imagination is nothing, nothing will come of it*'(*Imaginations*, p 36). In another of his glosses the narrator of *Kora in Hell* reiterates that improvisations are (and can only be) their own justification:

One may write music and music but who will dance to it? The dance escapes but the music, the music – projects a dance over itself which the feet follow lazily if at all. So a dance is a thing in itself. (*Imaginations*, p 47)

The ultimate balance to the heavy mockery in *The Great American Novel* is the narrator's assertion (that is, his argument but, more important, his immediate, improvisational *claim* or *demonstration*) of the 'flamboyant' self created by an imagination which, he says, 'must adorn and exaggerate life, must give it splendor and grotesqueness, beauty and infinite depth.' Williams's celebrated concern with 'things' (e.g., 'no ideas but in things') involves more than an existential demand for concreteness and newness; it should remind us also that his positive theme always affirms the primary thrust of identity. The self and its objects both 'live' in the intensity of their realization – in what amounts to a demonstration of energy. His discussion of flamboyance to which I have already alluded goes on to make this point: 'the imagination demands for satisfaction creative energy. Flamboyance expresses faith in that energy – it is a shout of delight, a declaration of richness' (*Imaginations*, pp 200–1). The flamboyant self creates what Williams calls elsewhere 'the enlivening scurry' (*Imaginations*, p 280), an extraordinarily vivid and apt phrase which describes at once the form, narrative substance, and essential meaning of most of his poetry and prose. For the writer the enlivening scurry is possible in an extravagant freedom of language. The language of the surrealists, for example, makes 'words into sentences that will have a fantastic reality which is false.' To the inevitable falsity of fantastic reality Williams opposes the avoidable 'falseness of the piecemeal,' where language is subservient to material and conventional ends (*Imaginations*, pp 280–1). Even conversation (in writing and in life) is 'actual' only to the extent that it is an expression of 'singleness,' of the self as pure design: 'it must have only the effect of itself ... It must have no other purpose than the roundness and the color and the repetition of grapes in a bunch, such grapes as those of Juan Gris' (*Imaginations*, pp 286–7). This kind of thematic statement, of course, itself exists primarily in a dramatic context; in addition to whatever inherent ironies it may contain, it takes only a momentary place among all the other fragments of associative and disassociative memory, narrative, and exposition that make up the 'scurry' of the personae of *The Great American Novel* and the rest of the early prose pieces. As the monologist reminds us at one point, such fragments are 'particles of falling stars, coming to nothing' (*Imaginations*, p 208).

Ends are either complex or non-existent, the ceaseless mock of desire. Nevertheless, gestures of desire are central to all Williams's personae. They are all, in Paterson's phrase, 'flagrant in desire' (P, p 71), and desire seeks to move towards the intensified expression of itself in heroic gesture, design, dance. Or we might say simply that the self seeks to become articulate; scurryings, that is, are the moment-by-moment articulations of the self, leading perhaps to an aggregate of moments but to no end or resolution. In his 'Overture to a Dance of Locomotives' Williams notes that train wheels 'repeating / the same gesture remain relatively / stationary: rails forever parallel / return on themselves indefinitely' (SP, p 19). The artist hears and records these articulations (as Williams describes the process in 'Desert Music') in a way which itself intensifies and finally authenticates them: the verbal self (kinetic, energized, seeking self-realization) becomes the 'verb' of the 'made poem.'[15] Art is both the prototype and the apotheosis of self-realization, and the illusionist paradox is complete: the fictions of the self (including the self of the artist) achieve their fullest 'reality' in the fiction of art. The artist 'fixes' (designs, articulates, intensifies) the energized moment in an act that is an intensification of his own desire and a general affirmation of life. According to Williams, 'it isn't what he says that counts as a work of art, it's what he makes, with such intensity of perception that it lives with an intrinsic movement of its own to verify its authenticity.'[16]

'Intrinsic movement' which is self-authenticating: this is what Williams strives to create, both in those works where the persona is the self-conscious monologist and in those where the personae are more objectively drawn and dramatized. Many of the short lyrics deal with an action, or, even more often, a *poise* for action in which kinesis is momentarily arrested in form. Williams's 'Bird,' for example,

> with outstretched
> wings poised
> inviolate unreaching
>
> yet reaching
> your image this November
> planes
>
> to a stop
> miraculously fixed in my
> arresting eyes   (PB, p 41)

Here the bird's own self-realization, its movement towards articulation of energy (qualified, to be sure: 'unreaching / yet reaching / your image'), is explicitly augmented by the intense imaginative perception of the artist; aesthetic 'fix' or arrest, in other words, takes place on at least two levels. Or there is Elaine (in one of three dramatic sketches significantly called 'Stances') 'poised for the leap she / is not yet ready for / – save in her eyes' (PB, p 18); or the blue jay 'crouched / just before the take-off / caught / in the cinematograph – / in motion / of the mind' (this blue jay, Williams adds, is 'serving art / as usual' [PB, pp 48–9]); or in 'The Bitter World of Spring' the red elms 'that lift the tangled / net of their desires hard into / the falling rain' and the shad ascending 'water-headed, unrelenting, upstream' (CLP, p 75). At the centre of such poems is literally the articulating verb. In life, as in poetry, art is 'the agony of self-realization' (as Williams calls it in 'Desert Music') actualizing itself in form.

Actualization, it must be emphasized, is far more the form of desire than the form of consummation; it is tenuous, ephemeral, a 'cinematograph' at best, finding its source in pain as much as pleasure. It is simply whatever 'measure' we make or find in the arduous, hopeless pursuit of our dreams. In the later poetry particularly Williams focuses strongly on the traditional stoic qualities of courage, acceptance of suffering, and the relentless commitment to effort in the face of non-existent ends and sure failure – the qualities of the elms and shad described above. In book 4 of *Paterson* it is effort, of course, which emerges as the central theme: '*La Vertue est toute dans l'effort*' (P, p 184). There is also the effort of the music teacher and his pupils in Williams's poem 'Lesson from a Pupil Recital.' He remains 'blinking from his dreams' as his gross and awkward pupils attempt to release the music within them. Pupils and teacher (the 'creator' of the pupils just as the arresting eye 'miraculously fixed' the bird) fail to achieve anything commensurate with the dream, but the very desire for music takes a certain form, creates a certain music of its own, 'cleansing from each / his awkwardness for him to blossom / thence a sound' (CLP, p 83).

We have already noted Williams's identification with birds; it reflects his quixotic commitment to the sheer act of flight itself as passionate pursuit of the unknown in a void of nothingness. 'To seek what?' he asks rhetorically in another poem, 'The Woodpecker,' and the answer, as we might expect, is that 'there is nothing / there.' Even the unknown, he notes, if known, is no longer the unknown. Our only relevant 'knowledge' is of falling, pain, the consummation of failure: 'we never knew the earth so solidly as when we were / crushed upon it.' Or there is perhaps the formal knowledge of desire itself, so palpable as to be sustaining. As Joseph Riddel, the most acute recent critic of Williams, puts it, 'creative acts, efforts toward virtue, become in themselves the only virtue.'[17] Williams's comment on the woodpecker's pursuit of beetles sums up the mock-hero's most optimistic possibilities (which, in his earlier treatment of the swallow in *The Great American Novel*, were themselves mocked):

> Flight
> means only desire and desire the end of flight,
> stabbing there with a barbed tongue which *succeeds*!   (CLP, p 122)

PATERSON

Paterson brings together Williams's tendency in his other poetry to create dramatized personae who are avatars of the poet-hero and the use of a self-conscious monologist that was characteristic of the experimental fiction. Even the monologist is here given more generic reference (presumably Williams reflects the influence of

Joyce, Eliot, and Pound) and thus is himself kept at a somewhat greater dramatic distance from the author. In any case, he remains Williams's central version of the epic quester 'walking' the landscape in search of wonders, someone who (as he describes those he represents) 'craved the miraculous' (P, p 10). Or, to state the case more accurately, this is the role Paterson *tries to play* in an age of iron which yields wonders grudgingly if at all. Critics have noted that his is not 'pater' but 'pater-son,' but this distinction is not simply a sign that he represents rebellion, youth, hope, and renewal. Its ironic dimension suggests diminishment, attenuation, a less than fully adequate version of the father, someone who perhaps essentially models himself on a memorialized ideal – someone whose basic role (not necessarily his approach to that role) is foreign and anachronistic to the environment in which it must be realized. Clearly Paterson's *desire* to be romantic quester is heroic, but the context of reality mocks its fulfilment. His own awareness of his precarious situation and thus his self-mockery is acute. From the beginning his intentions are stated in the most tentative terms, his personal 'defectiveness' made clear: he is '*hard put to it*'; his major hope is less action itself than '*an identification and a plan for action*'; he is 'just another dog / among a lot of dogs – a lame one at that (P, pp 2–3; italics are Williams's). Significantly, he is not even allowed by the city to wander 'at large' in the park, which is the only natural landscape available to the modern hero (P, p 61). Paterson's middle name, 'Faitoute,' describes the fundamental quality of the epic hero in his world, but its ironic echoes in the poem are as insistent as its hint of possibility. Paterson, in fact, *does* almost nothing; even his walking is largely aimless strolling in a sterile void, 'foot pacing fast outward / into emptiness' (P, p 63).

Of the three other personae in *Paterson* who are the most obvious avatars of the poet-hero, two are even more ineffectual than Paterson himself. Corydon, for instance, is the mock-heroine of what is explicitly a mock-pastoral, the parody (or perhaps travesty) in this case so savage as to reduce both Corydon and her environment to a monochrome of despair and death. Attenuation has suffered almost total loss of substance. 'No more woods and fields. Therefore / present, forever present': this is the refrain of Corydon's modern pastoral of a 'pterodactyl'-like helicopter searching the Hellgate current for a corpse while the gulls circle in 'vortices of despair' (P, p 161). But even her message, like her entire modern pastoral, indeed, like Corydon herself, is an imitation of an imitation – bad T.S. Eliot, and worse Dante. 'It stinks,' she admits candidly in one of those moments which reveals her pain and her futile but continuing struggle to give some sort of coherence and articulation even to her despair of life, not to mention any possibilities that a 'new' present might have. Her authentic language (or, more precisely, the authentic language of her inauthenticity) is the barest 'chatter,' as Paterson elsewhere describes the nature of his own voice (P, p 39). In book 4 her identification with Paterson is substantial and deliberate (they are both made inept lovers of the same person).

Cress is another chatterer, and she also reinforces our sense of the poet-hero as failure, not only by her revelation of her own personal misfortunes but, of course, in the accusations she makes against Paterson.

At the other extreme as model of the poet in *Paterson* is Madame Curie (Allen Ginsberg, a promising beginner, is also paired with her in a positive sense). Like Daniel Boone, Curie experiences the consummation of the romantic hero in so far as she finds and releases (brings to form) in matter a power commensurate with her will and imagination. Her success is a paraphrase of Emerson's classic formulation of the transcendental quest and goal: 'That which was unconscious truth, becomes, when interpreted and defined in an object, a part of the domain of knowledge – a new weapon in the magazine of power.'[18] But as a historical figure she is something of an anomaly, perhaps a lingering echo of the great heroes of the past, more probably a genuine saint, authentically miraculous, essentially out of time. Williams emphasizes her uniqueness by drawing an amusing but significant comparison between the French couple and Mary and Joseph.

Paterson is, in effect, defined by the other personae of the poem, and he, in turn, articulates their natures as dimensions of himself. Together these personae constitute a scale of heroic possibility ranging from the extreme of Corydon's situation to that of Madame Curie. The first two sections of book 4 juxtapose these extremes: the opaque present as ultimate despairing mock or the continued possibility of 'a luminosity of elements, the / current leaping!' (P, p 176). Section 3 then characteristically 'resolves' them by returning to the full tension of mock-heroic as it manifests itself in the main body of the poem – by putting the focus, that is, neither on final failure nor major achievement but on unremitting *effort*. I have already alluded to Williams's major theme as it finds expression here:

> Virtue is wholly
> in the effort to be virtuous.
>   This takes connivance,
> takes convoluted forms, takes
>   time!   (P, p 189)

Despair is simply loss of will to effort. It is not a question of consummations; a steady commitment to effort is itself the heroic task, a failure of effort the major peril:

>   Weakness,
>   weakness dogs him, fulfillment only
>   a dream or in a dream. No one mind
>   can do it all, runs smooth
>   in the effort: *toute dans l'effort*   (P, p 191)

Walking – steady walking – is the articulating verb of the poem and the 'design' of its hero. A description of the 'form' of walking ('The body is tilted slightly forward,' P, p 45), quoted by Williams from *The Journal of the American Medical Association*, makes this clear from the beginning. Book 5 strongly reiterates the centrality of the poet's walk in the world but now in a context where it is seen as a sufficient and sustaining design, the highest possibility for the modern hero. For Paterson a continuum of heroic gesture will be his closest approach to formal order, the only possible 'measured dance' (P, p 239) on the ground of his desire.

As I have already noted, what Paterson *dreams* of being is an epic explorer of the wonders of the New World. His dream is as impossible of fulfilment as it was for the great explorers before him – as impossible, in fact, as Don Quixote's attempt to perpetuate the Age of Chivalry and Pierre Menard's to write Cervantes's novel. He is a defective hero in a defective world, or perhaps a world simply 'gone,' as he describes it at one point (P, p 79), and without renewal: 'Who is it spoke of April? Some / insane engineer. There is no recurrence' (P, p 142). Not only is this quester without an adequate environment for his quest; he is without any real sense of direction:

There is no direction. Whither? I
cannot say. I cannot say
more than how. The how (howl) only
is at my disposal (proposal).   (P, p 18)

He has some sense of the proper method of questing, but even this method is less fixed plan than existential cry of pain and need (howl), less under his present control (disposal) and thus some sort of end mastered, than what he calls elsewhere a 'plan' (proposal). The irony in Williams's major poem is insistently limiting and inherent to every dimension of its form. *Paterson*, in short, involves a futile quest relentlessly pursued, its narrative form that of the *blocked* quest or what I have been calling Cervantean mock-heroic. Williams, of course, realizes this; as his persona says at one point: 'Blocked. / (Make a song out of that: concretely)' (P, p 62).

More precisely, the quixotic song is a song of both freedom and blockage, in fact of freedom and blockage in irreconcilable, complex tension. Anticlimax is endemic to the poem – in the structural movement from section to section, even from passage to passage, and in the actions of the personae. Sam Patch's great dive is a metaphor of the whole: he plunges boldly towards the stream, his body wavers in the air, he disappears in the water, and the following spring turns up frozen in an ice-cake (P, p 17). Paterson's monologue, like that of the earlier personae of the experimental prose, alternates between hope and despair, possibility and denial, visions of renewal and of wasteland (or marriage and divorce), between willed commitment to self-realization – 'I must / find my meaning and lay it, white, / beside the sliding water' (P, p 145) – and bitter mockery of himself and others – 'Give up / the poem. Give up the shilly- / shally of art' (P, p 108). But he does not surrender his will and imagination and is willing, on the whole, to pay what he calls the 'cost' of loving; one recalls Paterson's vision in book 5 of the Jew in the extermination pit, smiling and comforting his companions as they are sprayed with machine-gun fire (P, p 223).

We are left, in the end, with the living ('concrete') shapes of desire in defeat. This is what Paterson articulates in himself and others. Cress, for example, takes this shape in her letters; so does the evangelist in the park; so, even, does Corydon. For Williams this is the shape of Maxwell Bodenheim, of Poe, of the particular heroics of modern stoicism. In this sense desire *is* fulfilled in the form of its own expression or self-realization. For Williams, as for Cervantes, the environment still offers some sort of dimension of adventure, some opportunity for the pursuit of dreams in which the pursuit at least allows the self to create (live) its fictions and the poet to give them further shape in naming. This is the most optimistic hope of mock-heroic narrative, the one expressed by Stevens through the towering figure of Chocorua: 'The air changes, creates and re-creates, like strength, / And to breath is a fulfilling of desire ...' At the same time Chocorua is simply the 'singular' spokes-man ('megalfrere') of the 'common self,' the latter called by Stevens a 'political tramp with an heraldic air.'[19] His punning on 'air' reminds us of the fragility of the mock-heroic environment, of the degree to which it offers, *at best*, only the opportu-nity for play or pretence. We cannot possess dreams but they can perhaps possess us. This at least is where Paterson has come out in book 5:

> Dreams possess me
> and the dance
> of my thoughts
> involving animals
> the blameless beasts   (P, p 224)

MELVIN BACKMAN

Death and Birth
in Hemingway

I sought my death and found it in my womb.
('Tichborne's Elegy')

If one were asked to name the American author most stoic in his philosophical
outlook, the most likely answer would be Ernest Hemingway. The Hemingway
code, with its insistence on courage and endurance, discipline and control, seems to
epitomize the stoic outlook. What establishes and measures the manhood of the
Hemingway hero – Nick Adams, Jake Barnes, Frederick Henry, Harry Morgan,
Robert Jordan, Colonel Cantwell, and Santiago – seems to be his stoic capacity to
endure pain and confront death. However, the confrontation with death generally
isolates the Hemingway hero, creating a situation in which he is actually or essentially uprooted from life and from others. His inner state, about which he tends to be
defensively silent, is the centre of his world and seems bound up with death anxiety.
Since it is this anxiety which constitutes, according to Paul Tillich,[1] the basic anxiety of mankind and which has brought into being religion and philosophy, the real
measure of Hemingway's stoicism will be the kind and degree of control the code
exercises over the *Angst*. From the stoic point of view control of the passions and
anxieties is based on a relating of self to the universe and on participating in the
divine power of reason. This power or governing principle of the cosmos is the *logos*.
Whether the Hemingway hero attains belief in the *logos* or, to use Tillich's words,
achieves the 'courage to be' is a question to be explored. But first one must explore
death in Hemingway's stories and novels, to see how it works both in and beneath
the events and actions and the characters' feelings and state of mind.

Hemingway, Malcolm Cowley has noted, belongs to the nocturnal writers who
have 'dealt in images that were symbols of an inner world,'[2] and writes of 'nightmares at noonday, accurately described, pictured without blur, but having the
nature of obsessions or hypnagogic visions between sleep and waking.'[3] It is the
submerged and unformulated feelings, as well as the unexorcised obsessions, that

may reveal the psychic reality of Hemingway's world. The most profound and obsessional feelings seem connected with death, but also with its apparent opposite – birth. It is with birth that Hemingway's first major work, *In Our Time*, begins. On the quay at Smyrna in the Greek evacuation of 1922 the women, as a British Officer recalls, were screaming at night. There were women with dead babies, who wouldn't give them up, some of the babies dead for six days. There was an old woman who died 'and went absolutely stiff,' her legs drawn up in a birth or foetal position. And there were other 'nice' things he remembered and dreamed about.

> You didn't mind the women who were having babies as you did those with the dead ones. They had them all right. Surprising how few of them died. You just covered them over with something and let them go to it. They'd always pick out the darkest place in the hold to have them. None of them minded anything once they got off the pier.
>
> The Greeks were nice chaps too. When they evacuated they had all their baggage animals they couldn't take off with them so they just broke their forelegs and dumped them into the shallow water. All those mules with their forelegs broken pushed over into the shallow water. It was all a pleasant business. My word yes a most pleasant business.[4]

The unnatural conjunction of birth and death is repeated in 'Indian Camp,' except that we have moved back about a dozen years and crossed the ocean from war-torn Europe and Asia Minor to peaceful America up in Michigan. As Nick Adams and Dr Adams were rowed across the lake to the Indian camp, Nick's father's arm was around him as if to protect him from what was to come, though even the doctor could not have anticipated the outcome. In the camp the screaming of the pregnant squaw repeats, for the reader, the screaming of the women on the quay at Smyrna, and the result is essentially the same: death and birth are jack-knifed into one double bunk, with death on top. Nick's father knifed the woman's womb open to get at life while the Indian razored his own throat to get at death.

> 'Why did he kill himself, Daddy?'
> 'I don't know, Nick. He couldn't stand things, I guess.'
> 'Do many men kill themselves, Daddy?'
> 'Not very many, Nick.'
> 'Do many women?'
> 'Hardly ever.'
> 'Don't they ever?'
> 'Oh, yes. They do sometimes.'
> 'Daddy?'
> 'Yes.'
> 'Where did Uncle George go?'
> 'He'll turn up all right.'

'Is dying hard, Daddy?'
'No, I think it's pretty easy, Nick. It all depends.'

They were seated in the boat, Nick in the stern, his father rowing. The sun was coming up over the hills. A bass jumped, making a circle in the water. Nick trailed his hand in the water. It felt warm in the sharp chill of the morning.
In the early morning on the lake sitting in the stern of the boat with his father rowing, he felt quite sure that he would never die.   (P 95)

In the boat being rowed by his father away from the death scene Nick trailed his hand in the warm water as if to establish some unconscious connection with life, while his conscious mind blocked out the reality of death. But the next vignette returns to reality, to the evacuation in the rain at Adrianople:

No end and no beginning. Just carts loaded with everything they owned. The old men and women, soaked through, walked along keeping the cattle moving. The Maritza was running yellow almost up to the bridge. Carts were jammed solid on the bridge with camels bobbing along through them. Greek cavalry herded along the procession. Women and kids were in the carts couched with mattresses, mirrors, sewing machines, bundles. There was a woman having a kid with a young girl holding a blanket over her and crying. Scared sick looking at it. It rained all through the evacuation.   (P 97)

In both scenes there is an evacuation, a jam-up, death commingling disturbingly with birth. The Greek woman giving birth under a blanket held against the rain stirs associations, like a bad dream, not only with the squaw screaming in the pain of giving birth to a breeched child but of the father cutting his throat under the blanket. If, underlying Hemingway's matter-of-fact details, there is a kind of Beckettian feeling about death – 'they give birth astride of a grave, the light gleams an instant, then it's night once more'[5] – there is something else, something that connects death with the womb.

'Indian Camp' begins and ends with the image of Nick in a boat moving over the water – an ancient symbolic image (like the ark of Noah or Moses) signifying the foetal life in the uterus, unafflicted as yet by the trauma of birth. 'Indian Camp' is centred on birth trauma but framed or circled by water, out of which Nick comes and to which he returns, as if symbolizing the amniotic fluid of the intrauterine existence. The book itself, filled with womb images, tells of all kinds of blows, representing variations on the birth trauma. In terms of the book's dynamics there are two opposing forces: one pulling Nick back to the womb, the other throwing him out into a painful and threatful situation. The feelings towards the womb are ambivalent, associated, on one hand, with the birth trauma, and, on the other hand, with refuge and security. For example, the Indian father in the upper bunk, like Ole Anderson in his bed in 'The Killers,' rolled over against the wall to signify his turning to death, his withdrawal to the closed dark wall of the womb. Soldiers were shot climbing walls, cabinet ministers were shot in the rain against the wall of a hospital (an institutional womb no longer functioning in the chaotic post-war world to support life), and one of the ministers too sick to stand was shot sitting down in the rain with his head on his knees. In 'The Battler' Nick was knocked out of a caboose by a brakeman into the dark and onto a track which led into swamp; making his way to a fire, Nick found a mutilated, crazy ex-fighter who welcomed him and then turned on him. Although young Nick was saved a beating then, he was promised he had a lot coming to him and that he too would end a 'beat up crazy.' In the next scene, a First World War vignette, Nick got some of what was coming to him: a spinal wound that left him, legs sticking out awkwardly (as in the breech birth of the papoose), helpless against a church wall, ready to make his separate peace. But there was no peace to be made ... only the far country in Michigan to return to.

Even the far country however had been burned over, so Nick had to hike deep into the woods to find a good place for his fishing camp. High by the river and overlooking the swamp, he pitched his tent.

> Inside the tent the light came through the brown canvas. It smelled pleasantly of canvas. Already there was something mysterious and homelike. Nick was happy as he crawled inside the tent. He had not been unhappy all day. This was different though. Now things were done. There had been this to do. Now it was done. It had been a hard trip. He was very tired. That was done. He had made his camp. He was settled. Nothing could touch him. It was a good place to camp. He was there, in the good place. (P 215)

Nick was withdrawing as far as he could from the war, the pain, the threat of death, the stresses and complications of the world – going back to a womblike refuge. Yet as Nick slept, curled up under his blanket, in his new old home, five frightened men waited in Chicago to be hanged, one of them with a blanket wrapped around his head; Sam Cardinella, who lost control of his sphincter muscle, was hanged, strapped tight into a chair and sitting in his own excrement. Up in Michigan Nick knew nothing about this death in Chicago; he did know, however, that the world into which he had been thrown was no kingdom of God, as his mother, living in her darkened room, would have him believe. By retreating to the Big Two-Hearted River he was putting the world away, for a time. Now he gave himself up to the early morning, the river, and the fishing. Baiting his hook with a grasshopper he waded into the rushing current and cast his line out. All morning he fished, catching two big trout, which he kept alive in 'the long sack that hung from his shoulders in the water' (p 228); one very big trout had got away from him, the excitement making him feel a little sick then. At noon he stopped to eat his sandwiches; afterwards, sitting on a log in the cool of the shade, he watched the river.

> Ahead the river narrowed and went into a swamp. The river became smooth and deep and the swamp looked solid with cedar trees, their trunks close together, their branches solid. It would not be possible to walk through a swamp like that. The branches grew so low ... He did not feel like going on into the swamp ... Nick did not want to go in there now ... In the swamp fishing was a tragic adventure. Nick did not want it. He did not want to go down the stream any further today. (Pp 230–1)

The changing width of the river may stir associations with Fossalta. The swamp signifies blocked passage and may stir memories of the blocked evacuation of the Greeks at Adrianople and, further back in time, of the blocked passage of the papoose in the birth canal, the screams of the mother undergoing the jackknife Caesarian birth without anaesthesia, and the suicide of the father above. The trout fishing, as Philip Young has convincingly demonstrated, provides escape and refuge for Nick from trauma.[6] It serves Nick too as a way of linking up with life – of going back before birth to the intrauterine stage of existence when the embryo-foetus, connected by the umbilical cord to its mother, lives like a fish in her dark fluid-filled sack. The analogy in 'Big Two-Hearted River' is rather explicit: Nick with his fishing line out in the water, waiting to feel the life of the trout at the other end of the cord, catching the trout and putting it into the sack where it swam and would be joined later by another trout. The title of the story, after all, is the 'Big Two-Hearted River.'

Nick Adams is the Fisher King of *In Our Time*. Rendered sick and helpless by too much exposure to death, Nick was seeking life and strength. The need to connect with life's wellspring becomes dominant and urgent when the threat of annihilation and the fact of non-being break through the ego's defenses, disturbing the rhythms of one's life and nullifying the very reason for being. With Nick Adams this happened at his wounding at Fossalta, in 'Now I Lay Me':

> I myself did not want to sleep because I had been living for a long time with the knowledge that if I ever shut my eyes in the dark and let myself go, my soul would go out of my body. I had been that way for a long time, ever since I had been blown up at night and felt it go out of me and go off and then come back. I tried never to think about it, but it had started to go since, in the nights, just at the moment of going off to sleep, and I could only stop it by a very great effort. So while now I am fairly sure that it would not really have gone out, yet then, that summer, I was unwilling to make the experiment.

I had different ways of occupying myself while I lay awake. I would think of a trout stream I had fished along when I was a boy and fish its whole length very carefully in my mind; fishing very carefully under all the logs, all the turns of the bank, the deep holes and the clear shallow stretches, sometimes catching trout and sometimes losing them. I would stop fishing at noon to eat my lunch; sometimes on a log over the stream; sometimes on a high bank under a tree, and I always ate my lunch very slowly and watched the stream below me while I ate.   (P 363)

'Now I Lay Me' makes explicit that Nick's fear of the dark was fear of dying, that yielding oneself up to sleep was felt as the losing of one's identity to death, to nothingness; light was a way of holding off darkness, staying awake at night a way of holding off death. Implicitly the story is about the early years of Nick: his boyhood fishing and childhood fears. The title 'Now I Lay Me' evokes the image of a child's night prayer against death. That Nick's fear of death began in his early life is confirmed by the deleted opening of 'Indian Camp,' which describes the boy's fear at night:

He was not afraid of anything definite as yet. But he was getting very afraid. Then suddenly he was afraid of dying. Just a few weeks before at home, in church, they had sung a hymn, 'Some day the silver cord will break.' While they were singing the hymn Nick had realized that some day he must die. It made him feel quite sick. It was the first time he had ever realized that he himself would have to die sometime.[7]

The feeling of death generated for Nick by the image of the breaking of the cord suggests the birth trauma: that is, the foetus suffers death and separation anxieties in being forced by the mother out from her womb, forced out of its familiar aquatic home into a strange land-world.[8] The connection between the new world and the old having been cut, the foetus-child is thrust into a new existence and slapped into breathing with its own lungs – in effect, the traumatic transition from a symbiotic to a separate existence. Nick's fishing at night in 'Now I Lay Me' and at day in 'Big Two-Hearted River' constitutes his response to the disturbing threat of death actuated by war; it represents on the unconscious level a regressing to his aquatic, antenatal existence or reunion with the womb. We are, in a sense, circling back to 'Indian Camp' and the feeling of death generated by the birth trauma, to 'On the Quai at Smyrna' and its women and dead babies and the baggage animals with broken forelegs drowning in the water. Death, Hemingway seems to be saying, is not born at war but in birth or in the womb; and death anxieties, though actuated by the war, have their beginnings in the womb.

Whereas Nick Adams, the American soldier returned from Europe, is characterized by withdrawal, the Americans in post-war Europe in *In Our Time* are characterized by impotence. The American males in 'Mr. and Mrs. Elliot,' 'Cat in the Rain,' and 'Out of Season' could not consummate their sexual relations; in fact, the American male in 'Out of Season' could not even go fishing. Interspersed among these stories of sterility are the vignettes describing violence in the bullring: generally aborted violence in which bullfighters were gored or killed, a horse disemboweled, a bull exhausted by too much bad sticking, matadors self-shamed or drunk. Isolated in the midst of the impotence and indiscriminate violence is the description of Villalta's killing of the bull:

> When he started to kill it was all in the same rush. The bull looking at him straight in front, hating. He drew out the sword from the folds of the muleta and sighted with the same movement and called to the bull, Toro! Toro! and the bull charged and Villalta charged and just for a moment they became one. Villalta became one with the bull and then it was over. Villalta standing straight and the red hilt of the sword sticking out dully between the bull's shoulders. Villalta his hand up at the crowd and the bull roaring blood looking straight at Villalta and his legs caving. (P 181)

This killing is Hemingway's moment of truth: by a single thrust of controlled aggression man gratifies his need to achieve union and to retaliate and kill.

These feelings and needs have found their best creative expression in *The Sun Also Rises*, which takes the form of a twentieth-century version of the Waste Land myth. Jake Barnes is the maimed Fisher King, Brett Ashley the profaned grail and corrupting Queen, Robert Cohn the false knight, Pedro Romero the warrior-priest performing the ancient fertility rites. When the King arranged for the warrior-priest to fornicate with the Queen, the spirit of the rites was violated and the corruption spread. Both Brett and Jake sought water: she to cleanse herself, he to search for retreat and for life itself. Although the river and the sea provided Jake with temporary refuge, they could not make him whole or rid the Waste Land of its blight. Because of her unsexing by the War Brett's union with any male remains sterile and destructive. So the novel ends as it began, with Jake and Brett riding in a taxicab in a circle, the circle representing not the renewing cycle of nature but the repetitive aimless movement of sick beings. Separate and together, Brett and Jake survive in their malaise, she to pursue her empty hedonism, he to hold on to his unsustaining stoicism.

In terms of the Hemingway psychology Jake and Romero, taken together, represent the maimed and retaliating male; Brett the injured and injuring female. The emasculation of Jake may be associated with the death-castration depicted in 'Indian Camp'; according to Freud the fear of death is an analogue of the fear of castration. By making love to Jake's woman and by killing the bull, Romero functions as an *alter ego* to provide release for Jake's erotic and aggressive needs – enabling Jake in a subconscious way to re-enter the womb, since his war wound prevents him from entering the womb-genitalia with his own body. In his recoil from and attraction to the womb-genitalia Jake may, in a sense, have been reacting to the trauma of birth in which woman is felt as both destroyer and sustainer of life.

The first wounded Hemingway hero to enter the womb-genitalia is Frederick Henry. When Henry first began to make love to Catherine, she pretended that he was her lover who had been killed in the war, and she had Frederick say: 'I've come back to Catherine in the night.'[9] Although Henry made love to her at first as if it were a game, he did not fall in love with her until after his wounding. Henry's wounding by the big trench mortar shell exploding in the dugout is another variation on the birth trauma in 'Indian Camp' and on the wounding of Nick Adams in 'Now I Lay Me' and 'A Way You'll Never Be' – the wounding along the water, entangled legs and smashed legs, the squaw having become 'mama mia,' the birth-death sensations of being forced or exploded out into nothingness and of wanting to come back:

> ... then there was a flash, as when a blast-furnace door is swung open, and a roar that started white and went red and on and on in a rushing wind. I tried to breathe but my breath would not come and I felt myself rush bodily out of myself and out and out and out and all the time bodily in the wind. I went out swiftly, all of myself, and I knew I was dead and that it had all been a mistake to think you just died. Then I floated, and instead of going on I felt myself slide back. I breathed and I was back. The ground was torn up and in front of my head there was a splintered beam of wood. In the jolt of my head I heard somebody crying. I thought somebody was screaming. I tried to move but I could not move. I heard the machine-guns and rifles firing across the river and all along the river. There was a great splashing and I saw the starshells go up and burst and float whitely and rockets going up and heard the bombs, all this in a moment, and then I heard close to me someone saying 'Mama Mia! oh mama Mia!' I pulled and twisted and got my legs loose finally and turned around and touched him. It was Passini and when I touched him he screamed. His legs were toward me and I saw in the dark and the light that they were both smashed above the knee. One leg was gone and the other was held by tendons and part of the trouser and the stump twitched and jerked as though it were not connected. He bit his arm and moaned, 'Oh mama Mia, mama Mia,' then, 'Dio te salve, Maria. Dio te salve, Maria. Oh Jesus shoot me Christ shoot me mama Mia mama Mia oh purest lovely Mary shoot me. Stop it. Stop it. Stop it. Oh Jesus lovely Mary stop it. Oh oh oh oh,' then choking, 'Mama mama mia.' Then he was quiet, biting his arm, the stump of his leg twitching. (Pp 54–5)

The wounding causes Henry to retreat to a romanticized foetal existence in the hospital where he was cared for and loved by his nurse Catherine. Although Catherine has been compared to one of Kipling's 'submissive infra-Anglo-Saxon women that make his heroes such perfect mistresses,'[10] she acts in a maternal as well as a sexual role. She demonstrates a physical and psychological need to incorporate herself into Frederick, like mother and foetus: 'There isn't any me. I'm you. Don't make up a separate me' (p 115). Frederick was pulled back to her, like a hurt child to the womb, in a romantic variation of Nick Adams in 'Big Two-Hearted River.'

> I loved to take her hair down and she sat on the bed and kept very still, except suddenly she would dip down to kiss me while I was doing it, and I would take out the pins and lay them on the sheet and it would be loose and I would watch her while she kept very still and then take out the last two pins and it would all come down and she would drop her head and we would both be inside of it, and it was the feeling of inside a tent or behind a falls.   (P 114)

This romanticized foetal state constitutes the separate peace to which Henry wished to return; the war constitutes, of course, the threat of death, which culminates in the battle police's summary decision to shoot him. He escaped by plunging into the river and by hiding under the canvas covering the guns being transported by rail, but the gun in effect destroyed 'the good place.' There would be no separate peace in Italy as long as the war was on. Across the lake was Switzerland; so, blown by the wind and rowing the bartender's boat, Catherine and Frederick made their way to this European womb of peace. Yet even in Switzerland there would be no real refuge for them because death, as in 'Indian Camp,' would attend the Caesarian birth of Catherine's child, and the foetus would be strangled by its own umbilical cord.

The love of Catherine and Frederick was a narcissistic pact against the others – the 'they' of the outside world: 'there's only us two in the world and there's all the rest of them. If anything comes between us we're gone and then they have us' (p 139). It is a defensive narcissism shadowed by death which induces Frederick to project onto the world the threat he felt besetting them from the outside: 'The world breaks everyone ... those that will not break it kills. It kills the very good and the very gentle and the very brave impartially' (p 249). The threat is felt by all the wounded Hemingway heroes of the twenties; yet Frederick, who ironically is the least helpless and most fully recovered of the three (Nick Adams, Jake Barnes, and Frederick Henry), is the first to verbalize the feeling that man is the victim of a hostile universe and that he is attended by the threat of death from the beginning to the end of his life. Jake is more stoically silent, largely because the nature of his wound has forced him into a vicarious existence so that Pedro Romero becomes his heroic *alter ego*, Robert Cohn his scapegoat *alter ego* of self-centredness and self-pity. Henry's philosophical outlook, partly because of the narcissism underlying his pessimism, seems less defensible than Jake's 'I did not care what it was all about. All I wanted to know was how to live in it' (p 148). Nevertheless, Henry's very indictment of the world points to an evolving aggressiveness necessary to supplant the wounded protagonist's powerlessness.

In the twenties Hemingway wrote about the maiming of the young American in body and spirit, about the slow healing of the wound, and the helplessness induced by the malaise. In the thirties the victim turned agressive with a vengeance, and the killings Hemingway describes in *Death in the Afternoon* (1932), *Green Hills of Africa* (1935), and *To Have and Have Not* (1937) evince a ritualized, compulsive, hysterical destructiveness, which is another phase of the sickness. This unleashed aggressiveness seems originally a defensive reaction triggered by the self-preservation instinct against the threat of death experienced at birth and in war, but it becomes connected with the need for self-affirmation through the mastering of fear by courage, the converting of impotence into virility, and the transforming of being killed into killing. The overmastering anxiety of having experienced too much pain and death and of having been rendered helpless actuates the need to strike back, to kill. The overexposure to pain and death and decomposition is very clear in 'A Natural History of the Dead,' with its curious blend of belligerence and horror and with its grim finale. The captain doctor, having tossed iodine into the artillery lieutenant's eyes and disregarding his screams, prepared to operate on him, ordering: '"Hold him tight ... He is in much pain. Hold him very tight"' (p 449). It is a war episode reminiscent of another time when Dr Adams had men hold the squaw down and he, disregarding her screams, knifed her womb open. There was pain, all right: the pain of the mother, the pain of the breeched child, the pain of the father above. No wonder the father killed himself, no wonder the child in Catherine Barkley's womb strangled itself, and no wonder the old man in 'A Clean Well-Lighted Place' tried to hang himself.

The Hemingway world of the twenties and thirties was no clean well-lighted place; it was rather a kingdom of *Nada*. In place of the primordial feeling of being protected in and outside the mother's womb, there was nothingness ... and there was no father above. 'The small boy who shouted "Fraid o'nothing,"' Carlos Baker has noted of Hemingway, 'became the man who discovered that there was plenty to fear, including that vast cosmic nothingness which Goya named *Nada*.'[1] The old waiter in 'A Clean Well-Lighted Place,' knowing well this feeling, uttered the Lord's Prayer to *Nada*. Although the waiter denied the existence of the Lord, he responded with compassion to the plight of the old man who had tried to commit suicide, for the old waiter was of those who need a light for the night, of the gentle kind – like the priest in *A Farewell to Arms*, the old man at the bridge, and Anselmo in *For Whom the Bell Tolls*. In Hemingway's kingdom of *Nada* and suffering the pull to death is very strong. The other way which most of the Hemingway heroes of the thirties take is that of anger and aggression. Hemingway has written of his own need to kill: 'Since he was a young boy he has cared greatly for fishing and shooting. If he had not spent so much time at them ... he might have written much more. On the other hand, he might have shot himself.'[12] Hemingway would rationalize killing in *Death in the Afternoon* as 'the feeling of rebellion against death which comes from its administering. Once you accept the rule of death thou shalt not kill is an easily and a naturally obeyed commandment. But when a man is still in rebellion against death he has pleasure in taking to himself one of the Godlike attributes; that of giving it' (p 233). The particular killing that Hemingway was sanctifying was the killing of the bull, almost as if by killing the bull the matador provided a primitive, mystical way of incorporating the bull's male power into oneself. The archetypal matador and hero of *Death in the Afternoon* is Manuel Garcia, Maera, who also serves as the prototype for the Manuel Garcia of 'The Undefeated.' Maera is described as killing the bull – the 'f--king bull made out of cement' that dislocated his wrist and that he did not kill till his seventh charge over the horns of the bull – with the same kind of rage and perseverance and *pundonor* with which he fought death in a Seville hospital: 'with a tube in each lung, drowned with pneumonia that came to finish off the tuberculosis. When he was delirious he rolled under the bed and fought death under the bed dying as hard as a man can die ... Era muy hombre.'[13]

In bullfighting Hemingway was apparently fighting not only death and powerlessness, but also society and woman. Society was felt to be the maker of war, woman the maker of birth – both the makers of man's traumas. Although the traumas of war have received more overt attention from Hemingway in his work, it is woman who has been the subject of the greater animosity. Despite the fact that war caused the emasculation of Jake and the wounding of Nick, it is woman who was felt to be the castrator and threat. Nick's mother, he remembered in his sleepless nights at the hospital (in 'Now I Lay Me'), had tried to destroy his father's arrowheads and Indian weapons. Brett, by using Jake as pimp and confidant for her love affairs with others, reinforced the damage already done to his manhood. Margot Macomber shot her man as soon as he discovered his manhood; and Harry, in 'The Snows of Kilimanjaro,' preferred to believe that his rich wife had destroyed his ability to write. In terms of the emotional needs of the protagonist, and apparently of the author, the bull is both symbol of male power that the matador fights and kills and incorporates, and symbol of woman that he dominates and enters and kills. The bull is the sacrifice; the matador is the warrior-priest effecting the sacramental union of Eros and Thanatos; the purpose is renewal of life and restoration of power.

The aggression of the Hemingway men of the thirties would probably, by its very nature, have exhausted itself in time; however, towards the end of the decade circumstances provided the event, the Spanish Civil War, which effected a change and seemed to strike a balance between aggression and love in Hemingway. *For Whom the Bell Tolls* is remarkably free of the malaise, anxiety, and tension of the early works; relatively expansive and relaxed, it discourses on duty, courage and brotherhood in long-winded introspection by Robert Jordan, as if he were lecturing to himself and the reader. Not only would many of the topics have been taboo for the early Hemingway but the endless thinking out of feelings and ideas would probably have been dismissed as phony or certainly have merited Hemingway's 'You'll lose it if you talk about it.' Nevertheless, a significant change did take place: Hemingway was moving from narcissism, pessimism, nihilism, and existential stoicism towards a somewhat self-conscious humanism and stoicism, group solidarity, and, in varying degrees, love and faith. There was a new awareness of other people, other egos, and the other sex. Pilar and Maria are testaments to this awareness.

Pilar – there is no other woman like her in all Hemingway's works. Dependent on no man, despite her relationship with Pablo, she exists in her own right: tough, courageous, loyal, reliable, generous-hearted, foul-mouthed, passionate, intuitive, and wise with a down-to-earth blend of wisdom and mysticism. She is the gypsy sibyl who, knowing of Jordan's approaching death and caring about Maria, arranged for the Jordan-Maria love to happen. Almost against her will Pilar drew from their love a vicarious sexual gratification, because she was a passionate woman resisting her change of life and because she loved both Maria and Jordan, differently, in her own erotic maternal way. As much man as woman, she was the centre of the guerilla band, their leader and mother, a matriarchal figure for whom, strangely enough, Hemingway seemed to feel an affinity. This affinity may have been the result of the war, of their shared interest in death and the Spanish cause, and, more important, of Hemingway's readiness at this time to acknowledge a feminine aspect of his own being.

In *For Whom the Bell Tolls* Hemingway would seem to have split woman in two, separating the ruling element from the submissive element. Maria is the first of Hemingway's women to elicit from her lover a tender, deeply felt concern for her well-being. Despite Frederick Henry's professed love for Catherine, his narcissism kept him from developing the kind of tenderness which characterizes Jordan's love for Maria. If Maria, as innocent victim of the rape of war, embodies the wounded psyche of the early Hemingway hero, then Jordan's love for her is motivated by a deep need to restore the body and spirit maimed by war, and, by an act of will, to reconcile the self to life and humanity.

> 'Thee, they cannot touch. No one has touched thee, little rabbit,' he comforted ...
>
> 'If we do everything together, the other maybe never will have been,' ... she appealed, and told him what Pilar had said: ... 'That nothing is done to oneself that one does not accept and that if I loved someone it would take it all away. I wished to die, you see.'[14]   (Pp 71–3)

They retreated at night to their womb, the sleeping bag under the pines, where he made love to her as if he knew that she was the last of life to be given him in the race against death. When they made love in the sun-warmed heather, with the sun beating down on them and uniting its pulsing energy with theirs, the earth moved for them. For him the consummation was felt in an ecstatic release of consciousness after the plunging down into the dark of the earth, then an upward soaring as if released from earthly bonds. It was like dying – like dying unto the womb:[15]

> Then there was the smell of heather crushed and the roughness of the bent stalks under her head and the sun bright on her closed eyes and for all his life he would remember the curve of her throat with her head pushed back into the heather roots and her lips that moved smally and by themselves and the fluttering of the lashes on the eyes tight closed against the sun and against everything, and for her everything was red, orange, gold-red from the sun on the closed eyes, and it all was that color, all of it, the filling, the possessing, the having, all of that color, all in a blindness of that color. For him it was a dark passage which led to nowhere, then to nowhere, then again to nowhere, once again to nowhere, always and forever to nowhere, heavy on the elbows in the earth to nowhere, dark, never any end to nowhere, hung on all time always to unknowing nowhere, this time and again always and to nowhere, now not to be borne once again always and to nowhere, now beyond all bearing up, up, up and into nowhere, suddenly, scaldingly, holdingly all nowhere gone and time absolutely still and they were both there, time having stopped and he felt the earth move out and away from them.   (P 159)

Maria, with her short-cropped sun-gold hair and gold-flecked skin, was like the sun, like life itself, to which Jordan held tight, as if to hold off the darkness of death. Yet Maria stirs associations too with the *Virgen* to whom men prayed – Joaquin, Anselmo, Lieutenant Berrendo – at the hour of their death. For Joaquin too the earth would move when the bombs exploded on him as he was praying to the Holy Virgin. The Blessed Virgin of Pilar was also invoked by a sister to protect her brother, the young cavalryman from Tafalla, whom Jordan, rising up from the sleeping bag of love, shot dead. Maria symbolizes, paradoxically, life and death.

For Whom the Bell Tolls is constructed of paradox. Robert Jordan's objective was to destroy the bridge – for the sake of building other bridges for mankind. For the sake of brotherhood in Spain Jordan killed the young soldier from Tafalla,[16] whom in another time he might have joined in running the bulls at Pamplona. Jordan, and Hemingway, claimed to believe in the family of man, the 'continent of Mankinde'; yet he admitted that the necessity to kill, as Agustin put it, was like the desire of a mare in heat waiting for the stallion (p 286). Jordan's humanistic rationalizations and struggle with his conscience about killing do not seem to tap the authentic being of the protagonist or the author. Closer to the authentic life is what Hemingway said about Kashkin, which applies to Jordan too: 'There was something wrong with Kashkin evidently and he was working it out in Spain' (pp 231–2). Early in the novel the gypsy sang a song beginning with '*I had an inheritance from my father*' (p 59); it was an inheritance that Jordan would have ultimately to confront, but not till the end of the novel. After Jordan was wounded, he sent Maria away:

> 'Listen. We will not go to Madrid now but I go always with thee wherever thou goest.
> Understand? ... Thou wilt go now, rabbit. But I go with thee. As long as there is one of us
> there is both of us. Do you understand?'
> 'Nay, I stay with thee.'
> 'Nay, rabbit. What I do now I do alone ... Each one must do it alone.   (P 463)

Then he got Pilar to take her away, and refusing Agustin's offer to shoot him, he made his farewells and prepared – alone, his back against a pine tree – to deal with the reality of death. The make-believe was over.

For Jordan the real decision had come: to be or not to be, to kill another or to kill himself. Holding tight against the pain, he called upon his grandfather to help him not to kill himself. Father – there was no father. His father, like the castrated boar of a Pablo, was discredited ... *cobarde* ... no *cojones* ... shot himself. Robert Jordan 'lay very quietly and tried to hold on to himself that he felt slipping away from himself as you feel snow starting to slip sometimes on a mountain slope, and he said, now quietly, then let me last until they come' (pp 470–1). Then he integrated himself; and lying stomach down in the pine needles, his gun ready, he looked down at the road, the bridge, the stream, and prepared to kill the enemy when he came into sight.

> Lieutenant Berrendo, watching the trail, came riding up, his thin face serious and grave.
> His submachine gun lay across his saddle in the crook of his left arm. Robert Jordan
> lay behind the tree, holding onto himself very carefully and delicately to keep his hands
> steady. He was waiting until the officer reached the sunlit place where the first trees of
> the pine forest joined the green slope of the meadow. He could feel his heart beating
> against the pine needle floor of the forest.   (P 471)

We have come full circle from the planning of the bridge's destruction at the novel's beginning to the explosive tension within the cave to the love in the sleeping bag to death in the pines. The end was in the beginning, the beginning in the end. Death was inside Jordan all the time, waiting for the right moment: Jordan knew it, Pilar knew it. Death, one might say, is the principal actor in *For Whom the Bell Tolls*, or, in the Heideggerian sense, death is present in each moment of life. Jordan's stoic confrontation of death marks a significant growth from the shellshock and regression of Nick, the impotence and malaise of Jake, the narcissism and withdrawal of Henry, and the compulsion to kill of Harry Morgan. Or was Jordan really courting death and, as his name suggests, seeking the promised land across the river and into the trees, blowing the bridge that would connect him to life? Was Maria angel of life or angel of death? There is another way of looking at the matter which may throw some light on the question. In changing the original triangle of Dr Adams–Mrs Adams–Nick to Pablo–Pilar–Jordan, Hemingway has substituted good mother for bad; however, the fathers of both Nick and Jordan have been depicted as *cobardes* who commit suicide, and Pablo, too, has been branded as *cobarde*, and even as a Judas, so that he has had to be replaced by Pilar. Another triangle of Pilar–Jordan–Maria is formed; in this trio Pilar is both father and mother, Jordan and Maria her son and daughter. Although Pilar could not save Jordan from death, she could, with the help of Jordan, save Maria from trauma and death. The thrust of *For Whom the Bell Tolls* is towards the sun, towards life, away from the cave of death. There is plenty of death in *For Whom the Bell Tolls* and there is the larger defeat of the war itself despite the victory of the bridge. Nevertheless, General Golz takes the defeat in stoic spirit:

'*Nous sommes foutus. Oui. Comme toujours. Oui. C'est dommage. Oui.*' (P 428)

'*Rien a faire. Rien. Faut pas penser. Faut accepter.*' (P 429)

For the first time in a Hemingway novel victory does not really belong to Death.

All the rivers run into the sea. It is by the rivers and the canals that the wounds and trauma of birth and war were received; it is to the canals and to Fossalta that Colonel Cantwell returned in *Across the River and Into the Trees*. But the Colonel – in coming to Venice, city of the seas, and to Renata, portrayed as rising from the sea, her name signifying rebirth – was ultimately seeking the sea. More ancient than the land, the sea is primal mother and source of life, figuring deeply in man's dreams and neuroses, as Ferenczi has noted:

Individual observations of the symbolism of dreams and neuroses reveal a fundamental symbolic identification of the mother's body with the waters of the sea and the sea itself on the one hand, and on the other with 'Mother Earth,' provider of nourishment. Now such symbolism might be expressive of the fact not only that the individual lives on the mother before birth as a water-inhabiting endoparasite and then for a longer time after birth as an air-breathing ectoparasite, but also that sea and earth were actually the precursors of the mother in the development of the species, and at this stage took the place, in that they protected and nourished these animal ancestors, of the maternal protective adaptations which were acquired later. In this sense the sea symbolism of the mother would approach a more archaic, more primitive character.[17]

Under a blanket in the black gondola moving over the waters of the canal the Colonel made love to Renata – as if to exorcise for Hemingway memories of the river and canal that ran in Nick Adams's nightmares in 'A Way You'll Never Be,' of the canal that was too narrow for the birth of the baby in 'Indian Camp,' and of the blanket which a girl crying in the rain at the Adrianople evacuation held over a woman having a baby. The memories of the trauma were more real than the love, for the love, like the 'secret order' ritual of the Colonel and the Gran Maestro, consisted of mawkish fantasy and bellicose egotism. Nevertheless, just as the canal would not lead to the sea, so Cantwell's return to the past would bring no restoration of life, leaving him to bitterness and death. Cut of the same cloth as Harry Morgan, Richard Cantwell resorted to anger as a defence against repressed anxiety and despair. The only Hemingway hero who would reach and become one with the sea of life would be Santiago of *The Old Man and the Sea*.

The Old Man and the Sea resolves more successfully than *For Whom the Bell Tolls* the earlier anxieties and compulsions, such as the anxieties of birth and death, and the compulsions to kill or be killed. However, since *The Old Man and the Sea* is Hemingway's only novel in the last two decades to provide such a resolution,[18] though admittedly he was not producing much in those years, one must conclude that the resolution was Santiago's rather than Hemingway's. Santiago – with his natural Spartan existence sustained by simple stoicism, faith, and acceptance of life – represented, in all probability, a component of the author's being that could not be translated into Hemingway's own existence. Too much of the other fisherman, Nick Adams, may still have been part of Hemingway even though The Big Two-Hearted River had long since given way to the Caribbean Sea, and twenty-seven years of changes and happenings had occurred in the interval between *In Our Time* and *The Old Man and the Sea*. The river was Nick's retreat from struggle, but the sea was Santiago's natural arena in the struggle for existence. As Santiago said,

> ... he was born to be a fisherman and the fish was born to be a fish. The killing of fish is an old accepted livelihood. And the setting for Santiago's struggle is the most natural in the world: overhead move the sun and the stars and the moon; beneath sways the sea, *la mar*; and about the boat move the birds and fish. The sea is the old man's home and the others are his friends and brothers. The old fisherman himself – his skin blotched brown by the friendly sun, his eyes 'the color of the sea,' the scars on his hands 'old as erosions in a fishless desert' – is part of this natural universe. It is a complete and closed universe, a friendly one – its Creator neither hostile nor beneficent but mysteriously just. And the old man talks to the fish and birds and the stars just as primitive man might have done long ago.[19]

La Mar, in terms of the birth-death theme, is the waters of the womb to which the old man returned every day to fish, going back to the intrauterine existence where one was never alone and was part of a primordial, harmonious world. But his purpose, his fate, was to catch the big marlin. Once he caught the big fish and joined their lives together with the line, he was reliving, in a sense, the birth trauma: the fish becoming the mother from whom Santiago drew strength, yet whom he battled with love and fortitude and resolution. Like Christ on the Cross, Santiago took his suffering against the wood, staying with the fish till the second day when finally, though faint with pain and weariness, he turned the fish close to the boat for the kill.

> He took all his pain and what was left of his strength and his long gone pride and put it against the fish's agony and the fish came over onto his side and swam gently on his side, his bill almost touching the planking of the skiff and started to pass the boat, long, deep, wide, silver and barred with purple and interminable in the water.
>
> The old man dropped the line and put his foot on it and lifted the harpoon high as he could and drove it down with all his strength, and more strength he had just summoned, into the fish's side just behind the great chest fin that rose high in the air to the altitude of the man's chest. He felt the iron go in and he leaned on it and drove it further and then pushed all his weight after it.
>
> Then the fish came alive, with his death in him, and rose high out of the water showing all his great length and width and all his power and his beauty. He seemed to hang in the air above the old man in the skiff. Then he fell into the water with a crash that sent spray over the old man and over all of the skiff. (P 52)

Though faint and sick and tired, the old man pulled the fish in and lashed him to the boat; then, lashed side by side, man and fish sailed together homeward.

Santiago's killing of the marlin is related to but different from Manuel Garcia's killing of the bull in 'The Undefeated' and *Death in the Afternoon*, for Santiago killed without anger, hate, defiance, or lust for killing – doing what he was born to do and had to do again and again. The old man talked to himself about the killing of the fish: 'You killed him for pride and because you are a fisherman. You loved him when he was alive and you loved him after. If you love him, it is not a sin to kill him. Or is it more?' (p 59). If in his experience with the fish Santiago was reliving both the foetal relationship with the mother and the trauma of birth, then the killing of the fish represents both his birth and confirmation of manhood, to prove once again that the trauma had not unmanned him. Santiago mastered the death anxiety by experiencing the birth trauma as a crucifixion,[20] making it back on the third day to port, to his shack, to bed, to sleep, to the boy and another day. Although the sharks destroyed the body of the fish and hurt Santiago, they did not destroy the meaning of the experience, his renewal of body and spirit. The focus of the story moves from the old man and the sea and the fish to the old man and the boy Manolin; from mother and foetus, so to speak, to father and son. The Nick Adams who relived in his nightmares the wounding at the 'long, yellow house with a low stable and the river'[21] by Fossalta has been metamorphosed into the old man who dreamt happily of the lions and the 'long yellow beach' (p 45) of his youth.

The lions and the long yellow beach of Santiago's dreams of youth suggest some wishful thinking in Hemingway's characterization of his hero, as if the author wished to expunge Nick's trauma and restore a healed Nick Adams to life as the old Cuban fisherman. However, in terms of the background of Nick's and Santiago's lives, the two characters cannot be one and the same. From the realistic point of view the old fisherman is not Hemingway's 'strange old man'; the 'strange old man' is the Hemingway who felt compelled to return to Spain and Africa in the fifties – not just for the sake of a nostalgic recapture of past glories and happiness, but out of a driven need to re-encounter death. As in the thirties there was again a preoccupation with killing, which may trace back to the primitive hunter's incorporating of the killed life into himself but, more importantly, to a decline in Hemingway's creativity. Even less than the author of *Death in the Afternoon* and *Green Hills of Africa* was Hemingway able to convert the killings into literature. The artist had broken down ... broken down because Hemingway's special genius seems to have been rooted not in the killing but in the being killed. Although killing as a sport seems to have served Hemingway as a quick release of bound up tensions and anxieties, the creating of life through art seems to have disarmed or metamorphosed death in a less destructive and psychically more valid way for Hemingway. The major creative period of Hemingway's writing was concentrated in the twenties, when, out of the compelled and profound response of his conscious and unconscious being to the experience of death, he gave life to the death situations of Nick Adams, Jake Barnes, and Frederick Henry. The artist was born out of death, his writing serving not only to exorcise anxieties but, by creating another reality, to justify his being.

The return to the womb seems to have been a subconscious and unconscious way of mastering death and separation anxieties by reliving the birth trauma and by going back to the intrauterine condition. At the centre of almost all the Hemingway heroes is *Angst*. Projected onto the outside world the *Angst* has created, in effect, a hostile and bleak universe in which man is subjected to death, infected by malaise, and rendered powerless. The Hemingway code, which developed as a means of holding tight against pain and death, has enabled the hero to function and survive without surrendering his essential pride. Only partly effective in dealing with anxieties, the code did not work with existential anxiety, the anxiety of non-being and meaninglessness, because it could not give meaning to life or modify the destructiveness and nihilism of the twentieth-century world. So it is that the code, for all its stoic character, did not and could not provide a belief in the *logos* to counter death and *Nada*. For in the very beginnings of life there was unreason – undermining existence, estranging and traumatizing man. Nor could the reliving of the womb experience undo the trauma or negate the unreason.

The centrality of the trauma in the psychic life of the Hemingway hero led to a shrinking of the emotional, intellectual, and spiritual elements of his being in order to defend against internal and external threats. Hence the dictum – Don't think about it – constituted his attempt to reduce vulnerability as well as his desire to concentrate life in physical being. His desire to live by the body was the result of both fear of psychic disturbance and joy in the body's senses and responses. Because of the psychic withdrawal brought about by the trauma of war and birth, the Hemingway hero has remained a loner at heart, unable to give authentically of himself to others. The feeling of primal rejection lies at the root of the *Nada* in the Hemingway world and severely limits the religious experience, reducing it essentially to an outcry for help in time of need. Even Santiago, who brings to his suffering the quality of a simple stoic Christ, is limited in his religious experience. Locked within the wounded self, the Hemingway hero is not able to make the kind of authentic relationship to others or to a divine power which would give purpose to life and sustain the human spirit in its struggles.

The closest that Hemingway was to come to such an ideal is, of course, Santiago, who, though womanless and old and alone, lived in hope and resolution and quiet rapport with a natural universe. But the ending of *The Old Man and the Sea* was not the ending of Hemingway's life. Although no one can say for sure what was taking place in Hemingway during the years that followed the publication of *The Old Man and the Sea* in 1952, it seems apparent now that his body and spirit were badly deteriorating and that the artist in him, like the artist in Mark Twain of the late years, could no longer create. Under those conditions stoicism may no longer have applied. 'He had held for years,' Carlos Baker tells us, 'to his maxim: "*il faut (d'abord) durer.*"' Now on the first Sunday in July 1961 that maxim was succeeded by another: '"*il faut (après tout) mourir.*" The idea, if not the phrase, filled all his mind. He slipped in two shells, lowered the gun butt carefully to the floor, leaned forward, pressed the twin barrels against his forehead just above the eyebrows, and tripped both triggers.'[22]

DUANE J. MACMILLAN

His 'Magnum O':
Stoic Humanism in
Faulkner's A Fable

The early 1940s were difficult years for Faulkner; he was forced for financial reasons to sign an unfortunate seven-year contract with Warner Brothers and, by 1945, all seventeen of his books were out of print. Film commitments prevented completion of a work (tentatively entitled 'Who?') which, in April 1946, Faulkner predicted would be his '*magnum o.*' That novel became *A Fable.*[1] Letters to Malcolm Cowley and Harold Ober indicate that, by the end of 1947, work on a *A Fable* had ground to a halt. Five books, the Nobel Prize for Literature, Membership in the French Legion of Honour, commencement-day orations, scripts for Howard Hawks, a conference with Robert Frost in Brazil, and the impending marriage of his daughter Jill further delayed the novel until its publication on 2 August 1954.[2] *A Fable* won Faulkner his second National Book Award and a Pulitzer Prize; it also unleashed a torrent of reviews, and has continued to command more critical attention than any other Faulkner novel set outside Yoknapatawpha.

Concerning the composition of *A Fable*, Faulkner told Robert Linscott: 'I am writing and rewriting, weighing every word which I never did before.'[3] Such painstaking care, according to Cowley, can be seen even in the evolution of the novel's title: 'Instead of carrying the usual title, illustration, and descriptive text, it would show nothing but a cross – with perhaps below it in the right-hand corner, and not in large type, the two words "A Fable."'[4] The rebus idea was discarded, but Faulkner presumably considered not only his novel but also the Christian myth to be a 'fable.' Faulkner was not writing a Christian allegory, *per se*, any more than he was delivering a polemic against war: 'you don't really have time to identify yourself with a character ... you're not trying to preach through character ... you're too busy writing about people.'[5] Moreover, Faulkner saw his work as all of one piece, and *A Fable* is linked with the totality of his canon: Faulkner said as much to Cowley almost ten years before the publication of *A Fable*; he repeated the idea at Nagano; and he specifically explicated the advantages of using the Christian myth as a literary tool to Jean Stein in New York:

In *A Fable* the Christian allegory was the right allegory to use in that particular story ... No one is without Christianity ... It is every individual's individual code of behavior by means of which he makes himself a better man than his nature wants to be ... Whatever its symbol ... [it] is man's reminder of his duty inside the human race ... Writers have always drawn, and always will draw, upon the allegories of moral consciousness, for the reason that the allegories are matchless ... the trinity of conscience: knowing nothing, knowing but not caring, knowing and caring. The same trinity is represented in *A Fable*.[6]

After receiving the Nobel Prize in 1950 Faulkner changed his approach towards his public, neither shunning publicity nor insisting upon his personal and professional privacy. He toured Japan in August 1955, was Writer in Residence at the University of Virginia in 1957–8, and visited West Point Military Academy in April 1962. He also accepted several invitations for public lectures and, understandably enough, *A Fable* figured large in such interviews and public statements.[7] It seems surprising, then, that most critics have not been prepared to take seriously Faulkner's explicit evaluation of this novel. By 1954 Faulkner had become a consummate stylist, able to control his medium and mould it to his purpose. He was especially concerned with getting into print what he considered to be important about life 'before he had to set down the pen and die,' and he had laboured diligently for an unusually long time over every line of the book. There is, furthermore, a deliberate and overt relationship between the *credo* of *A Fable* and Faulkner's Stockholm address.[8] If one approaches *A Fable* as Faulkner presumably would have wished – i.e., as his literary *magnum opus* – many 'shortcomings' in matters such as thematic content, characterization, imagery, symbolism, and tone shrink in proportion or become positive assets in appreciating this novel as Faulkner's masterpiece, for that well may be what *A Fable* is. This suggests, to paraphrase Faulkner's comment on *Ulysses*, that one should approach *A Fable* as a Southern Baptist preacher approaches the Bible – with faith – and, to a certain extent, this is true. No single reading of *A Fable* will ever exhaust its implications, yet it is also true that there is a basic simplicity about the book that even a first reading makes clear. *A Fable* presents Faulkner's view of the human condition and his eye is ever and consistently on the infinite variety of this piece of work called man, and on the virtue and the continuous efficacy of sacrifice in ensuring man's endurance so that he may eventually prevail. *A Fable* is a magnificent *exemplum* on the *credo*, 'I believe in Man.'

Faulkner's deliberate use of the Christian myth as part of the 'lumber-room of experience' of the western world results in several obvious biblical analogues in *A Fable*; the Corporal as Christ-figure, numerous 'trinities' of one kind or another, thirteen 'apostles,' a Magdalen, a Marya, and a Marthe, a 'last supper' with its Polchek-Judas, its 'Saviour'-denying Peter, and its Paul, several 'miracles,' a 'temptation' scene, and a 'crucifixion' involving a 'crown of thorns' and two thieves.

The blatant clarity of such parallels should indicate that Faulkner did not mean them to become ends in themselves; they are simply metaphors for Faulkner's broader theme. Several details in *A Fable* support this latter argument. The Corporal is not the only Christ-figure in the novel. A mysterious stranger who is depicted as an advocate for all mankind and as a 'Man of Sorrows' offers the 'Bread of Life' to Marthe (F, pp 8–12). A divisional Judge Advocate General recognizes that it takes courage to pity mankind and he sacrifices his life for others (F, pp 45–6). These virtues are highlighted, of course, in the execution of the Corporal (F, pp 385–6), but they are also present in the Federal Deputy's offer to use his father's estate to ransom the racehorse, even though he, also, is tempted to 'take the world' (F, p 162). Gragnon's abortive attack has overtones of a crucifixion and he is made a scapegoat, if not a sacrificial lamb (F, pp 21–3, 36, 54–5, 377): if Gragnon is also a Judas (F, p 135), the implication, surely, is that everyman is, potentially at least, a composite of Christ and Judas. The Runner, too, is Christlike on occasion (F, pp 65, 208); so is the Groom (F, p 147); so also is Tobe Sutterfield (F, p 165).

Of course, the Corporal is *the* Christ-figure in *A Fable*. The references and parallels, above and beyond the terribly moving crucifixion scene and Brzewski's 'resurrection' into the Tomb of the Unkown Soldier, are unmistakable. Critics of *A Fable* have repeatedly commented upon the Corporal-as-Christ symbol. The implications of the other Christ-figures in the novel, however, suggest that Faulkner was neither retelling the Passion story in the idiom of 1918 or that of the post-Hiroshima era (see F, pp 352–4), nor that he wanted to make the Corporal the only sacrificial character in the book. If, for instance, the dinner of the thirteen can be seen as a proto-eucharist, so do characters like Levine (F, p 324), Marthe (F, p 222), the Generalissimo (F, pp 245 ff), and Gragnon (F, pp 47–8), have 'last suppers' before the most momentous events of their lives. Ironically, even the Generalissimo, the Antichrist of *A Fable*, can, in certain respects, be seen to be Christlike: in the face of published criticism, this observation requires some explication.

General Lallemont had once said of the Generalissimo: '*If I were evil, I would hate and fear him. If I were a saint, I would weep. If I were wise, and both or either, I would despair*' (F, p 230). Saints presumably would not weep for God: He needs nothing, not even the tears of saints, and His Son is restored to Him in the Resurrection. Nor would they weep for Satan, for he is beyond hope, and powerless before God. But they would weep for Christ who has to endure crucifixion. Evil men could not hate omnipotent and ubiquitous God; and they would, supposedly, worship Satan. But they would hate Christ because He provides a particularized example or paradigm of virtue which they have deliberately discarded from their own lives. Wise men, recognizing the inevitability of the crucifixion, might well despair. The Quartermaster-General tells his superior in the desert that his (the Generalissimo's) 'hour is not yet come'; that time when he must deliver, 'with Christ in God,' not merely

France, but *man* (F, pp 261–4). But the Generalissimo has sacrificed the desert murderer (himself an ironic or, at least, 'inverted' Christ [F, p 268]), so that the entire garrison may be saved and a war averted: when the Quartermaster-General recognizes and realizes the fallibility of his hero as a man, the tall Norman weeps: '"Yes, he [the murderer] was a man. But he [the Generalissimo] was young then, not much more than a child. These tears are not anguish: only grief' (F, p 271). In this instance both leaders are 'men of sorrows' (although later the Quartermaster-General will reverse his charitable evaluation of the Generalissimo when he accuses him of sacrificing Brzewski in order to begin a war). From his earliest school days the Generalissimo was looked upon as no mere man, no mere youth, no mere Parisian: he was *the* man, *the* youth, *the* Parisian: the chosen *one* to be the revered son of 'that city which was the world too, since of all cities it was supreme, dreamed after and adored by all men ...' (F, p 247). The messianic implications are indisputable. The Quartermaster-General explicates them in detail when he tenders the Generalissimo his resignation (F, p 328). The fact that the Quartermaster-General is disappointed is central to an understanding of *A Fable*. Like the Israelites of the Old Testament, he expected the Messiah to be a great warrior who would sweep aside the earthly enemies of the world (France-Israel): like them, he was wrong. The Generalissimo is not divine. He is of the world, and in it. He is man. So is his natural son, the Corporal. There is no divine Christ, but man – in stoically enduring even his own pitiable, fallible vices and limitations, and in effecting his pity and compassion and love, and pride and honour and sacrifice – can perform divine acts.

This theme is seen in many aspects of *A Fable* (in the thematic intent of the racehorse episode or in the negative implications of the deaths of Levine and the young priest, for example); but mostly it is manifested in the fantastic array of characters which Faulkner has described in his novel. There are thumbnail sketches, perfect in every detail, such as those of the Generalissimo's batman, the federal deputy, blind Angelique and her ancient husband, Monaghan (of 'Honor'), and Sutterfield's grandson, who speaks the French of the Sorbonne. There are small groups of perfectly contrasting characters, such as the German General and the Allied Chiefs of Staff, Levine's flight crew, or Marthe's 'family,' either with the Generalissimo or in their closing scene at the farm. There are magnificent descriptions of crowds (reminiscent of the great Negro migration of 'Raid' in *The Unvanquished*), which are limned with the perfect control of a master craftsman. Finally, there are the 'giants' of *A Fable*: the Generalissimo, the Quartermaster-General, the Sentry-Groom, Tobe Sutterfield, the Runner, and the Corporal.

Much has been written about 'Mistairy,' the Sentry-Groom, of *A Fable*. Most critics recognize that he is used by Faulkner to provide a link between the racehorse episode and the major plot of the novel, and he is usually described by the following oft-quoted passage:

... the foul-mouthed white one to whom to grant the status of man was merely to accept Darkness' emissary in the stead of its actual prince and master.   (F, p 158)

But this Popeye-like description, when accepted as a character portrait of the Groom, does him much disservice on at least three counts: first, the description is given in conjunction with the mobs seeking the Groom, Sutterfield, the horse, and the 'incredible and unbelievable ... tens of thousands of dollars' they had supposedly won at races and, therefore, it can hardly be an objective evaluation of the Groom; secondly, it ignores the fact that, at this time, the Groom is a practising Baptist and Mason (F, p 154); and thirdly, it does not 'see the Groom's heart' (irrespective of his foul vocabulary), which is clearly recognized by Tobe Sutterfield. Like Saul of Tarsus, the Groom is a blasphemer and sinner who 'kicks against the pricks' of his 'conversion' and the conscience-jibes of the Runner: indeed, he tries to kick off the head of the Runner (F, pp 84–5). His association with the racehorse, however, has permanently changed the Groom: he is a 'new man' in a spiritual sense, whether he wished the transformation or not (F, pp 151–3). Mosaic-Messianic implications are suggested by the Groom's influence on the horse, his return 'on the dawn of the third day' with the necessary gear for the 'salvation' of the animal, and his ultimate sacrifice of the beast in order to ensure its purity and fabulous immortality (F, pp 151–4, 162–3). Like other major characters in *A Fable*, the Groom, by implication at least, has stoically accepted his lot as an orphan and a pariah, a social outcast 'despised and rejected of men'; like Moses, in particular, he spends a 'diaspora' in the wilderness before he is ready for his final apotheosis in No Man's Land (F, pp 315–21). When the Groom is destroyed in the holocaust, his 'role' is carried on by Pauline Runner. Perhaps this explains his unusual and terrible scar: he (the Runner) is half a dead man (the Groom) and half himself, a proto–St Paul for the Corporal's 'church': 'the Runner's voice crying out of the soundless rush of flame which enveloped half his body neatly from heel through navel through chin: "They cant kill us! They cant! Not dare not: they cant!"' (F, pp 321–2).

Reverend Tobe Sutterfield, the 'blackamoor minister from America,' is a more easily grasped character than is the Groom, but he is by no means a simple, two-dimensional portrait of 'man waiting – no mere Simeon-as-stoic figure. His very Christian name implies symbolic connotations – (Tōbe or To-be): this inference gains strength when he changes his surname to Tooleyman or Tout le Monde (F, p 150), and it becomes especially portentous when one considers him as the leading figure of

... the rich and organ-rolling [named] organization, committee, which he headed: *Les Amis Myriades et Anonymes à la France de Tout le Monde* – a title, a designation, so embracing, so richly sonorous with grandeur and faith, as to have freed itself completely from man

and his agonies, majestic in its empyrean capacity, as weightless and palpless upon the
anguished earth as the adumbration of a cloud. (F, p 146)

He is not an ordained minister, but he 'bears witness' – witness not to God only, but
more especially to man: 'To man. God dont need me. I bears witness to Him of
course, but my main witness is to man ... Man is full of sin and nature, and all he
does dont bear looking at, and a heap of what he says is a shame and a mawkery. But
cant no witness hurt him. Some day something might beat him, but it wont be Satan'
(F, p 180). Critics who see the Generalissimo as Satan or the Antichrist should take
this comment into account. Sutterfield's witness is instrumental in clarifying the
Runner's mission to and for himself, but of much greater import is the fact that
Sutterfield's faith in man is no mere recognition of a Manichean dichotomy in man's
nature, although that is there too: '"Evil is a part of man, evil and sin and cowardice, the same as repentance and being brave. You got to believe in all of them, or
believe in none of them. Believe that man is capable of all of them, or he aint capable
of none. [So, when the Runner replies], "Maybe what I need is to have to meet
somebody. To believe. Not in anything: just to believe"' (F, p 203), he comes to
realize that, after all, Sutterfield's and all men's (*Tout le Monde*'s) salvation lies in a
faith in man and in his potential for self-realization. In effect, Sutterfield's faith rests
in man's ability *to be* man. It is a totally realistic, unromantic, and stoic perspective,
tempered by Faulkner's inveterate humanism.

The Quartermaster-General is a man who is disillusioned by what he considers to
be a catastrophic and treacherous piece of political expediency: he believes that the
Generalissimo deliberately promulgates the evils of war by arranging a continuance
of hostilities through a meeting of the German General and the Allied Chiefs of Staff
and by setting down the barrage which destroys the battalion containing the Groom
and Sutterfield. Such an interpretation is accurate and justified, as far as it goes, but
it presents a limited perspective on the Quartermaster-General in that it does not
manifest the essential flaw in his character. There are reasons – beyond those of
wealth, family connections, and examination results – why the Quartermaster-
General should stand second to the Generalissimo at St Cyr. The *hamartia* in the tall
Norman's perspective is that he sees the world as a romantic rather than as a realist:
he views man as what he thinks man ought to be rather than what he is. In one sense
the Quartermaster-General is the logical antithesis to Tobe Sutterfield. As early as
their graduation at the military academy, the Quartermaster-General looks upon the
Generalissimo not as a man, but as the Saviour of France and, ultimately, of the
western world. Even the childhood and early career of the Quartermaster-General
are sketched in terms of his relationship to and his hopes and aspirations for his
classmate. When the Quartermaster-General follows the Generalissimo into the desert outpost, it is in terms of a Gethsemane or a diaspora that he sees the necessity

for such a posting: so, too, the Generalissimo's sojourn in the Tibetan monastery. The Saviour of France and of man must purge himself of the flesh so that he may fulfil his immortal and predestined role (F, pp 246–7, 254–5, 258–62). Moreover, it is the Quartermaster-General – *not* the Generalissimo, as some critics claim – who states that rapacity does not fail:

> Rapacity does not fail, else man must deny that he breathes. Not rapacity: [the world's] whole vast glorious history repudiates that. It does not, cannot, must not fail ... Not rapacity, which, like poverty, takes care of its own. Because it endures, not even because it is rapacity but because man is man, enduring and immortal; enduring not because he is immortal but immortal because he endures: and so with rapacity, which immortal man never fails, since it is in and from rapacity that he gets, holds, his immortality – the vast, the all-being, the compassionate, which says to him only, Believe in Me; though ye doubt seventy times seven, ye need only believe again. (F, pp 259–61)

That the Quartermaster-General could believe that the Generalissimo, as man, could be free of the very factor which ensures man his immortality is an index of the romantic astigmatism of his cosmology. Because he tries to make the Generalissimo into something more than man, the Quartermaster-General's expectations are inevitably doomed. Therefore, in the scene in which he tenders his resignation to his superior (F, pp 326 ff), his own perspective is the major cause of his disillusionment: he must learn both that the Generalissimo is only man, and that being man is enough, is sufficient, to ensure the immortality of the race. The Quartermaster-General learns, also, that either the Corporal or the Generalissimo makes a far greater sacrifice than the mere resignation of a commission (F, pp 331–2). Finally, having reached a maturity of perception and perspective on man – including the Corporal, the Generalissimo, and himself – the Quartermaster-General is in a real position to hold the wounded head of the Runner in the closing scene of *A Fable* (F, p 437). Now, when he weeps, these are tears of neither grief nor anguish, but of compassion, sympathy, love, understanding – of stoicism in the Faulknerian sense.

The Runner is undoubtedly one of the more enigmatic characters of *A Fable*. Symbolically he stands about equidistant between the almost purely mundane intellect of the Generalissimo and the almost purely mundane faith of Tobe Sutterfield. The Runner is certainly a cut above David Levine, yet he is less than the Corporal in certain respects. He is directly responsible for catalysing the battalion (and especially the Groom) into action by leaving the trenches in order to embrace the martyrdom and the horrors of the holocaust in No Man's Land; but the Runner is also guilty of a peculiar kind of misanthropy which results in his deliberate evasion of responsibility in getting himself demoted from a lance corporal to a private. In a very real sense the Runner is an example, *par excellence*, of Sutterfield's definition of man, alluded to above. If he upstages the Corporal in the novel, it is because Faulkner has more clearly depicted and defined (although not resolved) a wider spectrum of inner conflicts and contradictions in this character than in his Christ-figure Corporal. Actually, the Runner wants to despair: in this he is like Levine who does despair. Presumably this is why Faulkner has two of the Runner's superior officers suggest that, like Levine, he commit suicide in a latrine (F, pp 62, 65). Ironically the results of his loss of rank are exactly the opposite to what the Runner expects. As a private he learns 'about the thirteen French soldiers almost at once' – he 'who five months ago had been an officer too, by the badges on his tunic also forever barred and interdict from the right and freedom to the simple passions and hopes and fears' common to the brotherhood of man (F, p 66). The basic idealism which underlay his original cynicism and despair is revitalized to the extent that he recognizes that 'even ruthless and all-powerful and unchangeable Authority would be impotent before that massed unresisting undemanding passivity' of united mankind (F, p 68). He has only to await the 'discovery' of the thirteen men by the military hierarchy. In this act, and in his ultimate faith in the common man, the Runner is like the Deputy Marshall who awaits 'Authority's' ultimate capture of the racehorse, the lawyer who speaks for democracy, and Tobe Sutterfield. The real crux of the Runner's ultimate awareness occurs when he recognizes both that the mutiny must take place and that it is doomed to failure before it ever starts: yet the sacrifice of the battalion (like that particularized by the execution of the Corporal or the racehorse) must be made, if only to manifest the indomitable spirit of the common man, each individual man. The hierarchies of institutionalized civilization (social, religious, military, or political) inevitably rob man of his individuality: this is their real crime against mankind, and this philosophical insight is understood and acted upon accordingly by the Runner. The implication and significance of his new awareness lie in the fact that he discards the egocentric 'masturbation' of despair, renews his dormant hope in man, stoically endures until he leads his battalion into the self-fulfilling immolation in No Man's Land – with full knowledge that it will be sacrificed to man's ineluctable folly, yet with total faith in the inherent value of the act (F, pp 73, 311–22). Such stoic perception enables the Runner, both in the midst of the barrage and in the Paris street at the Generalissimo's funeral, to cry out against the oppressors of individual man: '"They cant kill us! They cant! Not dare not: they cant! ... Tremble. I'm not going to die. Never"' (F, pp 322, 437).

The Corporal in *A Fable* has been found by many critics to be too ephemeral and two-dimensional to be an effective central character in the novel. Faulkner has been faulted – almost unanimously by those who suggest that this novel is a failure – for treating the Corporal superficially or even slightingly, expecially when one considers his symbolic import. But in insisting that *A Fable* be read in a 'Christ-reincarnated' tradition and mode, readers shift the centre of interest onto the

Corporal's shoulders when, in fact, neither Faulkner nor the novel suggests such a focus at all. In his public interviews Faulkner makes only one specific reference to the 'Corporal as Christ,' and this only after he has already indicated that the novel is concerned with telling the story of the father who is forced to choose between the sacrifice and the saving of his son. Faulkner also says that the idea for the novel came incidentally out of speculation concerning who might be buried in the Tomb of the Unknown Soldier, and that if it had been Christ, He would have been re-crucified in 1918. In other words, the idea of the 'Corporal-as-Christ' may have ranked *third* in order of Faulkner's conception of the novel. Naturally enough, any book which uses the Christ story metaphorically, and expecially one which contains a crucifixion and a resurrection, is likely to be misconstrued by readers simply because of the tremendous weight such a figure is given in occidental thought. It may be impossible to write a novel using the Christ myth primarily as metaphor: if this is the case, then *A Fable* can justly be called a failure.

A Fable, however, is a resounding success. If there is a central character in the novel, it is the Generalissimo, not the Corporal:

> As I see it, the writer has imagined a story of human beings that was so moving, so important to him, that he wants to make a record of it for his own satisfaction or, perhaps, for others to read, that story is a very old story, it's the story of human beings in conflict with their nature, their character, their souls, with others, or with their environment ... The novelist is talking about people, about man in conflict with himself, his fellows, or his environment ... That [the writing of *A Fable*] was again the writer who had imag- ined, who had heard of a story that was so moving, so true to him, that he had to put it down. I was primarily telling one of the oldest and the most moving tragic stories of all as it had been written thousands of times, that is, the father who is compelled to choose between the sacrifice or saving his son. [In addition to the Christian myth, one immedi- ately thinks of Lucius Junius Brutus who sacrificed his sons for Rome, Abraham and Isaac, and Captain Vere and Billy Budd.] It came, incidentally, out of speculation which a lot of people besides me have probably wondered at: Who might be in the tomb of the Unknown Soldier? And if that had been, if Christ had appeared again in 1914–1915, he would have been crucified again. To tell that story, the thought was if I could just tell this in such a powerful way that people will read it and say this must not happen again, that is, if Providence, Deity, call Him what you will, had tried to save the world once, save men once by the sacrifice of His Son, that failed, He tried it again and that failed, maybe He wouldn't try to save us again that way. *Though that was incidental, I was primarily telling what to me was a tragic story, of the father who had to choose between the sacrifice or the saving of his son.*[9]   (Italics added)

Faulkner did not have to develop the Corporal as a Christ-figure any more than he did the St Paul-figure or the Judas-Polchek character. He could rely on the cultural consciousness of the western world to grasp the significance of the Corporal as a Christlike man. This concept is a kind of *donnée* in *A Fable*; and this literary gambit is not, necessarily, a weakness in the novel for at least two reasons. First, as Christ-figures obviously tend to dominate their literary compositions, an overly detailed and scrupulous correlation of the Corporal's role with the Christ metaphor would undoubtedly have thrown the novel into a different, essentially Christian, perspective, and Faulkner's stoic humanism is invariably Christian only to a coincidental degree. Secondly, Faulkner could, presumably (in different context, of course), have used a Dedalus, a Prometheus, an Ishmael, a Ulysses, or a Galahad figure, without having to explain in detail the relative metaphoric significance of such a character. As many critics have noted, Brzewski possesses many un-Christlike characteristics: the significant implication of these 'differences' (which surely must have been deliberately intended by the author) may well be that Faulkner has attempted to play down the role of the Corporal as Christ in *A Fable*. The fact that many readers insist upon seeing the Corporal as the centre of interest in the novel is a weakness in their own preconceptions regarding Christ-symbols in general. In the tradition in which Faulkner says that he conceived *A Fable*, the psychological emphasis of the stories invariably rests with the father figure. Even in the Christian tradition it is written that 'God so loved the world that He gave His only begotten Son' to the end that all might not perish. This argument does not suggest that Faulkner has not given Brzewski Christlike attributes, nor does it deny the validity of those references which link the Corporal with the Christ myth: this reading of *A Fable* simply suggests that a too rigidly applied preconception will both limit and misconstrue the philosophical and aesthetic values and implications of the novel.

Perhaps the most positive interpretation that can be attributed to the Corporal's Christliness is that he is, indeed, a sacrificial figure; but it should be kept in mind that Christianity holds no monopoly on hecatombs. He represents the best of one attribute of man – the willing and wilful abnegation of self in the cause of perpetuating, through individual, significant example, the intrinsic worth of each and every man in the face of overwhelming institutionalized and traditional odds. As one example of man at his best, the Corporal and his passion are not too dissimilar from the racehorse story: the horse interlude exemplifies a magnitude, a kind of natural decorum, a 'Yoknapatawpha commentary' on the non-Yoknapatawpha fable of Brzewski and the war in Europe. An interesting marginal linkage between the Generalissimo and the racehorse plot is provided by the symbolic implications of his office decorations: 'two bronzes which sat at either end of the otherwise completely bare desk – a delicate and furious horse poised weightless and epicene on one leg, and a savage and slumbrous head not cast, molded but cut by hand out of the amalgam by Gaudier-Brzeska' (F, p 283).

The Generalissimo is not only the central character of *A Fable*; he is also certainly the most enigmatic figure in the novel. He towers over his staff at Chaulnesmont, over the crowds assembled to await his decision regarding the mutineed battalion, over the entire population of France, the massed armies of Europe, like some monolithic, all-wise, all-powerful, yet benevolent dictator. He is more a force, an influence, an abstraction, than any mere man. Faulkner has described him as 'a fallen angel,' magnificent to such a degree that even God feared him.'[10] This 'Saviour of France, of the world' does not pity man, does not fear him, for he understands and respects him. The Generalissimo is totally dispassionate and completely without compassion. (In this respect Tobe Sutterfield is a more humane character and, probably, is closer to voicing Faulkner's personal faith in mankind than is the Generalissimo.) The Generalissimo is as awesome as Satan in all his glory but, without any diabolical qualities, for there is nothing vicious or malevolent in the old General. He does not love man. He does not hate man. He simply understands the species with an objectivity and an attitude of benevolent uninvolvement that is neither subhuman nor superhuman, but simply unhuman. Despite all his power, he does not play God in any traditional sense of that term, but simply permits men to enact their several and inevitable fates. He allows the desert-outpost murderer, General Gragnon, and the Corporal to choose their respective deaths and never once does he seem either elated or depressed by what happens. The death of his son seems merely to reinforce his own private estimation of the race – he makes no overt judgment regarding the Corporal's execution, save telling his son that he can and will destroy him (F, p 349). Yet the Generalissimo is human to the extent that he is fallible. In the desert outpost he 'loses a camel' (F, p 257) in preventing a local war: for this reason (ironically, not for the death of the beast's rider), the Generalissimo fails at his mission, resigns his post, and goes into seclusion in a Tibetan lamasery. He is human, too, in that from his earliest school days, he wears 'a locket – a small object of chased worn gold, obviously valuable or anyway venerable, resembling a hunting-case watch and obviously capable of containing two portraits' (F, p 245): presumably, it contains portraits of his parents, although this fact is not established absolutely. He also administers a kind of human patronage in selecting his old schoolmate as Quartermaster-General once he (the Generalissimo) is given charge of the armies of France. In at least one scene Faulkner presents him as positively human – a 'boy, a child, crouching amid the golden debris' of his various decorations (F, pp 236–7). The Generalissimo remains an enigma in *A Fable*; but in a very real sense the Generalissimo provides a psychological, philosophical, and aesthetic centre of interest in the novel – a kind of static constant around which the action whirls and flows. Yet, in another sense, the author's concern in *A Fable* is *not* the Generalissimo: it is the nature of man and the human condition itself to which Faulkner has addressed himself in this novel.

The first time the Generalissimo appears in *A Fable* he is represented as the apex of a trinity of generals and as a man with a basic trinity of beliefs: 'the slight gray man with a face wise, intelligent, and unbelieving, who no longer beieved in anything but his disillusion and his intelligence and his limitless power' (F, p 13). This *credo* is modified slightly when he is described as 'the old gray inscrutable supreme general with the face of one who long ago had won the right to believe in nothing whatever save man's deathless folly' (F, pp 232–3), but the characterization remains curious to the extent that, although almost every day of the Generalissimo's life is eventually described through a series of brilliant Faulknerian flashbacks, the reader never learns how or when or why the man has become disillusioned. Indeed, he seems, from his entrance into St Cyr to his funeral procession through the streets of Paris, to be perpetually beyond both illusion and disillusion. (Equally curious is the instant, quiet 'shock of recognition' that passes between the Corporal and the Generalissimo at Chaulnesmont, even though the two have never met or seen each other previously [F, p 17].) This quiet old man apparently understands civilians with a degree of perceptivity equal to that which he manifests towards military problems. After asking his aide to leave open the windows at his Chaulnesmont headquarters, so that the wailing of the assembled multitude can be heard clearly within, the Generalissimo observes, 'They dont want to know ... They want only to suffer' (F, p 236).

There remain two scenes involving the Generalissimo which must be examined in some detail, for they are central to this reading of *A Fable*. The first is the one involving the Quartermaster-General's proffered resignation. He wishes to resign for two reasons; he feels morally responsible for the shelling of the troops in No Man's Land, and, secondly, he believes – as we have noted above – that the Generalissimo is deliberately executing Brzewski in order to promulgate war and the continuing necessity for a military hierarchy. In one sense, at least, the Quartermaster-General is like the Corporal in believing that man is capable of stopping war through the simple expediency of refusing, *en masse*, to fight. In this light the entire scene ironically foreshadows the temptation scene between the Generalissimo and his son; but the Quartermaster-General is unlike the Corporal inasmuch as the former believes that the military establishment has negated the last possible chance man has on earth for peace and self-responsibility (F, pp 327–9). It is interesting (although explainable in terms of his particular psychological myopia) that the Quartermaster-General seems to assume the same kind of fatality about the Generalissimo's actions as does Marthe (F, pp 286 ff), and that, like the Corporal, the Quartermaster-General takes for granted that the Generalissimo is afraid of man (F, p 352). Both the Quartermaster-General and Marthe (though perhaps not the Corporal) fail to see the logical inconsistency of their respective perceptions: if the Generalissimo is fated to act as he does, either he cannot be held morally culpable for his decisions or, like Oedipus, he must be held tragically responsible. Both the Quartermaster-General and Marthe apparently blame the Generalissimo and imply that matters could have been different if he had chosen to act otherwise. In some sense, at least, the Generalissimo is either (or both) a supremely tragic figure as a man, or (and) entirely above tragedy in his 'unhuman' role as a force, explicated above. Both the Quartermaster-General and the Corporal fail to understand the fact – and its implications – that the Generalissimo is *not* afraid of man:

> 'I am not afraid of man,' the old general said. 'Fear implies ignorance. Where ignorance is not, you do not need to fear: only respect. I dont fear man's capacities, I merely respect them.' (F, p 329)

The difference in perception and understanding between the Generalissimo and the Quartermaster-General (and, ironically, between the Generalissimo and the Corporal) is indicated in the implications of his final answer to the tall Norman's request for resignation:

> 'A man is to die what the world will call the basest and most ignominious of deaths: execution for cowardice while defending his native – anyway adopted – land. That's what the ignorant world will call it, who will not know that he was murdered for that principle which, by your own bitter self-flagellation, you were incapable of risking death and honor for. Yet you dont demand that life. You demand instead merely to be relieved of a commission. A gesture. A martyrdom. Does it match his? ...
> 'If he does ... [accept] his life, keeps his life, he will have abrogated his own gesture and martyrdom. If I gave him his life tonight, I myself could render null and void what you call the hope and the dream of his sacrifice. By destroying his life tomorrow morning, I will establish forever that he didn't even live in vain, let alone die so. Now tell me who's afraid?' (F, pp 331–2)

In other words, the Generalissimo has the power to save the Corporal – an act which would be judged 'humane' or 'Christian' or 'benevolent' by the majority of mankind. In doing so, however, the Generalissimo would absolutely negate the possibility of his son's sacrifice for those very virtues and attributes for which he is apparently willing to die. The saving of the Corporal's life would utterly destroy his purpose in living. Such an apparently dispassionate, yet absolutely stoic and tragic choice on the Generalissimo's part is the keystone of *A Fable*'s plot and its psychological and philosophical implications. The fantastic moral implications of his *not* saving the Corporal to this world are most effectively underscored by the simplicity of the Generalissimo's final question: '"Now who's afraid?"'

The second scene which is of utmost importance in understanding the General-issimo (or the Corporal, or *A Fable*) is, of course, the oft-cited temptation scene between the old general and his natural son (F, pp 343–54). The setting is an old Roman citadel, high, overlooking the night lights of Chaulnesmont, and here, in a manner somewhat similar to the biblical account of Satan's temptation of Jesus, the old man offers the Corporal freedom, power, and life – if he will but deny and betray his reasons for leading the mutiny. This scene marks both the structural climax of *A Fable* and the culmination of its psychological and philosophical import. But with respect to the biblical parallel, the differences are more important and relevant to Faulkner's book than are the similarities. A comparison between *A Fable* and Matthew 4 or Luke 4 evinces the following distinctions: in the novel there are absolutely no external or supernatural factors, such as the ministering of angels; no citing of scriptural precedents as answers to specific temptations; no beginning of a ministry but, instead, an acceptance of imminent death; no 'victory over Satan' – despite critical commentary to the contrary – because on at least four occasions the old general reiterates that he has not 'misread' his son: that is to say, the father is, from the beginning, totally aware of his son's character and the choice that he will inevitably make. This idea is reinforced by the Generalissimo's parting comment to the Corporal: '"Remember whose blood it is that you defy me with"' (F, p 356). As was his father before him in the Tibetan lamasery, so is the son at the Roman citadel 'tested' in order to understand and put away forever the weakness of catering to the flesh and to the world – and it is worth noting that both settings are more closely related symbolically, at least, to the stoic than to either the Judaic or the Christian traditions. This weakness is the 'window' the old man repeatedly tells his son to close and be himself discharged. But the major implication of the differences between the novel's scene and the Bible's is that the former presents a thoroughly secular and mundane version of man in conflict with himself and his environment, whereas in the latter the divinity of Jesus plays a major role in the story.

The scene is important with respect to an understanding of the Generalissimo in at least four different ways. First, he explicates his personal understanding of war as an objective and innate factor in man's nature:

> ... the most expensive and fatal vice which man has invented yet, to which the normal ones of lechery and drink and gambling which man fatuously believes are capable of destroying him, stand as does the child's lollypop to the bottle, the courtesan and the playing card. A vice so long ingrained in man as to have become an honorable tenet of his behavior and the national altar for his love of bloodshed and glorious sacrifice. More than that even: a pillar not of his nation's supremacy but of his national survival. (F, p 344)

This passage negates the Quartermaster-General's limited estimation of the Gener-alissimo's 'deliberate proliferation' of war. The Generalissimo accepts war as he does every other aspect of man's nature (including his natural propensity for self-sacrifice); as such, he decides that it is better to have men like himself than the Gragnons of the world oversee man's affairs (cf F, p 352).

Secondly, he offers his son the same kind of choice regarding the traitor Polchek that he (the Generalissimo) was offered by life with respect to the desert-outpost murderer. Again, the choice presents a kind of microcosmic representation of the overall theme of the novel: the father having to choose between the sacrifice and the saving of his son: the son does not make the same choice as his father did because he cannot do so and still remain true to his nature as his father did to his (F, p 346). This observation is important, also, in the light of the next aspect of the scene's import.

Thirdly, the Generalissimo does, indeed, recognize that the Corporal, *per se*, is not the enemy he must defeat – indeed, 'enemy' is an inappropriate term, because the Generalissimo and the Corporal are but individualized, concretized, related examples of antithetical, abstract forces in the world:

> ... 'we are two articulations, self-elected possibly, anyway, elected, anyway postulated, not so much to defend us as to test two inimical conditions which, through no fault of ours but through the simple paucity and restrictions of the arena where they meet, must contend and – one of them – perish: I champion of this mundane earth which, whether I like it or not, is, and to which I did not ask to come, yet since I am here, not only must stop but intend to stop my allotted while; you champion of an esoteric realm of man's baseless hopes and infinite capacity – no: passion – for unfact. No, they are not inimical really, there is no contest actually; they can even exist side by side together in this one restricted arena, and could and would, had yours not interfered with mine.' (F, pp 347–8)

This passage illustrates not only that the Generalissimo and the Corporal are, in one sense, two sides of the same coin – and a Roman one, at that – but also that the two men must and will remain true to their respective perceptions of the human condition. That is to say, if either gave in to the precepts of the other, he would be guilty of ignominious conduct; he would betray his innermost nature for the sake of self-interest or political expediency.

Fourthly, the scene makes clear that the Generalissimo does *not* fear the Corporal. The son is simply a single example, an instance, of what the race can become, can produce – must produce – periodically, when the occasion demands a voice to stand up for the prevalence of the humane virtues of mankind. But let there be no mistake. Given the human condition as it is recorded in the entirety of history, mankind also needs the Generalissimos of the world: they, too, make possible the continuance of the human race. They, like the Corporals, are called upon to make the periodic and supremely tragic choices, and, in the world of *A Fable*, it is difficult to decide who makes the harder decision, the Generalissimo or the Corporal:

'Are you afraid of me?' [asks the Corporal].

'I already respect you; I dont need to fear you. I can do without you. I shall; I intend
to ... Afraid? No no, it's not I but you who are afraid of man: not I but you who believe
that nothing but a death can save him. I know better. I know that he has that in him which
will enable him to outlast even his wars; that in him more durable than all his vices,
even that last and most fearsome one; to outlast even this next avatar of his servitude
which he now faces: his enslavement to the demonic progeny of his own mechanical curiosity ... in this case the vice of war and that other one which is no vice at all but instead is the
quality-mark and warrant of man's immortality: his deathless folly.'   (F, pp 349, 352)

In addition to these aspects of the temptation scene, the Generalissimo describes
the ultimate, absolute result of man's 'enslavement' alluded to in the quotation immediately above, in a terrifying, science-fiction vision of a totally mechanized,
atomic world (F, pp 352–4) – yet even here the Generalissimo believes that man
will not only survive and endure, man will prevail. The old man's perspective on the
world is supremely tragic and stoic:

'I dont fear man. I do better: I respect and admire him. And pride: I am ten times prouder
of that immortality which he does possess than ever he of that heavenly one of his delusion. Because man and his folly– '
'Will endure,' the corporal said.
'They will do more,' the old general said proudly. 'They will prevail.'   (F, p 354)

The old man also enunciates the wisdom of his vast experience which stipulates that
the greatest single aspect of living is simply breathing, merely being aware that one
is alive. It is an idea that is repeated in *A Fable* (cf F, pp 203, 350, 358), and
perhaps it is the hardest, certainly the most poignant temptation which the Corporal
must overcome. His father's reiterated, '"Remember that bird ... Take that bird,"'
particularizes in a most moving and tempting way the theme of freedom and life that
is associated throughout the novel with larks and nightingales.

There is no satisfactory solution or outcome to this temptation scene in that the
antitheses represented by the Generalissimo and the Corporal remain forever in
opposition. This paradox is absolutely necessary, for the one could not exist without
the other: man must have both extremes in his nature for his continued existence.
Tragedy always presents unresolved tensions, held momentarily in unequal balance
until the protagonist is crushed between them; but the issues themselves are never
really resolved because the tragic opposites themselves are eternal. The enigma of
the Generalissimo remains, also, in that he can recognize the problem presented by
his son and still permit the sacrifice of Brzewski to take place; recognize both the
necessity and the futility of the act, and still be a man. The Generalissimo

approaches Sutterfield's *credo* that one has to believe in all aspects of man or none at all: nevertheless, the Generalissimo and Tobe, like the Generalissimo and the Corporal, remain opposed. The respect and admiration and pride which the Generalissimo claims to have for man is never externalized in any of his acts except in his permitting his son to become a martyr. Ironically, the fact that the Corporal sees only the endurance possible in man's destiny while his father sees the potential for man's prevailing marks the essential difference in their respective natures and philosophical outlooks. The son sees that his personal sacrifice enables man to endure anything, even death, in order to perpetuate certain verities. The father recognizes that such sacrifices must be allowed to take place so that man may one day prevail.

Recalling the implications of Malcolm Cowley's epistolary comment concerning Faulkner's intended rebus title for this novel, *A Fable* can be seen as a deliberate attempt to present truth in fabulistic terms. In this sense the book partakes of certain characteristics of myth, of parable, and of fable. Because of this tendency, there is often an aura of unreality or a lack of precise definition about the main characters and about the action. Such artistic gambitry on Faulkner's part will tax the credulity of the reader only if he insists on judging the novel by naturalistic or realistic criteria. One short incident in the novel illustrates Faulkner's technique in this respect rather well. In the great temptation scene the Generalissimo's final 'bribe' to his son is the gift of life itself. He couches the temptation in terms of a parable about an execution in Mississippi (F, pp 350–2). Realistically, there seems little or no reason why the Supreme General of all France should know such a story, or why it should be especially relevant to the mountain-born Eastern European Brzewski. Yet – in terms of *A Fable* the parable is totally effectual: it presents the final temptation in a poignant, moving, and meaningful manner; it contributes to the unity of the novel by having the setting in common with the racehorse section of the story; and, most importantly, in the reading of the book the incident does not seem unnatural or out of place at all.

The Generalissimo's aura of omnipotence and omniscience which often renders him more a force in the world than a human being naturally contributes to his fabulous nature. His name (which is never given in the novel) is synonymous with France, greater even than Napoleon's, or Joan of Arc's – with invincible man. Both the narrator in the novel and the Quartermaster-General specifically link the Generalissimo with a fable. Upon completion of his first two-year tour of duty in Africa the Generalissimo returns briefly to France: 'appearing now only the more durable because of the proven – no: reproven – fragility, at once frail yet at the same time intact and inviolable because of what in another country had been not merely ruin but destruction too: like the saint in the old tale, the maiden who without hesitation or argument feed in advance with her maidenhood the ferryman who set her across the stream into heaven (an Anglo-Saxon fable too, since only an Anglo-Saxon could seriously believe that anything buyable at no more cost than that could really be worth a sainthood – the hero' (F, p 252). When the Quartermaster-General relieves his superior at the desert outpost, his description of the future Saviour of France and of man becomes even more specifically fabulistic in character:

> [You will be] ... a lay figure not only without life but integrated as myth only in mutual confederation: the property of no one ... because you will be the property of all, possessing unity and integration only when your custodians happen to meet from the ends of the earth ... and match fragments and make you whole for a moment ... after twenty years not you or even your two powerful kinsmen will be real, but only that old fading parchment, and it real only because your refusal of it incorporated it into your legend ... until at last those who feared you once will have watched you pass out of enmity to amazement: to contempt: to unreality, and at last out of your race and kind altogether, into the dusty lumber room of literature. (F, pp 262–3)

The Corporal, himself, is particularly depicted as a fabulous character. After the opening scene, where he is little more than the focus of narrator attention in the battalion of men who are brought to Chaulnesmont, he is not heard of again for some fifty-odd pages. He is then reintroduced only as one of the thirteen soldiers who have been preaching peace among the non-commissioned ranks. It is as a symbol of these thirteen men or of the entire batallion which mutinies that the Corporal functions through much of the plot of *A Fable*. In three set scenes, however, the Corporal emerges most as an individual (the last-supper sequence [F, pp 333 ff], the temptation scene [F, pp 343 ff], and as the central topic of discussion in the family scene between Marthe and the Generalissimo [F, pp 283 ff]): yet here, too, the Corporal is often presented with fabulistic connotations. The Corporal is part of a foretold, foredoomed, pageant piece of history in which, ultimately, no one, not even the Generalissimo, has any real power to alter the predestined order of events. The Corporal is but one factor in the fable of man.

It is in this latter sense that the entire plot of *A Fable* is exactly what its title implies. As Marthe suggests (F, pp 296, 299), all the characters merely play roles or are personae in a fable which must be enacted and re-enacted periodically in the history of man: it is part of the human condition that the dialectic never be resolved. The Corporal's sacrifice is no less valid, nor the implications of his act less effectually moral, because it is part of a fable: as the Runner says, only what happens afterwards is important (F, p 78). Depending upon the reader's religious perspective one may find solace in either the patience of Job, the faith of the Passion, or the readings of Epictetus and Marcus Aurelius Antoninus: I am convinced that *A Fable* clearly points to the latter alternatives as Faulkner's intent for his book.

Finally, no estimation of *A Fable* is complete without some consideration of the parallels and allusions in this novel to Faulkner's Nobel Award acceptance speech.[11] The entire work can be read as an *exemplum* on the central assertion of that address: 'I decline to accept the end of man ... I believe that man will not merely endure: he will prevail. He is immortal ... because he has a soul, a spirit capable of compassion and sacrifice and endurance.' As a text, this quotation can be read as the supreme statement characterizing the entire canon. But with respect to *A Fable* itself, the Nobel speech is particularly relevant because the novel apparently embodies what Faulkner considered to be the most important aspects of his literary philosophy, coming, as it does, four years after the Award and being designated by the author as his *magnum opus*.

Some critical confusion has resulted from the fact that those passages in *A Fable* which seem to paraphrase the Stockholm speech most closely are altered just enough to change the emphasis slightly or to make the meaning ambiguous when the two works are considered together. Furthermore, critics find it philosophically disturbing or psychologically distressing that these passages (especially those at the novel's climax) should be given to the Generalissimo, and not to the Corporal, to articulate; for the critics are then frustrated by the dilemma of identifying Faulkner with the Generalissimo as a kind of *alter ego*, when what the old general says seems to run counter to the pity and compassion and sacrifice which Faulkner extols throughout his work. The problem ceases to exist, however, when one approaches the novel, not any specific character (not even the Generalissimo), as Faulkner's exposition of his private and literary *credo*. Granted, the Generalissimo sees man ultimately prevailing over his own stupidity and folly in a way that is well beyond the comprehension of the Corporal; but the blind spot or the human fallibility of the Generalissimo's cosmology is that he may fail to see the possible efficacy of his son's sacrifice. The father understands the inevitability and, perhaps, the necessity for the recurrence of Christlike sacrifices by individuals who champion the absolutely selfless aspects of the human psyche; but he apparently feels that such sacrifices are eternally foolish and that man's nature remains (historically, at least) basically rapacious. Conversely, the Corporal intuitively knows that he must die; that his self-willed sacrifice is right; and that his death is probably – although he can never be sure – going to be of some use to the world. As a result of his particular astigmatism the Corporal sees man only enduring, never prevailing. But such a Manichean-like dichotomy as is manifested between the Generalissimo and the Corporal neither exhausts the philosophical implications or psychological ramifications of *A Fable* nor accounts for seeing the novel as an *exemplum* of the Nobel Award speech.

The major clue to Faulkner's magnificent achievement in *A Fable* is contained in Tobe Sutterfield's simple but beautiful and true statement of faith – a statement that is certainly more stoic than it is Christian, and amply warrants a final, close reading:

'Man is full of sin and nature, and all he does dont bear looking at, and a heap of what he says is a shame and a mawkery. But cant no witness hurt him. Some day something might beat him, but it wont be Satan ... Evil is part of man, evil and sin and cowardice, the same as repentance and being brave. You got to believe in all of them or believe in none of them. Believe that man is capable of all of them, or he aint capable of none.'   (F, pp 180, 203)

The implications of this *credo* finally encompass the entire cast of *A Fable*. Many of man's actions are blameworthy. Much of what he says is foolish, or stupid, or blasphemous. But man–Man–MAN writ large through the entire history of the world, contains his own ultimate salvation. The fable of man postulates not only the despairing Levines and the suiciding priests; not only the Gragnons and the murderous German Generals; not only the petty flunkies who perform heinous deeds and executions for mere pay; not only the life-denying Peters and the life-betraying Polcheks; but also the Runners who see, understand, and continue to kick against the pricks of the establishment; the Quartermaster-Generals who stop and pity and have compassion, even when the world runs over them; the Grooms who, against their wills, fulfil their natures; the Sutterfields who understand through faith only; and, ultimately, both the Corporal-Christs who must die and the Generalissimo-fathers who must decide between the tragic saving and tragic sacrificing of their sons. Man's ultimate endurance seems to be assured by his innate capacity for invention and exploration; his potential for prevailing against all odds; in his mere sufficiency to be all in all, the *alpha* and the *omega* of his own destiny. This world view is both humanistic and stoic. It is Christian only to the coincidental degree that it, too, advocates the virtues of pity and pride, and compassion, and sacrifice. But it *is* the *credo* that Faulkner presents in *A Fable*.

DANIEL FUCHS

Saul Bellow and the Example of Dostoevsky

It is no longer possible to say that all modern American literature comes from *Huckleberry Finn*. In a literal sense it was never possible, but Hemingway's famous hyperbole has had its *éclat*. In view of recent developments in the novel, however, it sounds with the resonance of another era. True, Salinger is oblique witness to the life of a tradition that includes Anderson, Hemingway, Lardner, and Faulkner, but the initiate, with his pastoral innocence, cannot be the iconographic centre of a literature which is focused on the adult genital ego in culture, and on its corresponding mental sweat. It was once possible to think of a pure adolescent heart as symbolic of hidden virtue still resident in the young country, a natural, redeeming reality deeper than all worldly appearances. But the difference between Huck and Holden Caulfield is instructive: solitude has become isolation, traumatic experience full-blown neuroticism, lighting out for the territory retiring to the mental institution. Adolescence is no longer an example but a case. Salinger is on Mark Twain's side, on his far side – civilized life is scarcely worth living – but we no longer have the freedom of the asexual idyll, we have urban, claustral impotence. Holden's grey hair symbolizes the end of an American myth, in a time when America comes of middle age.

There are, however, advantages to growing all the way up, fallen though that state may be; what is lost in innocence is gained in knowledge. Though this moral has often been full of possibility in American literature, the force of it is no longer considered to be dramatic in itself. America has moved closer to Europe and much, not 'all,' contemporary American literature comes from Flaubert or the Russians if it 'comes from' anywhere. We have seen what the Flaubert tradition affords; among recent writers John Updike seems to be its clearest exemplar. Bellow, on the other hand, seems to be the leading American exponent of the 'Russian' way. The idea of the writer as teacher rather than martyr, citizen rather than artist, journalist rather than aesthetician, the idea of a literature which is flexible enough to be tendentious and broad enough to be inspiring, a literature which refuses to adopt the pose of objectivity, detachment, and disenchantment with life in quest of the compensatory salvation of form and avoids comparing the artist with God, especially in point of indifference and cosmetic refinement (paring his fingernails) – all this bears witness to the Russian influence. The Russians would never think of art as religion, yet moral feeling in their work is charged with an energy, a yearning, a hope, that may finally be described as religious. Their art respects, indeed thrives, on mental effort and expresses, as Irving Howe has remarked, 'that "mania for totality" which is to become characteristic of our time.'[1] The post-modern Jewish writers have brought to American literature a dramatics of the mind which, generally speaking, recalls the Russians. V.S. Pritchett has suggested that there is an affinity between the American writers of Yiddish background and the Slavic. They know what the western writers have long ago forgotten, says Pritchett, 'the sense of looseness, timelessness and space.'[2] Pritchett's impressionistic remark acknowledges the essentialist affirmation, desperate though it may be, of irreducible moral truths defining a sort of rhythm of the ethical sphere. The artist-god comparison implies the need for a total subjective originality which denies that this timelessness is real. These generalizations may be illustrated by a comparison with the Russian master whose example is most vivid in Bellow's eye, Dostoevsky.

The central impetus in both writers, in periods marked by ideological confusion and in novels full of explainers, is the quest for what is morally real. Ivan Karamazov's 'if there is no God everything is permitted' is the sort of immoralist proposition that they must refute. When Dostoevsky says of the 'enthusiast,' Belinsky, 'He knew that the moral principle is at the root of everything,'[3] we have a statement in tune with Bellow's idea of 'axial lines.' To begin with a conventional illustration in both writers' works, an image of innocence is the child, sometimes offered with an unabashed naivety. We recall, for example, Augie's *après vu* of his fatherhood, or Myshkin's story of the peasant woman with a baby who says, '"God has just such gladness every time he sees from heaven that a sinner is praying to Him with all his heart, as a mother has when she sees the first smile on her baby's face."'[4] While such an image may embarrass the properly jaded reader, we know that a character like Myshkin could not exist without such sentiment. The contemporary reader has, perhaps, less difficulty with Ivan's conception of the child as victim, as symbol of unspeakable injustice, as is seen in incidents of child beating so vividly represented that even Alyosha agrees that a sadistic perpetrator should be shot. Similarly, a courtroom re-enactment of child beating is a blow sufficient to turn the civilized Herzog to murderous thoughts. Of course, child abuse has a seductive force in Dostoevsky, who is sometimes called the Russian Sade; but its thematic effect inverts Sade in order to expose nihilism, not to promote it. The poetry of crime – fully orchestrated and directly dramatized in Dostoevsky, muted and usually the subject of a lyric polemic in Bellow – comes to serve as a last-ditch proof of the existence of

God or, at least, of the existence of moral imperatives since, in modern literature, God appears typically at the back door. The creator of Raskolnikov might almost have written (though it was actually Bellow), that 'there are friendships, affinities, natural feelings, rooted norms. People do on the whole agree, for instance, that it is wrong to murder. And even if they are unable to offer rational arguments for this, they are not necessarily driven to commit gratuitous acts of violence.'[5]

To be sure, the words of the Grand Inquisitor to Christ – 'Dost Thou know that the ages will pass, and humanity will proclaim by the lips of their sages that there is no crime, and therefore no sin; there is only hunger?'[6] – carry great force in an age of environmentalism. We are familiar with Brecht's paraphrase of 'Feed men, and then ask of them virtue.' And it develops into the argument of Mailer's 'The White Negro' where he excuses the murder of a storekeeper by young killers. *Anomie* issuing in desperate boredom does link characters like Stavrogin and Mailer's Marion Faye. Stavrogin wishes to 'put powder under the four corners of the earth and blow it all up'[7] – as does Marion in similar words. The difference is that Dostoevsky, like Bellow, has ultimately a contempt for the immoralist Stavrogin, whereas Mailer's essential sympathy lies with the immoralist (now hipster) Faye.

Even greater is Dostoevsky's contempt for the radical Pytor Verkovensky, whose vision of the revolution come to pass is one of crime as the norm. Speaking to Stavrogin, he counts his troops: 'The lawyer who defends an educated murderer because he is more cultured than his victims and could not help murdering them to get money is one of us. The school-boys who murder a peasant for the sake of sensation are ours. The juries who acquit every criminal are ours. The prosecutor who trembles at a trial for fear he should not seem advanced enough is ours, ours.' Pytor concludes that 'crime is no longer insanity, but simply common sense, almost a duty; a gallant protest.'[8] True, in Czarist Russia any protest was credible, but what we get in Pytor is a prefiguring of Stalinist manipulators. On his part, Bellow has always been mistrustful of the clairoyance of radical solutions, but it is not until *Mr. Sammler's Plant* that he dramatizes a comparable political hysteria.

Dostoevsky's attack on nihilism, then, is political as well as ethical. Not confined to hysteria, the assault often expresses itself as comedy at the expense of ideology, which is seen to be utilitarian, socialist, individualist, western. The underground man is, perhaps, the most conspicuous illustration of this assult on the radicalism of the 1860s (as opposed to the more humanitarian radicalism of the 1840s with which he has some ambivalent sympathy, as did Dostoevsky himself), which is imaged as the wall, the piano key (determinism), the ant hill, the chicken coop (the urban mass and that utilitarian haven, the apartment house), and the Crystal Palace (the new cathedral of utilitarian perfection). As Ralph Matlaw says, Dostoevsky is attacking the utopia of Chernyshevsky, Fourier, and Saint-Simon which tried to reconcile Hegel and Rousseau, the world historic process and the man of feeling, historical determinism and individual will.[9] In *Notes from Underground* and elsewhere Dostoevsky makes no distinction between ideology and utopia, which he uses in its pejorative sense. The uncensored version had intimations of Christian belief; however, the censor seems to have done well in deleting them if his aim was the dramatic coherence of the work. Despite his brilliance and his authenticity the underground man is trapped in the atom of his ego, unable to love, unable to be more than a caricature of the 'freedom' he claims to represent. But with *Notes from Underground* the genre of ideological comedy is established. The ruthless, loud honesty, the intellectual acuity, the comic dramatization of mental suffering – all these appear earlier in Diderot's *Rameau's Nephew*, but the full head of self-consciousness, historical awareness, and philosophical depth is Dostoevsky's addition. The underground man knows more than the nephew and enjoys less; he is isolated and, generally, impotent.

Ideological comedy – which is to have an impact on Bellow – is not confined to *Notes from Underground*. In *Crime and Punishment*, for example, there is the marvelous Lebeziatnikov, a rarely noticed character. After describing the 'anaemic, scrofulous little man,' the usually neutral narrator tells us that he is 'really rather stupid; he attached himself to the cause of progress and "our younger generation" from enthusiasm. He was one of the numerous and varied legion of dullards, of half-animate abortions, conceited half-educated coxcombs, who attach themselves to the idea most in fashion only to vulgarize it and who caricature every cause they serve, however sincerely.' Lebeziatnikov is a theoretician and, in a wildly comic scene, expounds Fourier and Darwin to the smug bourgeois Luzhin who despises him as a man of no connections. Luzhin, ready for any praise, accepts Lebeziatnikov's praise for being ready to contribute to the establishment of a new 'commune,' for abstaining from christening future children, for acquiescing 'if Dounia were to take a lover a month after marriage, and so on.' Luzhin, who is the most tyrannical, self-absorbed, money-mad character in the book! When Luzhin asks to make certain that Sonia is a prostitute (later the sinister depth of this request is revealed), Lebeziatnikov says, in the tone of airy emancipation which Dostoevsky scorns, '"What of it? I think, that is, it is my own personal conviction that this is the normal condition of women. Why not? I mean, *distinguons*. In our present society, it is not altogether normal, because it is compulsory, but in the future society it will be perfectly normal, because it will be voluntary ... I regard her actions as a vigorous protest against the organization of society."' From Dostoevsky's point of view – and from her own – Sonia's life of prostitution is a martyrdom. This point of view is conservative, sympathetic to monogomy, privacy, Christianity, chastity. It is characteristic of Dostoevsky to scorn 'advanced' ideas, to characterize them as utopian schemes masking the self-interest of the idea-monger. (Lebeziatnikov does 'wait in hopes' of Sonia.) Dostoevsky often sees the cause itself as the caricature, profoundly mistrusting meliorist realism. Lebeziatnikov says, '"I should be the first to be ready to clean out any cesspool you like ... it's simply work ... much better than the work of a Raphael and a Pushkin, because it is more useful,"'[10] giving us the first statement of a theme which becomes major in *The Possessed*. Here, as elsewhere, Dostoevsky treats the ideologue as the buffoon. When, in his concern about the distraught Katerina, Lebeziatnikov tells Raskolnikov that '"in Paris they have been conducting serious experiments as to the possibility of curing the insane, simply by logical argument,"'[11] we have a delicious reduction of the excessive faith in rationalism which Dostoevsky condemns as western.

Dostoevsky's rare allusions to America suggest that he believes that the new land is about as western as you can get. In *The Possessed* it is for the fop, Lebyadkin, to sing its praises. He speaks glowingly of an American millionaire who 'left all his vast fortune to factories and to the exact sciences, and his skeleton to the students of the academy there, and his skin to be made into a drum, so that the American national hymn might be beaten upon it day and night.'[12] The experience of Shatov and Kirillov in America gives this rationalist optimism the lie. America, with its capitalism, its science, its utilitarianism, is, in Dostoevsky's mind, a desperate place, to which in comparison he must sometimes have thought that Russian culture was concerned with the smiling aspects of life.

In Bellow and Dostoevsky the world that we know is in good measure a world of ideas, positions, solutions. The letters of Herzog are only the most celebrated instance of the endless interplay of explanation which strikes Bellow as the most salient characteristic of an anxious age. Some of the ideas are worthy of Lebeziatnikov – like the theory of the Bulgarian aesthetician Banowich, who believes that telling someone a joke means that you want to eat him, or, more seriously, the various Sadean theories of negative transcendence which espouse creative criminality. Basteshaw, Dahfu, Bummidge, Lal are among those 'reality instructors' in Bellow in whom ideology is open to the charge of utopianism. Dostoevsky's attack is centred on the utilitarian and the revolutionary; while not excluding these, Bellow's is directed at more recent utopian attitudinizing, including the psychoanalytic, the technocratic, the modernist visionary. The mould is the same but the material has changed somewhat, partly because Bellow has a common-sense sympathy for a number of the liberal utilitarian propositions which Dostoevsky burlesques. For Dostoevsky suffering is the mother of human consciousness; granted, provided that one holds, as Bellow does, that pleasure is its father. Still, both writers reduce the Babel to a comic dimension from the point of view of a more traditional truth to be told. Both take confidence from older, 'obsolete' truths, residues of a religious tradition.

Bellow's outlook is analogous to that of certain social theorists. It sheds a clearer light on his aims, and on those of writers like him, to make a *précis* of their key arguments. Raymond Aron's *The Opium of the Intellectuals* implies in its title the downgrading of Marxist ideology and revolutionism which had great appeal to a number of the post-war liberal revisionist writers in America. Aron maintains that revolutionism had benefited from the prestige of aesthetic modernism, that the artist who denounces the philistines and the Marxist who denounces the bourgeoisie could consider themselves united in a battle against a single enemy. Aron notes, however, that none of the big literary movements was allied with the political left. Exceptions seem tangential and only prove the rule: 'Sartre's itinerary toward quasi-Communism appears to be dialectical. Man being a "vain passion," one is inclined in the last analysis to judge the various "projects" as all equally sterile. The radiant vision of the classless society follows on the description of the squalid society of today.'[13] Bellow shares his view not only of high culture but also of the mythicized proletariat, of whom Aron writes: 'Servant of the machine, soldier of the Revolution, the proletariat as such is never either the symbol or the beneficiary or the leader of any régime whatsoever ... The common source of these errors is a kind of visionary optimism combined with a pessimistic view of reality.'[14] As for the justification of such pessimism, Aron points out that in comparing the division of wealth and the standards of government of a century ago with those of today we can see that 'the growth of collective resources makes societies more egalitarian and less tyrannical. They remain, nonetheless, subject to the old, blind necessities of work and of power and, *ipso facto*, in the eyes of the optimists, unacceptable.'[15]

This 'doctrine of sustained tensions' with emphasis on 'the courage ... to endure,' as R.W.B. Lewis describes it, in a review of Lionel Trilling's *The Liberal Imagination*,[16] gives us what Lewis calls 'the new stoicism,' which is analogous to the Burkean view of history. Though the word has little of its original meaning, there is a similarity between the 'old' stoic rejection of Platonism in favour of sense perception and the late forties' stoic rejection of Marxism in favour of a pragmatic sense of possibility. Both posit a dignified self-sufficiency in a world of failed illusion. In Aron's dichotomy the essentialists and the utopians are at odds. We have seen Professor Herzog lecturing in a similar vein on the modernist '*new utopian history, an idyll, comparing the present to an imaginary past, because we hate the world as it is.*'[17]

Along with Aron, perhaps the clearest exponent of the stoical view is Edward Shils, a student of Karl Mannheim, sociologist and colleague of Bellow's at the University of Chicago. Bellow would seem to admire the tone that these men assume – totally unapologetic – in their critique of modernist utopianism. Like Aron, Shils must place the Marxist view in what he feels is its proper perspective. He points out that Trotsky thought 'the average human type will rise to the heights of an Aristotle, a Goethe or a Marx. And above this ridge, new peaks will rise.' But Shils feels that the working class, even where Communist, is uninterested in revolution, in the moral transformation of itself and the rest of the human race. Shils believes that all ideologists (e.g., Marxists, French monarchists, Southern agrarians) are hostile to human beings as they are. A revulsion against their own age makes intellectuals think of the elevated cultural life and dignified peasantry of a non-existent past (e.g., Tönnies, Simmel, Sombart, Marcuse). He denies the validity of the *Gemeinschaft Gesellschaft* distinction, since it assumes a small-scale, perfectly consensual, theological society which never existed. Shils does not believe that bourgeois individualism, urban society, and industrialism are an impoverishment of life. For him, as for Bellow since *Dangling Man*, the 'fundamental problems of humanity are the same as in antiquity.' He wants a pluralistic society rather than a completely integrated one, with a bow to British utilitarianism and Burke's critique of ideological politics, and with another to the British liberals, like Milton and Locke, who saw that society could be effective even if it had no uniformity of belief, no unifying ideology, and to Mill who, taking the next step, held that diversity of viewpoint was a necessity for a healthy society. Moreover, Shils believes that in mass society there is actually 'more of a sense of attachment to the society as a whole, more sense of affinity with one's own fellows, more openness to understanding, and more reaching out of understanding among men than in any earlier society of our Western history or in any of the great Oriental societies of the past'; that is, 'it is the most consensual.' Indeed, the 'uniqueness' of mass society is its 'incorporation of the mass into the moral order of its society.' Since the mass means more to the elites than in other societies, we see an enhancement of the dignity of ordinary life. Again, with a bow to Weber, 'the unique feature of the mass society is ... the dispersion of charismatic quality more widely throughout the society' (e.g., working class, women, youth, ethnic groups previously disadvantaged). Shils does attribute truth to the view which he is compelled to deny, saying alienation, yes, but there is another side to the conventional Marxist critique of mass society. The other side of alienation is disenchantment with authority; of egotism and hedonism, the growth of sensibility; of the decline of local autonomy, a more integrated society. Beyond all this dynamism the primordial attachments – kinship, locality, sexuality – will change but persist.[18]

Shils attacks 'ideology,' a term which he defines with strict constructionist precision. Ideology is a highly systematized pattern of belief integrated around a few pre-eminent values – salvation, equality, ethnic purity. Political coherence overrides every other consideration, with supreme significance going to one group or class – the nation, the ethnic folk, the proletariat, the party leaders. It has a Manichean cast, positing uncompromisable distinctions between good and evil, sacred and profane, left and right, we and they, the source of evil being a foreign power, an ethnic group, or a class (e.g., bourgeois). There is a distrust of traditional institutions – family, church, economic organizations, schools, conventional political alignments.

Shils distinguishes ideology from outlooks (e.g., Protestantism) which are pluralistic, containing creeds which shade off into ideology but do not take a sharply bounded and corporate form and have much less orthodoxy; and from systems and movements of thought which, like ideologies and unlike outlooks, are elaborate and internally integrated, but do not insist on total observance in behaviour, complete consensus among its adherents, and on closure *vis-à-vis* other intellectual constructions; and from programs, which involve specification of a particular limited objective, often in the form of a passionate rejection of one aspect of society.

Opposed to ideology is civility or civil politics; civility is the virtue of the citizen who shares responsibility in his own self-government. It is compatible with other attachments to class, to religion, to profession, but it regulates them out of respect for tradition and out of awareness of the complexity of virtue, awareness that every virtue costs, that virtue is intertwined with vice. With characteristic benignity Shils, writing in 1958, says that 'There is now in all strata, on the average, a higher civil sense than earlier phases of Western society have ever manifested.' In the manner of civility Shils does not believe that ideology should be 'completely dismissed' – the desire for greater equality, the distrust of authority, the need for heroism, all have 'some validity.' It is not the substance but the rigidity of ideological politics that does damage. Ideologies fail in their notions of global conquest. 'Normal' values assert themselves, compromises are made, and the world changes. As for the phrase 'end of ideology,' it applied only to a very specific time and in a very specific way; it did not mean that ideology could never exist. It was wrongly taken to mean that ideals, ethical standards, and general or comprehensive social views and policies were no longer either relevant or possible. Both sides failed, at times, to distinguish between ideology and outlook and between ideology and program. No society can exist without a cognitive, moral, and expressive culture; there can never be an end to outlooks and creeds, movements of thought and programs.[19]

It is worth briefly noting objections to these views which, like the views themselves, bear on a comprehension of Bellow and Dostoevsky. Needless to say, historical events of the late sixties represented an anger, a sense of injustice, that does violence to the tonality of these remarks and to a number of the propositions themselves. This is not the place for a weighing of arguments. It appears to an amateur observer, however, that Americans now and in the past have often been passionate about what Shils defines as programs and that ideology is a concept resonant with the struggles of *Mitteleuropa* from which a number of liberal and radical intellectuals derive perhaps too much of their vocabulary. Ideology, as Shils describes it, is as bad as he says it is. But it is difficult to gainsay Dennis Wrong's questioning of the total view: 'If "ideology" is by now, and perhaps with good reason, an irretrievably fallen word, is it necessary that "utopia" suffer the same fate? ... [Utopia] is the vision of a *possible* society, a vision that must deeply penetrate human consciousness before the question of how it might be fulfilled is seriously considered – and by that time we will already have advanced a long way towards its fulfillment.'[20]

The impatience or dislike shown by radical readers (adherents, say, of C. Wright Mills) for a book like *Mr. Sammler's Planet*, in which 'ideology' is presented as brutality, or a book like *Herzog*, whose hero feels that the 'occupation of a man is in duty, in use, in civility, in politics in the Aristotelian sense,' not in ideology or politics in the Marxist sense, is another way of drawing the lines. One recalls Lenin's view of *The Possessed*: 'great but repulsive.' Bellow has his own personalist, novelist's point of view, but his explicit utterances about ideology, by which he means what Shils means, are in the manner of Aron and Shils. 'Ideology is crippling to attention. It has no finite interests but makes a wholesale distribution of innumerable human facts. Its historical or biological schemes dispose of human beings by classification.' In support of a deeper contrary wisdom, he then quotes Dostoevsky who writes in accents Bellow comes to adopt: 'We cannot exhaust a phenomenon, never can we trace its end or its beginning. We are familiar merely with the everyday, apparent and current, and this only insofar as it appears to us, whereas the ends and the beginnings still constitute to man a realm of the fantastic.' The moral is then drawn by Bellow: 'Ideology commands an end, imposes a law, speaks the first and last words and abolishes confusion. But it has no interest in the miracle of being which artists endlessly contemplate.'[21] This 'mystery of mankind,' as Bellow is later to call it, this inexhaustibility, is indicative of the personalist, anti-ideological view. Even more so are Dostoevsky's critical remarks on *Anna Karenina*. Addressing himself to the question of Anna's guilt, Dostoevsky repudiates the 'physician-socialists,' saying that, for the Russian author, 'no ant-hill, no triumph of the "fourth estate," no elimination of poverty, no organization of labour will wave mankind from abnormality, and therefore – from guilt and criminality ... that in no organization of society can evil be eliminated, that the human soul will remain identical; that abnormality and sin emanate from the soul itself, and finally, that the laws of the human spirit are so unknown to science, so obscure, so indeterminate and mysterious, that, as yet, there can neither be physicians nor *final* judges, but there is only He who saith: "Vengeance belongeth unto me; I will recompense"' (the epigraph to the novel). This is deeper than environmentalism which says, 'inasmuch as society is abnormally organized, it is impossible to make the human entity responsible for its consequences. Therefore, the criminal is irresponsible and at present crime does not exist.' But, Dostoevsky continues, Tolstoy, knowing in this case the consequences of adultery and equal 'crimes,' expresses his older wisdom 'in a immense psychological analysis of the human soul.'[22]

It is one of the truisms of Dostoevsky criticism that the writer who excoriated the ideology of political radicalism himself embraced the ideology of pan-Slavism with its belief in the messianic mission of the God-bearing Russian people, the truth of

Russian orthodoxy, and the falsehood of western Roman Catholicism, the sanctity of the Russian soil, and the even more sacred quality of the Russian peasant; here we have the we-they, sacred-profane dichotomy, which Shils says characterized the ideologist. But Dostoevsky scarcely knew the peasants he idealized. And, as Philip Rahv has said, the manner in which he embraced orthodoxy was so apocalyptic as to undermine orthodoxy, subvert dogma, shatter the notion of institutionalized religion itself.[23] If, in *The Possessed*, he saw the failure of revolutionary ideology, he was too honest not to portray the nihilistic vacuum which revolution must fill. Perhaps anyone viewing political reality in Czarist Russia with a clear eye would see a chaos beyond the politics of civility to set right. Dostoevsky dreaded the anti-Christ whose arrival he intuited, which accounts for the gloom behind the comic balance of the book. As for his belief, does he ever really convince us of anything more than Shatov's 'I – I will believe in God'? And for all his sweet clairvoyance, the final point about Myshkin is that he fails.

Above all, the dramatic force of Dostoevsky's art often works against his didactic intention with a brilliance that illustrates the subtle uniqueness of literature – the exposition, in action, of ambivalence, the complex of feelings in the face of which any idea must be a simplification. The underground men, Raskolnikov, Ivan – all characters whom Dostoevsky fundamentally rejects – are creations of a child of light who saw best in darkness. But the metaphor should not confuse. Dostoevsky was nothing if not a personalist. In saying of him that 'nobody was less preoccupied with the empirical world ... his art is completely immersed in the profound realities of the spiritual universe,'[24] Berdyaev gives us what is, at best, a half-truth. How can one be a non-empirical psychological genius? More to the point is the description by Strakhov, who knew Dostoevsky intimately: '"All his attention was upon people, and all his efforts were directed towards understanding their nature and character. People, their temperament, way of living, feelings, thoughts, these were his sole preoccupation."'[25]

This personalism is consonant with the intellectual depth of his work; for he is, as Arnold Hauser puts it, 'a romantic in the world of thought' in that 'the movement of thought has the same motive power and the same emotional, not to say pathological, impetus in him as the flood and stress of the feelings had in the romantics.'[26] It is this lyricism of ideas combined with a centrist conception of character in which Bellow finds Dostoevsky the acknowledged master. Typically, in a Bellow novel, an essentially urban man, usually 'cracked,' often intellectual, portrayed in his solitude or isolation, usually unemployed in one way or another, whose business turns out to be personal relationships, is thrust forward at the moment of intense subjective crisis. Everyday apprehension is shattered by a welling up of the demonic. What George Steiner says of Dostoevsky also applies to Bellow: his 'characters – even the neediest among them – always have leisure for chaos or an unpremeditated total involvement.'[27] Virtuosi in mental suffering, these characters embody the heady balance of disequilibrium. When Dostoevsky, in his famous letter to Strakhov, wrote, 'I have my own view of art, and that which the majority call fantastic and exceptional is for me the very essence of reality,' he was pioneering, not aware that he was writing a motto for much of the literature of the future. It is this merging of realism and fantasy in a context of pained, obsessive, often funny subjectivity, this art, as Philip Rahv has it, of psychic distortion, moral agitation, and resentment,[28] the way of Gogol rather than the 'objective' way of Pushkin, which Dostoevsky and Bellow take as their aesthetic norm. Herbert Gold called the author of *Henderson the Rain King* the 'funniest sufferer since Gogol,'[29] to which one can only add, with the possible exception of the creator of *The Double, Notes from Underground*, and *The Eternal Husband*.

'All Dostoevsky's heroes are really himself,'[30] says Berdyaev, offering a version of the distinction between Doestoevsky, a writer of subjectivity and obsession, and Tolstoy, one of objectivity and proportion. This is a distinction of convenience, but it applies essentially to Bellow as well. Both present a theatre of self-realization where the heart is laid bare in the act of defining what is real. In this personal quest sociological categories are secondary to the spiritual. If this implies a distance between object and subject, society and self, action and temperament, it is a distance which both writers feel must be bridged. In both brotherhood is a refrain whose melody they are trying to recapture – trying and often failing. Both attempt to break out of what Edward Wasiolek has called '*the circle of hurt-and-be-hurt*,'[31] the network of sado-masochism, which appears to be a governing principle of the era of self-exaltation; there is Sonia, Myshkin, Alyosha – there is Wilhelm, Herzog, Sammler. But, in both, meekness or mildness is largely its own reward. *Caritas* is typically confounded by *Eros* in a scenario where man-woman relationships testify to the potency of moral tenuousness or disintegration. In Dostoevsky, as Berdyaev says, 'The mystery of marriage is not consummated,' and in Bellow the marriage is consummated but the mystery is not dispelled. For both, in Berdyaev's phrase, 'love serves only as an index of ... inner division.'[32]

Yet the delineation of similarities points significantly to differences, for Dostoevsky presents us with a drama of extremes, a moral *chiaroscuro*, an acting out in fact what in Bellow often remains fantasy or suggestion. Raskolnikov commits the murder, Herzog does not; Herzog thinks of and, in some ways, embodies the strength of mildness, Myshkin is its apotheosis; hit by a block of wood and his senses clarified, Henderson says, 'truth comes in blows,' but when Dmitri Karamazov says, 'I understand now that such men as I need a blow,' he has been condemned for a parricide he wished for. The self-willed in Dostoevsky are pathological, the meek incredibly self-effacing. It seems that Czarist Russia had a way of rendering fantasy literal, making for a dramatic, even operatic, quality which in a kindred contemporary spirit more nearly comes out as *opéra bouffe*. Dostoevsky's ideological preferences lent substance to an often Manichean opposition of forces. The outcome in Dostoevsky is typically tragic in overtone, a Dionysian coming to grips with the demonic, leaving one with a sense of waste nobler than the hidden cause. In Bellow even the Dionysian inspiration – e.g., Henderson, Herzog – is ultimately comic in that the painful, headlong quest is inseparable from a knowledge that is the self, the western, Dostoevsky-doubted ego, which is the last court of appeals; this self which, in its constant exposure, cannot be taken as seriously as it once was, and yet is most of what we have to take seriously. Where Dostoevsky dramatically records the disintegration of the self, Bellow tentatively assumes it, and the tragic is converted into the comic. In Bellow, accordingly, more often than in Dostoevsky, the soul is finally restored to a firm outline. The one point at which the writers would seem to be most widely apart is the apprehension of the self in its full sensual regalia. Here Bellow would appear to be positively Tolstoyan. A character like Stiva Oblonsky, in *Anna Karenina*, lives in the literary love of an author whose judgment is otherwise morally proscriptive of him. So many of Bellow's characters exist in this way. Ramona, for example, illustrates the delights of inner division. The observation of sensuousness implies the 'normal' world, but the dramatic situation implies the Doestoevskean 'extreme.' It is precisely this integration of opposites which describes a good part of the course of the literary *zeitgeist*, for what we see in Bellow, and in other recent writers, is the normalization of the extreme – making it comfortable, cosy, charming. 'If I'm out of my mind, it's all right with me,' says Herzog, and any reader of the book would understand him.

Bellow's work offers some extended illustrations of the Dostoevskean influence – unconscious or otherwise. It has not been noticed, for example, that the dialogue between Joseph and the Spirit of Alternatives in *Dangling Man* is a low-keyed recasting of the apparition of the devil to the hallucinated consciousness of Ivan Karamazov. Ivan recognizes that the devil is his double: 'You are the incarnation of myself, but only one side of me ... of my thoughts and feelings, but only the nastiest and stupidest of them' (BK, p 775). The devil appears as a shabby genteel Russian, whom Dostoevsky sees as a type. They 'have a distinct aversion for any duties that may be forced upon them, are usually solitary creatures, either bachelors or widowers. Sometimes they have children ... brought up at a distance, at some aunt's ... They gradually lose sight of their children altogether' (BK, p 773). That is, the devil is worldly self-absorption divorced from the essential ties. Child abandonment, while not quite the equivalent of child abuse, is closely related.[33] Yet this prince of darkness is a gentleman, 'accommodating, and ready to assume any amiable expression,' possessing, in Dostoevsky's view, the complete western veneer and the basic western wisdom. He does not know if there is a God; he knows only *je pense, donc je suis* and, Descartes's 'proof' of the existence of God to the contrary notwithstanding, its attendant solipsism, a sort of fantasy extension, in Dostoevsky's view, of the rationalistic, ego-oriented West: 'Does all that exist of itself, or is it only an emanation of myself, a logical development of my ego which alone has existed for ever' (BK, p 781).

Goethe was enough of a traditional humanist to create a Mephistopheles who desired evil but did only good, but Dostoevsky's Mephistopheles, operating in a universe much more attuned to the modern saturation of alienated consciousness, sees that he desires good but does only evil – which perfectly describes Ivan's predicament (culminating in his harrowing scenes with Smerdyakov, whose suicide he hears of immediately after the apparition vanishes). Ivan realizes at the outset that the devil embodies his 'stupidest' thoughts, yet so attractive are they that they threaten to destroy his 'intelligent' ones. 'God is dead,' 'the man-god,' 'will,' 'science,' 'all things are lawful,' 'the old slave man,' parade so tantalizingly before his hallucinated view that Ivan can dispel them only in the way Luther with his inkstand set the devil to rout – he throws his glass at him. If this is a breakthrough for Ivan, the devil himself remains *déclassé*. Konstantin Mochulsky notes that 'In his *Legend* Ivan represented the devil in the majestic image of a terrible and wise spirit, and here he has proved to be a vulgar hanger-on ... The spirit of non-being is an imposter: this is not Lucifer with singed wings, but ... the incarnation of world boredom and world vulgarity.'[34]

Precisely. And it is this note of boredom and vulgarity which Bellow strikes in his ostensibly reasonable, genteel, representative of non-being, the Spirit of Alternatives. There is no nightmare, no sickness here – at least in the first meeting. Consistent with the meandering movement of the work itself, the encounter is 'relaxed.' So reasonable is the Spirit, so plausible to the dangling man are his alternatives, that he is also called 'On the Other Hand' and '*Tu As Raison Aussi*.' Yet it is clear that in his equivocal manner, his indeterminacy, his inevitable drift to the negative, the alienative, his flirtation with ideology, his attitudinizing in a vacuum of conviction, above all, in his compulsion to the centre of indifference, to death, he is the dangling man's devil-double in the same sense that the apparition is Ivan's – as a representation of his own worst, his own 'stupidest' ideas and tendencies. (Joseph, we recall, is already separated from the older, benevolent, rational, Enlightenment Joseph.) This apparition is even quieter than Joseph; his point must be elicited, but when it is seen to be 'alienation,' Joseph retorts that 'it's a fool's plea.' Not that there is no alienation, but 'that we should not make a doctrine' of it. Trying another route, the Spirit suggests 'changing existence' through politics, but Joseph rejects the revolutionary and even politics *per se*. He does, however, admit to the value of 'a plan, a program, perhaps an obsession.' When the Spirit converts this typically American *ad hoc* impulse into 'an ideal construction,' Joseph notes the 'German phrase,' and wonders about the ideological exemplar or type. He concedes that an 'obsessive device' may be 'the only possible way to meet chaos' and sees the apparent 'need to give our-selves some exclusive focus, passionate and engulfing,' but the essentialist asserts itself in him: 'what of the gap between the ideal construction and the real world, the truth? ... Then, there's this: the obsession exhausts the man. It can become his enemy. If often does.' When the Spirit has no answer to this, apparently having no real convictions to defend, Joseph drives him out, flinging 'a handful of orange peel' at him (DM, pp 137 ff).

Like Ivan, Joseph seeks that which 'unlocks the imprisoning self,' and in order to escape being 'self-fastened' he himself is willing to entertain the 'highest "ideal construction,"' though, more or less, as a passing fancy. Still, he feels that *Tu As Raison Aussi* stands refuted; Joseph has confidence that the 'final end' of everyone is 'the desire for pure freedom,' which he defines in Dostoevskean fashion, not simply as free will but as will defining itself as spirit, 'to know what we are and what we are for, to know our purpose, to seek grace' (DM, p 154). This is as far as Joseph will go towards religion. But the resolution is offhand and represents only a moment of equilibrium. Joseph's depression worsens, and in the next encounter the Spirit ap-pears as an almost old-style Mephistopheles, the Spirit that Denies, tempting Joseph to 'give up,' to succumb to indifference, to die, to 'worship the anti-life.' Joseph recognizes his 'inability to be free,' and that this is the cause of his 'weariness of life.' Unmistakably, and despite his noble wish to share the pain of his generation, Joseph joins the army in the same way one joins the Grand Inquisitor's church: '"We soon want to give up our freedom ... we choose a master, roll over on our backs and ask for the leash"' (DM, pp 167 ff). When Joseph utters the hollow cry, 'Long live regimentation!' he is aware that he is 'relieved of self-determination, freedom can-celled' (DM, p 191). This conclusion has little of the ambiguity sometimes attributed to it. In the end Bellow's devil-double emerges as one who ascertains your doubt of selfhood, uniqueness, 'separate destiny.' Joseph is rendered almost as pale, sickly, chilled, and enervated at the end of his encounter with the double as Ivan is with his.

The dramatization of guilt leading to confrontation with the double is conspicuous in comparing Bellow's *The Victim* with Dostoevsky's *The Eternal Husband*. This comparison has not gone unnoticed, but the context of extended comparison of this essay affords us a wider view of its meaning. Actually, Dostoevsky's *The Double* is the precursor of both. A solitary spirit in a dreary urban landscape is the necessary beginning to each crisis of subjectivity. In *The Double* 'the damp autumn day, muggy and dirty, peeped into the room through the dingy window pane with such a hostile, sour grimace that Mr. Golyadkin could not possibly doubt that he was not in the land of Nod, but in the city of Petersburg, in his own flat on the fourth storey of a huge block of buildings in Shestilavotchny Street' (D, p 477). If the living is compartmentalized, so is the job, for Golyadkin is a result of the dehumanizing Russian bureaucracy. The crisis in his life breaks out when the moral qualities that the system exacts of its lesser lights, bootlicking, toadying, a fidgety, manipulative quality, a nastiness masking as playfulness, a choreographed self-interest, appears in the shape of Golyadkin Junior who, like Ivan's devil-double, is the embodiment of Senior's worst self. As the story begins, we see Golyadkin 'satisfied' with the 'insignificant' face and bald head he views in the morning mirror. He feels so good that he counts his money. Beware! – a sure sign of anal-retentive meanness in Dostoevsky is viewed here as a sign of life in the bureaucracy. A volatile mixture of self-esteem and self-abasement (before his superiors, or any other male authority figure), this isolated, hostile sado-masochistic urban bachelor is Dostoevsky's first underground man. He is 'sick' and goes to see a physician, palpitating before the meeting but greeting him with a schizoid 'figuratively crushing' glare. He is suffering from 'the perfumed compliment,' the 'masquerade' (D, p 485) and a sense of his own unimportance; this last is intensified when a rival in love, with better bureaucratic connections, wins out. In one of those scenes of comic humiliation of which Dostoevsky is in a class by himself, Golyadkin is rebuffed at the entrance to an important party only to stand in an obscure corner near the garbage – for three hours! Attempting to crash the party and dance with his beloved Klara, he is thrown out. Shaken, even his 'secure' office life seems to be disintegrating. At this point the *Doppelgänger* appears, full of Schilleresque sentiment. Raggedly clothed, he tells a three-hour story which makes Golyadkin sob, 'even though his visitor's story was the paltriest story' (D, p 530). Senior, on his part, confesses his personal torment, saying, 'It's from love for you that I speak, from brotherly love' (D, 532). But the very next day Junior is formal, official, self-important, a hypocritical mask-wearer, who usurps Senior's place and wipes his hand from Senior's handshake; later he condescendingly pinches Senior's cheek and finally has him committed. His attempt at *Brüderschaft* and all the worthy emotions a failure, it is no wonder that Senior goes crazy.

The Eternal Husband presents us with another comedy of self-exposure, another crisis in the life of an ostensibly well-ordered existence, another confrontation with the double. Where Golyadkin represented the harassed little bureaucrat, out of Gogol, Velchaninov is the smug bourgeois; in Wasiolek's terms, where Golyadkin was the 'mouse,' the underground man, the sexual loser, Velchaninov is the 'bull,' the sort who abuses him, the sexual winner. He is confident, muscle-bound and ego-bound, apparently immune to suffering or guilt. Mysteriously, he is smitten by an attack of 'higher ideas.' For a long time he had felt a vague malaise, a nervousness, a hypochondria; for an equal time aloneness has replaced his social life. The 'higher ideas' are the kind 'he could not laugh at in his heart,' but are forgotten the next day. Aware that his night thoughts are radically different from his day thoughts, he consults a doctor friend about his sleeplessness and is informed that being 'too conscious of the double nature of [his] feelings' is a symptom of approaching illness. Why is it that he forgets the recent past but remembers things that happened fifteen years ago? 'Why did some things he remembered strike him now as positive crimes?' (EH, p 348). His vulnerability to conscience, among other things, distinguishes him from unfeeling characters like Luzhin or Totsky. Like Ivan, like Golyadkin, he is pursued by the embodiment of his worst thoughts. This embodiment takes the elusive form of Pavel Pavlovitch Trusotsky, whom Velchaninov finally confronts, recognizing in this changed man the cuckold of nine years ago. Attempting a redemption of his idle life, Velchaninov is genuinely moved to do what he can for his natural daughter.

Pavel is the buffoon, the mouse, the sado-masochist, who had been cruel to the child – though his cruelty once took the odd form of hanging himself before her – out of resentment. *Ressentiment* is the key to his character, explaining his wallowing in bland *Brüderschaft*, alternating with intimations of revenge. As with Golyadkin and the underground man, he is seized by a compulsion to humiliate the humiliator. But between the guilty and the shamed there is some question as to who is the real predator. Pavel tells the story of Livtsov, the best man at Golubenko's wedding, who was insulted by Golubenko and who lost out in love to him; he stabs Golubenko (but does not kill him) at the wedding, saying, '"Ach! What have I done!"' When Pavel says, '"he got his own back,"' Velchaninov roars '"Go to hell!"' (EH, pp 405–6), and their understanding is clear. Pavel invites Velchaninov to meet what he hopes will be his fifteen-year-old bride-to-be and the situation threatens to be a repeat of their original one. Velchaninov pulls back: '"We are both vicious, underground, loathsome people"' (EH, p 443), he tells Pavel, recognizing a grim mutual dependency. Pavel later appreciates Velchaninov's not telling him about the girl's true feelings for him and nurses him with tea and compresses when he, exhausted and suffering from chest pains, seems to have a constitutional breakdown. '"You are better than I am! I understand it all, all"' (EH, p 455), says Velchaninov shortly before embarking on a sleep from which he is nearly never to awaken. Pavel attempts to murder Velchaninov with a razor in a not precisely premeditated act: he '"wanted to kill him, but didn't know he wanted to kill him."' Velchaninov sees that '"it was from hatred that he loved me; that's the strongest of all loves"' (EH, pp 460–1).

Though Bellow's *The Victim* is strikingly similar in certain respects, the emphasis is almost as much metaphysical as it is psychological. Whereas, for example, the child-victim of *The Eternal Husband* dies as a result of humiliation derived from the guilt of both men, the child-victim in *The Victim* dies from a fated physical disease. Accordingly, the double here is not so much a projecton of a particular guilt as it is a conception of suffering. In *The Eternal Husband* Velchaninov is clearly at fault; his subconscious wells up for release. With Bellow's Leventhal it is much more a question of obligation or responsibility, in that disillusioned, late forties sense. An illustration of the end-of-innocence stoicism of liberal ex-radicals – like Trilling's *The Middle of the Journey* and Mary McCarthy's *The Groves of Academe–The Victim* gives us a picture of the victim as victimizer, the tyranny of the disadvantaged and outcast. To complicate the tough-mindedness, *The Victim* also subverts the image of the benevolent Jew of popular fiction dealing with anti-Semitism.

The general scene of *The Victim* can fairly be called Dostoevskean: the hallucinatory, nocturnal, numinous quality, the unpromising urban backdrop, the steps, the room, the heat, the hide-and-seek beginning, the protagonist wishing to be decent but caught up in a petty bureaucracy which is a temptation to the contrary, the urban 'bachelor' (Leventhal is married but his good wife is necessarily out of town). But there are differences: where Velchaninov was directly guilty, Leventhal's real guilt is in unfeeling. His eyes are indifferent, not 'sullen but rather unaccommodating, impassive' (V, p 20). Physically large, he has none of the *amour-propre* of the Dostoevskean bull for, unlike him, he has not had a privileged life. On the contrary, it is not the softness but the 'harshness of his life [which] had disfigured him' (V, p 22). Meeting with the modest success of a respectable job and marriage, he tells his wife, '"I was lucky. I got away with it,"' having avoided 'the part that did not get away with it – the lost, the outcast, the overcome, the effaced, the ruined' (V, p 26). Allbee represents precisely this reality, as Leventhal comes to realize, but in a way that makes it very difficult for one to accept responsibility, even if direct in an attenuated way. Allbee is a victim of his own inadequacies and circumstances rather than any malicious action on Leventhal's part. Since Allbee is a determinist, his claim on Leventhal is more a gesture of revenge on conditions than it is an argument for individual agency. 'The day of succeeding by your own efforts is past. Now it's all blind movement, vast movement, and the individual is shuttled back and forth ... Groups, organizations succeed or fail, but not individuals any longer ... people have a destiny forced upon them' (V, pp 68–9). Determinism is the cuckoldry of thought, but we are far from the direct guilt of *The Eternal Husband*. (And even there one can argue that Pavel needs Velchaninov and feels a sexual attraction to the man who brings him such masochistic undoing.) For his part, Leventhal will accept responsibility. (Allbee was fired as an indirect result of a scene between Leventhal and his boss.) But Allbee plays so heavily on the sentiment of guilt that it comes out as self-righteousness, despite the fact that he is not so much Leventhal's psychological double as he is, so to speak, a metaphysical one; for, as the story develops, he comes to represent, in Leventhal's mind, a necessary allegiance to those who are not lucky, the ruined. This is the meaning of the two epigraphs to the novel. Responsible or not, we are responsible. There are, after all, these faces in a sea of suffering.

Allbee claims an ideal relationship with his ex-wife, but the more we know about it the more sentimental it seems to be. He cries when he sees the picture of Leventhal's wife because she reminds him of his own. It seems that their relationship was so good that she left him, because, he claims, he could not get a job. True love? Did Leventhal then break up his marriage as well? It turns out that Allbee had been fired at a number of places before. And that his drinking really is something like the problem that the excessively restrained Leventhal thinks it is. As for the depth of feeling he has for his wife, when she died he did not attend the funeral. (Pavel did not attend the funeral of his 'daughter.') They were separated; it was hot; he would have had to see her family. Surely this is one of those instances, common in Bellow and Dostoevsky, where fine sentiment is travestied by contrary action. For both writers it is a *spécialité de la maison*. In *The Eternal Husband* Pavel attempts to kill Velchaninov after effusiveness, tea, and hot compresses: 'it's just with a Schiller like that, in the outer form of a Quasimodo, that such a thing could happen,' says Velchaninov. 'The most monstrous monster is the monster with noble feelings' (EH, pp 46–7). Velchaninov might just as well be speaking of Allbee.

Part of Allbee's 'nobility' is hereditary. The depth of his *ressentiment* stems from his being the dispossessed Wasp, a *ressentiment* from above, deeper socially than Pavel's is from below. It explains his gloomy determinism, his excessive drinking, his difficulty in performing well at a job. When Allbee accuses Leventhal of ruining him 'out of pure hate' (V, p 74), we see an instance of pathology. Even more pathological is Allbee's virulent anti-Semitism; in New York 'the children of Caliban' run everything, whereas 'one of my ancestors was Governor Winthrop' (V, p 131). He asserts that his 'honour' tells him not to ask Leventhal for damages – though this is what he is doing, and then some – because he does not want to act like a 'New York type.' If things were not bad enough, books on Emerson and Thoreau are written by people with names like Lipschitz (V, p 131). Later Leventhal finds Allbee in his own bed with another woman, and the degradation of the sentimental widower proceeds apace. Ousted, the resentful Allbee sets the gas jet in Leventhal's apartment. He '"tried a kind of suicide pact without getting my permission first,"' thinks Leventhal; and in a rare judgmental remark, never quoted by those critics making a case for Allbee, the narrator says, 'He might have added, fairly, "without intending to die himself"' (V, p 249).

Leventhal does err on the side of suspicion – though Allbee shows that this is sometimes impossible to do. Leventhal has none of the charm and little of the energetic temperament of later Bellow central characters. *The Victim* is the only longer work of Bellow with no comic element to speak of. There is a scrupulous meanness in the description of the *milieu* – between father and son, brother and brother – which goes with the Flaubertian-Joycean texture of the whole. Leventhal notices that the lights over the Manhattan buildings are 'akin to the yellow revealed in the slit of the eye of a wild animal, say a lion, something inhuman that didn't care about anything human and yet was implanted in every human being too, one speck of it'

(V, pp 52–3). If this is the aura of sinister New York, it is also an intimation that the sympathetic heart is in danger of being lost.

Allbee is the double of Leventhal's impassivity – both are overcome, exorcised by Leventhal, finally. When Leventhal finds out that, because of the office dispute (his boss 'made [him] out to be a nothing,' something he could ill afford to hear), he was indirectly responsible for Allbee's losing his job, he wonders if he unconsciously wanted to get back at Allbee for some of his anti-Semitic jibes. Leventhal dreams of missing a train and of trying to catch the second section of it, from which men divert his path. His face is covered with tears. On awakening, 'he experienced a rare, pure feeling of happiness. He was convinced that he knew the truth ... everything without exception took place as if within a single soul or person.' Yet 'he knew that tomorrow this would be untenable.' Still he recalls the recognition in Allbee's eyes which 'he could not doubt was the double of something in his own' (V, p 151), a natural sympathy. Bellow, like Dostoevsky, does not end with a tearful wallowing in *Brüderschaft*. Despite the occasional closeness, even physical intimacy of a sort, the gain for Leventhal is in consciousness, not in new relationship.

Like *The Eternal Husband*, *The Victim* ends with a coda which affirms the dubious character of the double. In a scene which takes place a few years after the main action Allbee, like M. Trusotsky, seems to be reincarnated – fancy clothes, wealthy woman, and all. Cantankerous, accusing, Jew-baiting by habit, pushing his lady around but speaking of her in ideal terms, denying any guilt in the murder attempt – he is changed only in circumstance, and Leventhal notices an underlying decay. Unlike Leventhal, Velchaninov does not seem to have become different; money, good food, the creature comforts once again define his life. Pavel remains the eternal husband, subservient, harassed by infidelity, resentful of Velchaninov.

In a well-known speech in *The Victim*, which has no counterpart in *The Eternal Husband* but does have its counterpart in Dostoevsky's general outlook, wise old Schlossberg says, '"It's bad to be less than human and it's bad to be more than human ... I say choose dignity. Nobody knows enough to turn it down"' (V, pp 127 ff). These are sentiments to which the creator of Raskolnikov, the underground man, and Dimitri Karamazov would say Amen. 'More than human' is like that 'sense of Personal Destiny' leading to 'ideal constructions' for wisdom, bravery, cruelty, art, which the dangling man thinks about. The man Leventhal meets in the men's room during a Karloff movie comprehends the type: 'He really understands what a mastermind is, a law unto himself' (V, p 96). Similarly, Caesar is Schlossberg's illustration of 'more than human' in his idealized bravery (self-overcoming, casting out any human weakness) and his aspiration 'to be like a god' (V, p 121). There is an attraction-repulsion in both writers to the 'ideal construction,' the 'obsession [which] exhausts the man,' superman transcendence, as there is to underground-man envy, self-laceration, and unfeeling (Golyadkin and Pavel, Joseph and

Allbee). Leventhal, Bellow writes, 'disagreed about "less than human." Since it was done by so many, what was it but human?' He adds: 'he liked to think "human" meant accountable in spite of many weaknesses – at the last moment, tough enough to hold' (V, p 139). A nice touch this, recognizing as it does the common denominator of secular selfhood and its attendant anxiety, it establishes more-than-human/less-than-human as a continuum of gain and loss, up and down, in the struggle for subjective freedom. This is something of what Nietzsche meant when, as the story goes, he claimed that Dostoevsky's underman and his overman were the same. But Nietzsche misconstrued Dostoevsky's relation to his character, for his transvaluation of morals, unlike that of Dostoevsky, and of Bellow, was not related to Judeo-Christian roots. Did Nietzsche understand the anguished cry of the underground man – 'They won't let me – I can't be good' –?

LEWIS A. LAWSON

The Moviegoer
and the Stoic Heritage

Early in Walker Percy's *The Moviegoer* (1961) the patrician Aunt Emily sends her nephew, John Bickerson Bolling, the following note: 'Every moment think steadily as a Roman and a man, to do what thou has in hand with perfect and simple dignity, and a feeling of affection and freedom and justice. These words of the Emperor Marcus Aurelius Antoninus strike me as pretty good advice, for even the orneriest young scamp.'[1] Despite the forced levity of her application, the adjuration remains: Aunt Emily is proclaiming that the stoic way, after a three-hundred-year history in the South, still offers its aristocratic sons a sufficient philosophy.

It cannot be said that a reliance upon stoic texts to temper the prevailing Christian ecclesiastical structure was a telling distinction between North and South from the very beginning of the American colonies. Indeed, perhaps the earliest mention of the stoics is in John Harvard's will, in 1638, which left, among other books, a copy of Epictetus to the young college at New Towne,[2] in Massachusetts, which was happy enough to adopt the name of its benefactor. But the evidence does suggest that the stoic view did soon become a part of the set of ideas which motivated Southern patricians – such ideas as deism, squirearchy, and rationalism.[3]

A focus for the stoic view in the oldest colony was found in the College of William and Mary, which was begun in 1693, the second college in the colonies. Then, as now, one fruitful source of books for libraries was the benevolence of wealthy men, and the administration at Middle Plantation, shortly to become Williamsburg, made its appeal. The first to respond was Colonel Francis Nicholson, who left, in his bequest of 30 May 1695, a collection of books that included Meric Casaubon's *Marcus Aurelius*.[4] Such public support continued, for in 1739 the Reverend Emanuel Jones, rector of Petsworth Parish in Gloucester County, left at least part of his library to the college, including the only book to survive the library fires of 1859 and 1862, Arrian's *Enchiridion*, which Jones had acquired as a student at Oriel College, Oxford, in 1687.[5]

With its Anglican tolerance for the tenets of stoicism,[6] William and Mary continued as the Southern locus of that philosophy in the eighteenth century. There were, of course, the basic texts in the growing library. There is also evidence that members of the college board of visitors – those wealthy and influential men who set the tone of the intellectual community[7] – possessed such books in their private libraries. Ralph Wormeley, of Middlesex, had a copy of Seneca's *Morals* among the items of his estate in 1703,[8] while the library of the great Carter family included the *Enchiridion*.[9] The most distinguished man of letters in colonial Virginia, Colonel William Byrd, left Seneca, Aurelius, and Epictetus to his heirs.[10] The no less distinguished Richard Lee II, of Mount Pleasant, left both Epictetus and Seneca in his library when it was inventoried in 1714.[11] Indeed, London booksellers seem to have recognized the Virginian inclination to the stoic view, for Robert Beverley's *The History and Present State of Virginia* (1705) contained an advertisement for Seneca's *Morals* on one of its back pages.[12]

In time the Williamsburg book trade employed a much wider form of advertisement – *The Virginia Gazette*. To judge from the frequency with which they were offered, Seneca's works were perhaps the most popular books available during the period 1770–5.[13] But Marcus Aurelius was also so well known that certain public responses to the use of his name could reasonably be expected, for it was used as a newspaper pseudonym in 1768–9.[14] And, as would be expected, wills and inventories for the period reveal yet more private libraries which contained the key stoic texts.[15] The 1759 will of Daniel Parke Custis, whose widow married George Washington, listed two copies of Seneca's *Morals*.[16] Fittingly, in this time of wide stoic influence, the governor, Norborne Berkeley, Baron de Botetourt, was a reader of Aurelius and Epictetus, the latter in the popular new translation by Mrs Elizabeth Carter.[17]

It was during this period of widespread recourse to the stoics that Thomas Jefferson attended the College of William and Mary, where he graduated in 1762. When he first became acquainted with the stoic works is unknown, but once he had discovered them, he never ceased thinking that they provided a body of guiding principles that every educated person ought to possess. For that reason he on several occasions included them on reading lists that he provided for young people. In 1771, when he was twenty-eight, Jefferson drew up such a list for his friend and relative John Skipwith: among the fourteen titles under 'religion' were both Mrs Carter's *Epictetus* and Collins's *Antoninus*.[18] His advice to his nephew Peter Carr, in 1785, is much the same: 'In morality, read Epictetus, Xenophontis Memorabilia, Plato's Socratic dialogues, Cicero's philosophies, Antoninus, and Seneca.'[19] Forty years later he still possessed his respect for the Stoa, for he included Schweighauser's *Epictetus*, in six volumes, among the starting collection he was ordering for his creation, the University of Virginia.[20] Epictetus seems to have been his lifelong favourite of the school, for he wrote William Short, in 1819, that Epictetus had 'given us what was good of the Stoics; all beyond, of their dogmas, being hypocrisy and grimace.'[21] At the same time he stressed his dedication to Epictetus by implying that he had never been given the felicitous translation that would have won him a wider audience among those citizens who did not have the good fortune of a classical education: 'I have sometimes thought of translating Epictetus (for he has never been tolerably translated into English).'[22]

Through Jefferson the stoic bequest to the American experience was fully realized. Had stoicism provided only the concept of natural law that permeates Jefferson's *Declaration of Independence*, it would have left an indelible mark on American history.[23] But Seneca, Aurelius, and Epictetus are credited with an even greater effect on Jefferson and the other founders: 'From them came some thoughts and ideals that became part of the higher thought of Western civilization: nobiltiy of character, high ethical purpose, the ideal of self-sacrifice, belief in God and His divine providence, emphasis on virtue as the highest good and on action to make it effective, the need of bringing conduct into conformity with the law of Nature, and the realization of a high and stern sense of duty in public and private life.'[24]

It should be understood, though, that the claim is not being advanced that Jefferson was entirely and only a stoic. On the contrary, in the same letter to William Short he acknowledged: 'As you say of yourself, I too am an Epicurian. I consider the genuine (not imputed) doctrines of Epicurus as containing everything rational in moral philosophy which Greece and Rome have left us.' Then he appended his appreciation of Epictetus. But even then he had not sketched in the fullness of his conception of the moral faculty and role. For he continued: 'the greatest of all the reformers of the depraved religion of His own country, was Jesus of Nazareth. Abstracting what is really His from the rubbish in which it is buried, easily distinguished by its lustre from the dross of His biographers, and as separable from that as the diamond from the dunghill, we have the outlines of a system of the most sublime morality which has ever fallen from the lips of man; outlines which it is lamentable He did not live to fill up. Epictetus and Epicurus give laws for governing ourselves, Jesus a supplement of the duties and charities we owe to others.'[25]

Jefferson's distinction between the stoics and Jesus supports Adrienne Koch's conclusion about his religious philosophy: 'if one speculates on the historic function of Epicureanism and Stoicism and also upon their reintroduction into Europe in the sixteenth and seventeenth centuries, Jefferson's attitude may be better understood. In brief, they both functioned as systems of independent morality, needing no sanction from Church or State. This alone would have been sufficient to evoke some interest on Jefferson's part, since authoritarian religious morality was clearly repugnant to him at this period, as always.'[26] His opposition is clearly displayed in his feeling that one of his three most important accomplishments was authorship of 'The

Bill for Establishing Religious Freedom' in Virginia, even though that action dis-
established his own denomination, the Anglican Church. Jefferson, in sum, balanced
the pagans and Jesus to develop a view that honoured both the self and the other.

Later Southern patricians failed to maintain such a fine distribution of restraints.
Rather, they remained in the church with their Jesus, a Jesus who was a focus for
personal piety, rarely a goad to action that would shake the foundations of society.
And when they came out of the church and into the workaday world, they lived as
stoics, observing their world's steady decline: 'In the nineteenth century the Virginian, even more than other Southerners, was a deteriorationist. He believed in the
inevitable superiority of former times.'[27]

For many Southerners, then, the year 1861 brought no surprise. The fire-eaters,
conceiving themselves as Cavaliers, may have viewed the outbreak of the war as the
long-sought opportunity not merely to separate from the base Puritans, but to ad-
minister a deeply deserved drubbing as they took their leave. But many others, of a
fatalistic cast of mind, seemed to see the hostilities as only the latest calamity visited
upon the South. Such men may even have felt that defeat was certain; but such
knowledge would have made them even more energetic in their participation in the
Southern effort, once the war started: stripped of any opportunity for sordid success, Southern participation became the perfect vehicle for the display of unadulter-
ated virtue. Such psychology may explain, as readily as any other, the fact that so
many men fought on, long after the outcome was evident.

It is fitting that during the war the noblest Southerner of them all sought consolation in that other general's *Meditations*.[28] A devotion to Aurelius had been a part of
Robert E. Lee's inheritance from his father, a devotion revealed in behaviour more
than in direct reference. Such behaviour is apparent in his practice of committing
evening thoughts to paper when there was a moment to spare in camp. One of the
meditations which survived the dismal day at Appomattox, found in Lee's effects
after his death, stated his Aurelian vision as starkly as it might be presented: 'Private and public life are subject to the same rules; and truth and manliness are two
qualities that will carry you through this world much better than *policy*, or *tact*, or
expediency, or any other word that was ever devised to conceal or mystify a deviation
from a straight line.'[29]

Nor did Lee deviate from the straight line after the worst had come. Rather than
accept a titular position in business that would advertise his name or retire to write a
defence of it, he accepted the presidency of Washington College, there to serve the
last five years of his life. His statement to Valentine, the sculptor, as he sat for him,
sums up, as well as a single sentence could, Lee's sense of duty after the war:
'Misfortune nobly borne is good fortune.'[30] Only later, when he was reading the
Meditations, did Valentine discover the source of Lee's comment. The transcendent
indifference to the external world in Lee's code is in sharp contrast to Jefferson

Davis's response to the postwar world. His *Short History of the Confederate States of America* (1890) possesses a motto from Seneca which heralds the ironic vision that the stoic heritage has provided for the twentieth-century Southerner: '*Prosperum et felix scelus virtus vocatur.*'[31]

From Davis's mordant farewell it is but a step to the sundered world of the twentieth-century South. With separate spheres of high thinking and low acting, modern Southern literature offers few depictions of the man who combines the inner restraint fostered by stoicism and the will to selfless action derived from an imitation of Jesus. Jefferson and Lee fade from a commanding position in the foreground of the Southern imagination, to be replaced by the Snopeses. And against these invaders the patrician remnant offers a futile rear-guard defence. There seem to be no warriors among the band, but, rather, flaccid fathers too often given to the sententious, and thewless sons too often unwilling to pass through the rites of maturity in order to face the external world. Faulkner, in *The Sound and the Fury* (1929), offers the most widely known example of these types: Mr Compson, hiding his impotent virtue behind drunkenness and cynicism, and Quentin, cloaking his desperation to remain a child behind an exaggerated regard for his sister's chastity.

But there are other examples easily available. In Robert Penn Warren's *All the King's Men* (1946) these two: the aristocratic Judge Irwin, who plays at being the noble Roman as he constructs his models of catapults and battering rams and reads his Tacitus, until he achieves a semblance of Roman nobility by committing suicide at the revelation of his acceptance of a bribe; his son, Jack Burden, who self-consciously employs flight to the womb, until through the agency of his father's death he is enabled to enter the world of moral consequence. William Styron's *Lie Down in Darkness* (1951) presents Milton Loftis and his father. As Milton reveals the wreckage of his life on the day that he must bury the daughter who killed herself at least in part because of his failure to guide her, he often recalls the advice offered by his father, in preparation for the shock of maturity: '*Your first duty remember, son, is always to yourself*'[32]; '*My son, never let passion be a guide*' (LDD, p 41); '*My son, most people, whether they know it or not ... get on through life by a sophomoric fatalism. Only poets and thieves can exercise free will, and most of them die young*' (LDD, p 91); '*My son, pure frustration can lead to the highest understanding*' (LDD, p 151). However valid the advice may be, it is tinged with weariness and paltriness, and hence never becomes a vital presence in Milton's character. Nor does the curriculum at Jefferson's university set the concept of self-discipline, so Milton becomes a self-worshipping – rather than a self-respecting – man, in contrast to the old man he meets in Charlottesville who has come up 'to die near Mr. Jefferson' (LDD, p 181). Thus, Milton can never really recognize the needs of any other person. The most generous appraisal of his actions would be that they are thoughtless and immature.

In decisive contrast to the fictional picture of toothless heritage and triumphant materialism is the vision sketched in William Alexander Percy's autobiography *Lanterns on the Levee* (1941).[33] Perhaps in the realization of mortality brought on by declining health, Percy, after years of demanding from his frail body an active life (teaching, the law, military duty, and community obligation), offers, through his memoir, a meditation which will convey the values of the past to the future – his adopted sons and their generation. Descended from an aristocratic family which had been influential in community life in Louisiana and Mississippi since the eighteenth century, Percy (1885–1941) seems in many ways to be a remarkable conservator of the classic Southern stoic values. For, like Jefferson and Lee, he draws his strength from a dual tradition: 'I think if one would sit in the Greek theater above Taormina with the wine-dark sea below and AEtna against the sunset, and if there he would meditate on Jesus and the Emperor, he would be assured a god had made earth and man. And this is all we need to know' (LL, p 320).

Still like Jefferson, who created his own 'bible' by retaining the statements of Jesus while discarding the divine actions attributed to Him by the writers of the Gospels, Percy carefully winnows that which is unacceptable from the Christian heritage: 'The Gospels were written by simple men who earnestly and with a miraculous eloquence tried to report events which they themselves had never witnessed but of which they had been told. Even what these writers of hearsay set down we have never seen in the words they used, but only in later Greek translations. Consequently the narratives of the four Evangelists as we read them are full of misunderstandings and contradictions and inaccuracies – as every lawyer knows any human testimony aiming at truth is sure to be – yet they throw more light than darkness on the heart-shaking story they tell. They are pitifully human and misleading, but drenched in a supernal light and their contagion changed the dreaming world' (LL, p 316). Those 'misunderstandings and contradictions and inaccuracies' have been used by the churches, Percy feels, to pervert the genuine message offered by Jesus: 'I think of what is being offered to our young people in their need by the churches, and my heart is filled with anger and sorrow. I asked a clergyman recently why it was that so many prominent church-goers were crooks in business and hypocrites in private life. He replied: "They have been born again." This clarified nothing for me and I told him as much. He explained sadly: "When they are born again, they are certain of salvation, and when you are certain of salvation you may do what you like." But I urged, horrified: "People don't really believe that!" "Hundreds of thousands of them," he rejoined, obviously as grieved as I. "The ethics of Jesus do not interest them when their rebirth guarantees them salvation."' (LL, p 314).

Rejecting the abandonment of manners and morals that others justify by their acceptance of a religion preoccupied with eternal life, Percy looks elsewhere for his salvation: 'There is left to each of us, no matter how far defeat pierces, the unassailable wintry kingdom of Marcus Aurelius, which some more gently call the Kingdom of Heaven' (LL, p 313). With this orientation, one can face the world, where 'Nothing is so sad as defeat, except victory' (LL, p 145). From the *Meditations* can be extracted a sufficient belief: 'The self-communings of the Emperor, though often cold to clamminess, convince a man he never need be less than tight-lipped, courteous, and proud, though all is pain' (LL, p 316). Armed with such traits of behaviour, Percy can face the inevitable disappointments of his life like his grandfather: 'he never spoke of the war, it hurt so much, and besides, silence was General Lee's example' (LL, p 115).

But, though silent, Percy cannot avoid the ironic, Davis-like vision inherent in the possession of a heritage: 'In Russia, Germany, and Italy, Demos, having slain its aristocrats and intellectuals and realizing its own incompetence to guide or protect itself, had submitted to tyrants who laughed at the security virtues and practiced the most vile of survival virtues with gangster cynicism. In the democracies Demos had been so busy providing itself with leisure and luxury it had forgotten that hardihood and discipline are not ornaments but weapons. Everywhere the security virtues appeared as weaknesses and the survival virtues as strength and foresight' (LL, p 312). To such transmogrification Percy will not assent; rather, there is an eloquent appeal to his sons to cleave by the old truth: 'It is sophistry to speak of two sets of virtues, there is but one: virtue is an end in itself; the survival virtues are means, not ends. Honor and honesty, compassion and truth are good even if they kill you, for they alone give life its dignity and worth' (LL, p 313).

If *Lanterns on the Levee* is but the distillate of the living presence of William Alexander Percy, then how much more captivating would have been his creed embodied in action, especially upon someone during his impressionable adolescence? After the death of his parents Walker Percy discovered the charm of the man: 'to have lived in Will Percy's house, with "Uncle Will" as we called him, as a raw youth from age fourteen to twenty-six, a youth whose only talent was a knack for looking and listening, for tuning in and soaking up, was nothing less than to be informed in the deepest sense of the word. What was to be listened to, dwelled on, pondered over for the next thirty years was of course the man himself, the unique human being, and when I say unique I mean it in its most literal sense: he was one of a kind: I never met anyone remotely like him. It was to encounter a complete, articulated view of the world as tragic as it was noble' (LL, 'Introduction,' p x).

Writing over forty years after his first encounter with his 'Uncle Will,' Percy has tried to recapture his first impression: 'I can only suppose that he must have been, for me at least, a personage, a presence, radiating that mysterious quality we call charm, for lack of a better word, in such high degree that what comes to mind is not that usual assemblage of features and habits which make up our memories of people but rather a quality, a temper, a set of mouth, a look through the eyes.' Then the expansion upon the image: 'For his eyes were most memorable, a piercing gray-blue and strangely light in my memory, as changeable as shadows over water, capable of passing in an instant, we were soon to learn, from merriment – he told the funniest stories we'd ever heard – to a level gray gaze cold with reproof. They were beautiful and terrible eyes, eyes to be careful around. Yet now, when I try to remember them, I cannot see them otherwise than as shadowed by sadness' (LL, 'Introduction,' p viii).

Walker Percy must have felt those eyes following him as he went away, first to the University of North Carolina for undergraduate work, then to Columbia University for medical school. They must have reminded him not only of the sole parent, conduit to a family past, but also of a personification of the best of the Southern tradition. Their 'level gray gaze' must have provided a constant beacon, even during the years when he was away in the North, suffering from the debility of tuberculosis. And they must have seemed to grow larger when he acted upon his decision to return to Louisiana to live.

Once there, although his health denied him the career for which he had prepared himself, he discovered that he was not without resources. Writing later about the effect that rearing three boys may have had upon his Uncle Will's creation of poetry, Walker Percy said: 'At any rate, whatever he lost or gained in the transaction, I know what I gained: a vocation and in a real sense a second self, that is, the work and the self which, for better or worse, would not otherwise have been open to me' (LL, 'Introduction,' pp ix–x). That is to say, the example of a man sensitive to ideas and capable of conveying them through words was offered to him. Thus, Walker Percy devoted himself to reading, especially in those areas, such as existentialism, which had been ignored by his scientific education. In time he began a series of articles on language, that medium which seems most promising as a relief to the isolation celebrated by the existential philosophers.

But those eyes must have remained fixed on him, for an early essay was entitled 'Stoicism in the South.'[34] Having returned to the South to live, Percy may have been deciding how he could, or would, live there. For the essay is like so much of his writing, both non-fiction and fiction, in that it seems in a way to be a thinking out loud. The first style of life to come to mind could easily have been that of his adoptive father. The essay thus becomes a testing of the tradition of Southern stoicism against the demands of a new era. Percy's presentation of the Southern stoic heritage is an admirable realization: 'The greatness of the South, like the greatness of the English squirearchy, had always a stronger Greek flavor than it ever had a Christian. Its nobility and graciousness was the nobility and graciousness of the old Stoa. How immediately we recognize the best of the South in the words of the Emperor: "Every moment think steadily, as a Roman and a man, to do what thou hast in hand with perfect and simple dignity, and a feeling of affection, and freedom, and justice." And how curiously foreign to the South sound the Decalogue, the Beatitudes, the doctrine of the Mystical Body ... When [the Southerner] named a city Corinth, he did not mean Paul's community. How like him to go into Chancellorsville or the Argonne with Epictetus in his pocket; how unlike him to have had the Psalms' (ss, p 343).

Stoicism may have been the best practicable philosophy for patricians in the old South, given the primacy of the reality of slavery, Percy implies. Of course, if there had been a widespread, genuine, radical Christianity, slavery could not have existed. But it did, so that 'hierarchical structure' was the predominant factor in establishing human relations. That being the case, stoicism, with its emphasis upon 'the stern inner summors,' ensured that Southern slave-holding was at least leavened by restraint.

The war swept away the legality of absolute hierarchy. And the hundred-odd years since have witnessed social change, at an ever increasing tempo, as the black has claimed what is justly his. Such achievement does not depend upon the granting of favours by the patrician; hence the patrician has found himself ever more irrelevant and defensive. His mentality has thus developed a definite cast: 'Its most characteristic mood was a poetic pessimism which took a grim satisfaction in the dissolution of its values – because social decay confirmed one in his original choice of the wintry kingdom of self' (ss, p 343). And there the patrician waits for the *Götterdämmerung*: 'For the Stoic there is no real hope. His finest hour is to sit tight-lipped and ironic while the world comes crashing down around him' (ss, p 344).

The personality sketched in 'Stoicism in the South' vividly anticipates Emily Bolling Cutrer in *The Moviegoer*. Although she has a surviving older brother, Oscar, Emily seems to be the venerable figure of the family; not merely formidable in her own right, she acts as the repository of the past. Her nephew Jack, the protagonist, seems to see her as the still-living member of a series of larger-than-life figures that stretches back into history. As he stands in her living room, early in the novel, he faces the mantelpiece in an effort to address the household gods: 'One picture I never tire looking at. For ten years I have looked at it on this mantelpiece and tried to understand it. Now I take it down and hold it against the light from the darkening sky. Here are the two brothers, Dr Wills and Judge Anse with their arms about each other's shoulders, and my father in front, the three standing on a mountain trail against a dark forest. It is the Schwarzwald. A few years after the first war they had gotten together for once and made the grand tour. Only Alex Bolling is missing – he is in the third frame: an astonishingly handsome young man with the Rupert Brooke-Galahad sort of face you see so often in pictures of World War I soldiers. His death in the Argonne (five years before) was held to be fitting since the original Alex Bolling was killed with Roberdaux Wheat in the Hood breakthrough at Gaines Mill in 1862' (M, pp 24–5).

The crowning demonstration of a vital family virtue has been the death of a warrior in each generation. There had been Captain Alex Bolling in the Civil War, then his namesake in the First World War. By then the tradition was so well established that Dr Wills's son John lived a life of disquiet, apparently fearing that if he had no opportunity to live (and die) up to the family model, he would be condemned to live a life of everydayness. He thus regarded the outbreak of the Second World War as his opportunity to break out of personal insignificance; so he volunteered for the Canadian armed service, before the American entry into the war, thus to fulfil the ideal role, as his son Jack perceives: 'He had found a way to do both: to please them and please himself. To leave. To do what he wanted to do and save old England doing it. And perhaps even carry off the grandest coup of all: to die. To win the big prize for them and for himself (but not even he dreamed he would succeed not only in dying but in dying in Crete in the wine dark sea)' (M, p 157). Because of her sex Emily had been unable to engage in combat; she had achieved an honourable alternative, though, as a Red Cross volunteer during the Spanish Civil War. Thus, Jack sees that his Aunt Emily, despite the handicap of being a woman, has participated in ritualized family behaviour and in so doing become an eloquent voice in its behalf: 'It is as if, with her illustrious brothers dead and gone, she might now at last become what they had been and what as a woman had been denied her: soldierly both in look and outlook. With her blue-white hair and keen quick face and terrible gray eyes, she is somehow at sixty-five still the young prince' (M, p 27).

With an outlook formed by such military rectitude, she would rely upon Marcus Aurelius for inspiration, as her note to her nephew indicates. Even small actions, such as her fondling of the lion's head carved on her chair arm (M, pp 176, 182), become symbolic of her imperial assertion. Her brisk confidence evokes martial allusions, as when Jack imagines that she is telling him to 'hold the fort' (M, p 29). And she is prone to such imagery herself: 'The barbarians at the inner gate and who defends the West? Don John of Austria? No, Mr Bolling the stockbroker and Mr Wade the Lawyer' (M, p 33).

Indeed, Jack recalls, one of his earliest memories of his aunt is that when his brother Scott died, his aunt told him: 'I've got bad news for you, son ... Scotty is dead. Now it's all up to you. It's going to be difficult for you but I know that you're going to act like a soldier' (M, p 4). Such an injunction could be derived from Epictetus, who quotes Socrates about the duty of remaining at one's post like a soldier, or simply from family ethos; whatever its origin, Jack recalls that as an eight-year-old he felt it would be a simple order to carry out. And he had apparently grown up accepting his aunt's example, for he had, in his turn, become an army officer during the Korean War. Attempting to meet family expectation, he had written such sentiments to his aunt: 'Japan is lovely this time of year. How strange to think of going into combat! Not so much fear – since my chances are very good – as wonder, wonder that everything should be so full of expectancy, every tick of the watch, every rhododendron blossom. Tolstoy and St Exupery were right about war, etc' (M, p 87).

But Jack, when wounded, makes the mistake of experiencing fear – and surviving. Which, it should be stressed, is not saying that he acts in a cowardly way; rather, he discovers, through the intrusion of fear, that he is condemned to be an individual, not an idealized manikin in a gallant historical series. According to Martin Heidegger, whose ideas Percy utilizes in the novel, fear is one of those states of mind which discloses to the individual his actuality and its vulnerability – he is something which he did not create, even though he is responsible for his actions nevertheless, and those actions may result in his loss of life itself.[35] No longer will Jack be able to accept himself as an object, albeit glamorous with the achievement of ideal behaviour; no longer will he be able to conceive of himself as a self-contained consciousness isolated through proud aloofness from a tawdry world. Fear teaches the individual that the world can penetrate the strongest fort; hence the individual, rather than attempting to withdraw from the world, must thrust himself into it, confront it, quest for the fullness of being that it can yield.

Fear, then, is not negative, but positive. Through its agency the individual discovers possibility; he is what he is, but he is also what he can become. Jack thus returns from the war committed to a search. But the characte of the search he performs is self-defeating, literally. Seduced by the promises of the highly praised and widely employed objective-empirical point of view, he conducts a search for larger and larger generalizations, thinking that in understanding the world of matter and mass man, he will at some point arrive at an understanding of himself among them.[36] Quite the opposite is accomplished: as he accepts the concept that all significant knowledge is based upon generalization, so he experiences less and less understanding of himself as a datum identified by generalization. It does him no good to learn how he is like matter, or other forms of life, or even other men, when his quest has been to learn how he is unique (such as when he discovered himself as the I who am experiencing fear). In time, out of frustration he abandons his search, to fall into everydayness, that type of behaviour where all standards are developed by the mass. When the fall occurs, Jack acquiesces to the imposition of Heidegger's 'they-self,' the totally inauthentic self as commuter, as consumer, as moviegoer.

The world makes no sense, and throughout the novel Jack founders in it. Cut off from the sustenance provided by a myth, he cannot organize his world to resemble his aunt's: 'All the stray bits and pieces of the past, all that is feckless and gray about people, she pulls together with an unmistakable visage of the heroic or the craven, the noble or the ignoble' (M, p 49). For her, as well, although they lack the bold relief of the past, the present and the future still have a meaning, her admission to the contrary notwithstanding: '"I no longer pretend to understand the world." She is shaking her head yet still smiling her sweet menacing smile. "The world I knew has come crashing down around my ears. The things we hold dear are reviled and spat upon ... It's an interesting age you will live in – though I can't say I'm sorry to miss it. But it should be quite a sight, the going under of the evening land. That's us all right. And I can tell you, my young friend, it is evening. It is very late."' But Jack senses the difference between them: 'For her too the fabric is dissolving, but for her even the dissolving makes sense' (M, p 54).

When Aunt Emily speaks of the unfathomable world, she is of course addressing her irony at Jack, for his actions are especially mystifying in their failure to conform to the mould which she has cast for them. Already in this passage she is separating Jack from his status as a family member – 'my young friend.' But the absolute rupture of their relationship occurs when, in her eyes, Jack violates the chivalric code in his behaviour with her stepdaughter Kate: utterly overwhelmed with his own problems (which are of a type his aunt cannot apprehend), he allows Kate, who has a medically recognized history of mental instability, to accompany him on a trip to Chicago.

Jack is ordered to return to New Orleans, there to approach his aunt as if she were a military superior: 'There is nothing to do but go directly in to her and stand at ease until she takes notice of me. Now she looks over, as erect and handsome as the Black Prince' (M, pp 220–1). As she begins to upbraid him, she withdraws a metal letter opener in the shape of a sword from 'the grasp of the helmeted figure on the inkstand.' Thus armed, she is ready to speak of the stoic tradition: 'At the great moments of life – success, failure, marriage, death – our kind of folks have always possessed a native instinct for behavior, a natural piety or grace, I don't mind calling it' (M, p 222).

Then, waving the sword to the street, as if to defend Jack in his weakness from the corruption of the 'barbarians at the inner gate,' she makes clear what the traditional behaviour is: 'I did my best for you, son. I gave you all I had. More than anything I wanted to pass on to you the one heritage of the men of our family, a certain quality of spirit, a gaiety, a sense of duty, a nobility worn lightly, a sweetness, a gentleness with women – the only good things the South ever had and the only things that really matter in this life' (M, p 224). When she cannot understand his reasons for the behaviour which she regards as errant, she will not suffer his foolishness. Having been working in her account book when he entered, she now closes it, as she is closing the book on him: 'Smiling, she gives me her hand, head to one side, in her old party style. But it is her withholding my name that assigns me my new status' (M, pp 226–7). '" I do thank you so much for coming by," says my aunt, fingering her necklace and looking past me at the Vaudrieul house.' Immediately afterward Kate calls Jack a 'poor stupid bastard' (M, p 227), and in a sense he is – now without family in a society that places family before all other institutions and forms of identification.

In another generation thus to be disowned would be a staggering blow to a Southerner. But it is precisely Jack's predicament that he had not flourished within a calcified tradition; hence to be bereaved of it actually frees him to struggle for self-identity. The first small, but absolutely necessary, skirmish is Jack's ability to say that his aunt suffers from rightness and despair (M, p 228), unimaginative attitudes that preclude any possibility of openness and change. He, though, is at least stumbling towards a new form of confirmation of self: he will be that self which sacrifices itself in nurturing Kate's self. It is a small irony that when Kate meets Jack, after his dismissal by his aunt, she misunderstands what has occurred: 'She is certain that I have carried off a grand stoic gesture, like a magazine hero' (M, p 232). In reality Jack had himself despaired, concluding that Kate had abandoned him, and he is therefore trying to pick up a girl, any girl. When Kate does arrive, so great is Jack's relief that his action towards her has its source in that other Jeffersonian principle – 'Jesus a supplement of the duties and charities we owe to others.' To encourage such inference Percy has Kate and Jack make their first tentative commitment to one another as, in the background, a man enters the church to receive the ritual of imposition on Ash Wednesday.

If Jack is intended to be a representative character, then he would seem to personify Percy's contention, in 'Stoicism in the South,' that his countrymen must stop standing on the porch and go on into the church. Certainly Jack's action reflects one modern Southerner's decision, for Walker Percy converted to Catholicism about the time he returned to the South. But it should not be concluded that Percy, through the disguise of a novel, has thus rejected the totality of his uncle's example. Of Will Percy he has said: 'even when I did not follow him, it was usually in *relation* to him, whether with him or against him, that I defined myself and my own direction. Perhaps he would not have had it differently. Surely it is the highest tribute to the best people we know to use them as best we can, to become, not their disciples, but ourselves' (LL, 'Introduction,' p xi). *The Moviegoer* exists, then, because there was a force so impressive to inspire it; its dedication to 'W.A.P.' stands as testimony to the continuing vitality of stoicism in the South.

TOM MIDDLEBRO'

Marston LaFrance: A Tribute and Memorial Bibliography

Concluding a review-essay on four biographies of Hart Crane, Marston LaFrance wrote: 'The appreciation and study of conspicuous craftsmanship in poetry is never wasted, never lost.' It might have been a *credo*, for Marston valued and sought the craftsman's integrity, courage, and devotion in scholarship, literature, and life. He disdained sloppiness as a form of dishonesty, whether found in an incomplete bibliography, untidy fishing gear, a verbose memo, a self-indulgent writer, or an ill-prepared paper. He was always outspoken, and had the gift of the telling phrase, as when he once described the mind of an incompetent teaching assistant as 'a bucket of ping-pong balls dropped on a concrete floor.' He had a passionate bias for the traditional concept of academic excellence, a zealous respect for the intellectual functions of the university – 'to teach and to think,' in Sir William Osler's definition – and a complete loyalty to the welfare of his students. He was always detecting swan feathers on ungainly undergraduate ducklings. When he elicited a sign of the fervour that inspired his own work in the efforts of others, he gave his time and energy unstintingly to encourage and aid. Students seeking help at his office could count on Marston to set aside his own work, tamp down the tobacco in the large cracked bowl of his pipe with a blunt forefinger, and give them a judicious hearing. He expected a good deal of his students, and he often got it, for he set the example. He devoted the same disciplined energy to all his teaching, whether lecturing to first-year engineering students or giving a graduate seminar in American literature.

As a critic of literature, Marston was attracted to those writers, like Stephen Crane, William Faulkner, and Evelyn Waugh, for whom man's predicament as a compassionate being in a non-sentient universe was the point of departure. Artists who aspire to explore and sound the paradoxes must be masters of the form of consciousness, language. One of Marston LaFrance's great strengths as a critic was his sensitivity to the craft of language. He had an ear for the nuance and tone of word and context. This sensibility informed his own style, which was vigorous, flexible, lucid, and precise. Products of meticulous research and careful thought, his writings were yet permeated with his own encompassing zest.

Marston LaFrance's death was a bitter tragedy. It bore most heavily on his wife, Marie Ann, and their four children, for they were a devoted and loving family. Still, all who knew him share in the grief of deprivation. He served with tremendous gusto and integrity, and it was a privilege to know him. He will not be forgotten.

DEGREES

BA, Harpur College, June, 1953 (*magna cum laude*, Salutatorian of graduating class)
MA, Cornell University, June 1955
PHD, University of Wisconsin, January 1965

ACADEMIC APPOINTMENTS

Clarkson College: Instructor, 1956–8; Assistant Professor, 1958–63 (on leave for graduate study 1961–3)
Carleton University: Assistant Professor, 1963–5; Associate Professor, 1965–9; Professor, 1969–75 (Canada Council Leave Fellowship 1969–70); Dean of Arts I (Humanities), 1974–5

In addition, Professor LaFrance taught as visiting professor at Seattle University (Summer 1966), Columbia University (Summer 1968), and Dalhousie University (May-June 1974).

ADMINISTRATIVE APPOINTMENTS

Senate Committee for Summer School, 1964–7
Chairman, American Authors Lecture Series, 1965
Supervisor of graduate students in English, 1965–9
Graduate Studies Faculty Board, 1965–9
Chairman, Graduate Committee, Department of English, 1967–9
Building Advisory Committee, 1965–9
Chairman, Planning Committee for Arts I building, 1966–9
Planning Committee for new mathematics building, 1967–9
Appointments and Promotions Committee, Department of English, 1966–8, 1973–4
Graduate Faculty Committee to advise the President on the appointment of a new Dean of Graduate Studies, 1969
Admissions and Studies Committee, Department of English, 1971–2
Chairman, Senate Committee on Redundancy, 1972

Advisory Committee on Academic Planning, Department of English, 1972–4
Corresponding Member for Carleton, Humanities Research Council of Canada,
1971
Appointed to editorial board of *Emerson Society Quarterly: A Journal of the American
Renaissance*, 1971
Academic Freedom and Tenure Committee, Canadian Associateion of University
Teachers, 1973–4

PUBLICATIONS

Books

Editor, *Patterns of Commitment in American Literature*. Toronto: University of
Toronto Press 1967. 210 pp
A Reading of Stephen Crane. Oxford: Clarendon Press 1971. 272 pp
Editor, *John Steinbeck as Fabulist*, by Lawrence W. Jones, Muncie: Steinbeck
Society 1973. 35 pp

Articles

'Henry Wadsworth Longfellow and Archibald Alison,' *Colby Literary Quarterly*,
Series 6, No. 5 (March 1963), 205–8
'Longfellow's Critical Preferences,' *Colby Literary Quarterly*, Series 6, No. 9
(March 1964), 398–402
'Context and Structure of Evelyn Waugh's *Brideshead Revisited*,' *Twentieth Century
Literature*, 10:1 (April 1964), 12–18. Reprinted in *Evelyn Waugh*, edited by Robert
Murray Davis. St Louis: Herder 1969. Pp 57–68
'A Few Facts about Stephen Crane and "Holland,"' *American Literature*, 37:2
(May 1965), 195–202
'Stephen Crane's Private Fleming: His Various Battles,' *Patterns of Commitment in
American Literature*, edited by Marston LaFrance. Toronto: University of Toronto
Press 1967. Pp 113–33
'The Ironic Parallel in Stephen Crane's 1892 Newspaper Correspondence,' *Studies
in Short Fiction*, 6:1 (Fall 1968), 101–3
'Fielding's Use of the "Humour" Tradition,' *Bucknell Review*, 17:3 (December
1969), 53–63
'Crane, Zola, and the Hot Ploughshares,' *English Language Notes*, 7:4 (June 1970),
285–7
'Charles E. Linck's Bibliography of Waugh's Early Work, 1910–1930: Some Addi-
tions and Corrections,' *Evelyn Waugh Newsletter*, 4:2 (Autumn 1970), 8–9

'The Earliest Waugh Reference Known,' *Evelyn Waugh Newsletter*, 5:2 (Autumn 1971), 8–9
'The Year's Work in Waugh Studies,' *Evelyn Waugh Newsletter*, 6:1 (Spring 1972), 3–6, 7:1 (Spring 1973), 5–7; 8:1 (Spring 197[4]), 1–3.
'*George's Mother* and the Other Half of *Maggie*,' *Stephen Crane in Transition*: *Centenary Essays*, edited by Joseph Katz. Dekalb: Northern Illinois University Press, 1972. Pp 35–53
'Stephen Crane in Our Time,' *The Chief Glory of Every People: Essays on Classic American Writers*, edited by Mattew J. Bruccoli. Carbondale: Southern Illinois University Press, 1973. Pp 25–51, 263–5
'Stephen Crane Scholarship Today and Tomorrow,' *American Literary Realism 1870–1910*, 7:2 (Spring 1974), 125–35
Editor, 'Poison in the Cream Puff: The Human Condition in *Cannery Row*,' by Lawrence W. Jones, *Steinbeck Quarterly*, 7:2 (Spring 1974), 35–40
'*Sword of Honour*: The Ironist Placatus,' *Dalhousie Review*, 55:1 (Spring 1975), 23–53

Papers

'Private Fleming: His Various Battles,' presented at Carleton University, 9 November 1965
'Evelyn Waugh's Ironic Method of Perception,' presented to the Association of Canadian University Teachers of English at Memorial University, 29 May 1971
'Recurring Imagery in the Work of Stephen Crane,' presented at the University of Delaware, 9 May 1973

Reviews

'Olov W. Fryckstedt, editor, *Steven Crane: Uncollected Writings*, and T.A. Gullason, editor, *The Complete Short Stories and Sketches of Stephen Crane*,' *Modern Language Journal*, 49 (February 1965), 123–4
'T.A. Gullason, editor, *The Complete Novels of Stephen Crane*,' *Studies in Short Fiction*, 6 (1968), 221–2
'Donald B. Gibson, *The Fiction of Stephen Crane*,' *Stephen Crane Newsletter*, 3 (Spring 1969), 9–10
'Reynolds Price, *Love and Work*,' *Studies in Short Fiction*, 8 (Spring 1971), 345–6
'The Bridge-Builder' (review-essay on four books about Hart Crane), *Canadian Review of American Studies*, 2 (Fall 1971), 106–13
'The Revival of Crane. R.W. Stallman: *Stephen Crane A Critical Bibliography*,' *Times Literary Supplement*, 5 October 1973, p 1173

'Robert Wooster Stallman, *Stephen Crane, A Critical Bibliography,*' *American Literary Realism 1870–1910,* 7 (Spring 1974), 177–80
'Tetsumaro Hayashi, editor, *A Study Guide to Steinbeck: A Handbook to His Major Works,*' *Steinbeck Quarterly,* 9 (Winter 1976), 27–8

Notes

BUITENHUIS / THE STOIC STRAIN IN AMERICAN LITERATURE

1 R.D. Hicks, *Stoic and Epicurean* (New York 1962), p vii, J.M. Rist provides a more detailed analysis in his *Stoic Philosophy* (Cambridge 1969).
2 Hicks, *Stoic and Epicurean*, p 3.
3 Evelyn A. Hanley has made a study of *Stoicism in Major English Poets of the Nineteenth Century* (New York 1964). There is no equivalent in the field of American literature. Studies of individual authors include C.E. Pulos, 'Whitman and Epictetus: The Stoical Element in *Leaves of Grass*,' *Journal of English and Germanic Philology*, 65 (1956), 75–84; Sholom J. Kahn, 'Whitman's Stoicism,' *Scripta Hierosolymitana: Studies in Western Literature*, 10 (1962), 146–75; and C.B. Cox, 'Henry James and Stoicism,' in *Essays and Studies*, 8 (London 1955), 76–88.
4 In *The American Tradition in Literature*, ed S. Bradley, R.C. Beatty, and E. Hudson Long, revd shorter ed (New York 1962), p 21.
5 In *The American Tradition in Literature*, p 114.
6 In *Literature of the Early Republic*, ed Edwin H. Cady (New York 1961), p 357.
7 For his reading on the subject, see Ralph R. Rusk, *The Life of Ralph Waldo Emerson* (New York 1949), p 143.
8 Marcus Aurelius, *The Meditations* (London 1898), p 150.
9 Ralph Waldo Emerson, *The Complete Essays and Other Writings* (New York 1940), p 235.
10 In Henry David Thoreau, *Walden and Civil Disobedience: Authoritative Texts, Background, and Essays in Criticism*, ed Owen Thomas (New York 1966), p 265.
11 Ibid, pp 9–10.
12 Ibid, p 61.
13 Herman Melville, *Moby-Dick or the Whale* (Boston 1956), p 136.
14 Ibid, p 323.

15 In *The American Tradition in Literature*, p 511.

16 Walt Whitman, *Leaves of Grass, Authoritative Texts, Prefaces, Whitman on his Art, Criticism*, ed S. Bradley and H.W. Blodgett (New York 1973), p 299.

17 *The Complete Short Stories of Ambrose Bierce*, compiled with a commentary by E.J. Hopkins (New York 1970), p 340.

18 Ibid, pp 328–9.

19 Cox, 'Henry James and Stoicism,' pp 76–88.

20 Marston LaFrance, 'Stephen Crane's Private Fleming: His Various Battles,' in *Patterns of Commitment in American Literature*, ed Marston LaFrance (Toronto 1967), p 121.

21 Peter Buitenhuis, 'The Essentials of Life: The Open Boat as Existentialist Fiction,' *Modern Fiction Studies*, 5 (1959), 234–50.

22 Theodore Dreiser, *The Stoic* (New York 1947), p 231.

23 Ernest Hemingway, *The Sun Also Rises* (New York 1954), p 247.

24 Ernest Hemingway, *The Old Man and the Sea* (New York 1952), p 114.

25 William Faulkner, *The Sound and the Fury* (New York 1956), p 313.

26 Robert Pirsig, *Zen and the Art of Motorcycle Maintenance* (New York 1974), p 294.

STERN / TOWARDS 'BARTLEBY THE SCRIVENER'

1 *Sewanee Review*, 61 (1953), 602–27. This essay is one of the earliest and most comprehensive of the many articles that see 'Bartleby' as a story of the worker, particularly the literary worker, within the entrapments of a capitalistic, commercialized society.

2 *College English*, 6 (1945), 431–9. In the criticism that deals with literary parallels Oliver's is one of the most engaging examples, which is why I choose it to stand for a genre which, it seems to me, tends to lead to its own closed, walled-in world as far as 'opening up' a piece of literature is concerned.

3 Chapter 4 of *The Ways of Nihilism: Herman Melville's Short Novels* (California State Colleges Publications 1970), pp 91–125. Widmer's Gestalt is one of 'new left' nihilism, deriving strongly from Marcuse, especially from *One Dimensional Man*. Bartleby emerges as the nihilistic hero who refuses to participate in the lawyer's inhuman and philosophically blind world and thereby demonically points toward the true revolution beyond middle-class 'liberal' rationality.

4 In *Bartleby the Scrivener, Melville Annual 1965 Symposium*, ed Howard P. Vincent (Kent State University Press 1966), pp 113–39.

5 'Bartleby: The Tale, the Film' in Vincent, ed, p 47.

6 The psychologist-critic, Henry A. Murray, says that there is no psychiatric category for Bartleby. 'Bartleby is unprecedented, an invention of Melville's creative spirit, the author's gift to psychology, a mythic figure who deserves a category in his own name': 'Bartleby and I,' in Vincent, ed, p 23.

7 In Vincent, ed, p 49.

8 'A Bibliography of Criticism of "Bartleby the Scrivener,"' in Vincent, ed, pp 140–90, esp pp 151–90.

9 If we adopt the necessary luxury of detached hindsight and impose approximately a ten-year hiatus between ourselves and the twenty-year development of 'Bartleby' scholarship up to the beginning of the past decade, we can derive a chronological overview from a survey of some selected critics who see the tale as a parable of Melville himself and/or of the artist generally. These include, among others, Lewis Mumford, *Herman Melville* (New York 1929; rev 1962), pp 162–4; Alexander Eliot, 'Melville and Bartleby,' *Furioso*, 3 (1947), 11–21; Willard Thorp, 'Herman Melville,' *Literary History of the United States*, ed R.E. Spiller, et al (New York 1948; rev 1955), I, 463; Richard Chase, *Herman Melville: A Critical Study* (New York 1949), pp 143–9, 267, 280; also Chase's 'Introduction,' *Selected Tales and Poems of Herman Melville* (New York 1950), pp vii–viii; Newton Arvin, *Herman Melville* (New York 1950), pp 242–4; Eugene Current-Garcia and R.W. Patrick, eds, 'Introduction' and note, *American Short Stories* (Chicago 1952), pp xxiv, 109–10; Marx, n1 above; Norris Merchant, 'The Artist and Society in Melville,' *Views*, 4:3 (University of Louisville 1957), 56–7; Harry Levin, *The Power of Blackness* (New York 1958), pp 187–8; Jean-Jacques Mayoux, *Melville*, trans John Ashberry (New York 1960), pp 111–12, 158–86; Norman E. Hoyle, *Melville as a Magazinist* (Duke University Press 1960), pp 85–6, 89–94, 102; Hugh W. Hetherington, *Melville's Reviewers* (University of North Carolina Press 1961), pp 265–76; J.J. Boies, 'Existential Nihilism and Herman Melville,' *Transactions of the Wisconsin Academy of Science, Arts, and Letters*, 50 (1961), 307–20; Marvin Felheim, 'Meaning and Structure in "Bartleby,"' *College English*, 23 (1962), 369–70, 375–6; John Gardner, '"Bartleby": Art and Social Commitment,' *Philogical Quarterly*, 43 (1964), 87–98; Murray (see n 6 above), pp 3–24; and D'Avanzo (see n 4 above).

For a view of 'Bartleby' as a tale of existential alienation, isolation, or negation, some of the many essays to consult are F.O. Matthiessen, *American Renaissance* (New York 1941), p 493; R.E. Watters, 'Melville's "Isolatos,"' PMLA, 60 (1945), 1138–48; Alfred Kazin, 'Ishmael in His Academic Heaven,' *The New Yorker*, 24 (12 February 1949), 84–9; Newton Arvin, *Herman Melville* (New York 1950), pp 242–4; Jack Ludwig and Richard Poirier, 'Instructor's Manual,' *Stories: British and American* (Boston 1953), pp 6–8; Merlin Bowen, *The Long Encounter* (Chicago 1960), pp 133–4; William M. Gibson, 'Herman Melville's "Bartleby the Scrivener" and "Benito Cereno,"' *Die Neueren Sprachen*, 9 (1961), 107–16; James E. Miller, Jr, *A Reader's Guide to Herman Melville* (New York 1962), pp 13, 160–1; Roy R. Male, *Types of Short Fiction* (Belmont, California 1962), pp 438–9; Joseph Schiffman, ed *Three Shorter Novels of Herman Melville* (New York 1962), pp 229, 235–7; Maurice Friedman, *Problematical Rebel* (New York, 1963), pp 77–98; Norman Springer, 'Bartleby and the Terror of Limitation,' PMLA, 80 (1965), 410–18; John Haag, 'Bartleby-in for the Camera,' in Vincent, ed, pp 55–63; Maurice Friedman, 'Bartleby and the Modern Exile,' in Vincent, ed, pp 64–81; Marjorie Dow, 'The Attorney and the Scrivener,' in Vincent, ed, pp 94–103; Peter E. Firchow, 'Bartleby: Man and Metaphor,' *Studies in Short Fiction*, 5 (1968), 342–8; and Kingsley Widmer, see n3 above, as well as 'The Negative Affirmation: Melville's Bartleby,' *Modern Fiction Studies*, 8 (1962), 276–86.

10 Among several who assign a Christly role to Bartleby are Chase (see n 9 above); Nathalia Wright, *Melville's Use of the Bible* (Duke University Press 1949), p 128; G.A. Knox, 'Communication and Communion in Melville,' *Renascence*, 9 (1956), 26–31; Bowen (see n 9 above); H. Bruce Franklin, *The Wake of the Gods* (Stanford University Press 1963), pp 126–36, 150–3, 188–90, 205–6; Gardner (see n 9 above); and William Bysshe Stein, in Vincent, ed, pp 104–12.

11 See Robert D. Spector, 'Melville's "Bartleby" and the Absurd,' *Nineteenth Century Fiction*, 16 (1961), 175–7; and Firchow, n 9 above.

12 See also Stanley Edgar Hyman, 'Melville the Scrivener,' *New Mexico Quarterly*, 23 (1953), 381–415; and Richard Harter Fogle, 'Melville's *Bartleby*: Absolutism, Predestination, and Free Will,' *Tulane Studies in English*, 4 (1954), 125–35.

13 For the first, see Herbert F. Smith, 'Melville's Master in Chancery and His Recalcitrant Clerk,' *American Quarterly*, 17 (1965), 734–41. The main difficulty with Smith's thesis is that Melville most decidedly does not introduce the New York Court of Chancery in the context to which Smith wrenches it. For one thing, Bartleby refuses to engage in chancery work, the addition of which to his regular business causes the lawyer to hire Bartleby in the first place. Chancery in 'Bartleby' is used not as a model for ideal conscience but exactly as Dickens had used it in *Bleak House*. If one considers the dates of composition and publication of 'Bartleby,' the model provided by Dickens becomes extremely visible. *Bleak House* was serialized from March 1852 to September 1853. It was shipped to and read in the United States in 'parts,' the last of which was a double instalment. It was well known to Melville and his audience. It was reviewed in *Putnam*'s in November 1853, the same issue in which the first instalment of 'Bartleby' appeared.
    For Bartleby as death-wish, see Mordecai Marcus, 'Melville's Bartleby as a Psychological Double,' *College English*, 23 (1962), 365–8.

14 For one of the rare exceptions, see Patricia Lacy, 'The Agatha Theme in Melville's Stories,' *University of Texas Studies in English*, 35 (1956), 96–105. Lacy sees the narrator as sympathetic and a voice for Melville, and sees Bartleby as the long-suffering humanity exemplified in the Agatha letter to Hawthorne, in 'Cock-a-Doodle-Doo!" and in the sketch of Hunilla, the Chola widow, in *The Encantadas*.

15 In addition to Lacy, some representative points of view may be found in Marx (see n1 above); Chase (see n9 above); Robert L. Gale, 'Bartleby – Melville's Father-in-Law,' *Anneli Instituto Universitario Orientale, Sezione Germanica*, 5 (1962), 57–72; and Frank Davidson, '"Bartleby": A Few Observations,' *Emerson Society Quarterly*, no 27 (1962), pp 25–32.

16 Widmer, p 118.

17 Stein (see n 10), pp 104–12.

18 I am indebted for some of these observations to Irving Cummings of the University of Connecticut and Frank Hodgins of the University of Illinois. When Hodgins's long-awaited study of psychology and American literature appears, it will contain the kind of reading I call for in this essay.

19 R.H. Broadhead's *Hawthorne, Melville, and the Novel* (Chicago 1976) contains an excellent discussion of this problem. See esp pp 11–12.

20 I cannot resist the appositeness of Melville's warning in *Moby-Dick*. That book cautions repeatedly that because value and meaning are a projection of human perceptions, humans must be careful not to identify those values and meanings as objective, external realities, for all we discover is ourselves. The 'mild,' 'tormenting' Bartleby is a critical face seen in the mirror, into which some critics fall, thinking they are catching THE ungraspable phantom of single meaning. Ishmael warns that 'still deeper' is 'the meaning of that story of Narcissus, who because he could not grasp the tormenting, mild image he saw in the fountain, plunged into it and was drowned. But that same image, we ourselves see in all rivers and oceans. It is the image of the ungraspable phantom of life; and this is the key to it all.'

ALLEN / WALT WHITMAN AND STOICISM

1 Review reprinted by Whitman in *Leaves of Grass Imprints* (Boston: Thayer & Eldridge, 1860), p 20.

2 See index of Horace Traubel, *With Walt Whitman in Camden*: 28 March–14 July 1888 (Boston: Small Maynard 1906) [vol I]; 16 July–31 October 1888 (New York: Appleton 1908) [vol II]; 1 November 1888–20 January 1889 (New York: Mitchell Kennerly 1914) [vol III]; 21 January–7 April 1889 (Carbondale: Southern Illinois University Press 1959) [vol IV]; 8 April–14 September 1889 (Carbondale: Southern Illinois University Press 1964) [vol V].

3 Traubel, II, 332; III, 159.

4 Traubel, III, 186.

5 Traubel, II, 71.

6 Quoted by Richard Mott Gummere in 'Walt Whitman and His Reaction to the Classics,' *Harvard Studies in Classical Philology*, 60 (1951), 276.

7 J. Johnston and J.W. Wallace, *Visits to Walt Whitman in 1890–1* (London: Allen and Unwin 1917), pp 254–6.

8 Traubel, II, 71–2.

9 See David Goodale, 'Some of Walt Whitman's Borrowings,' *American Literature*, 10 (1938), 205–8; also Traubel, II, 204.

10 Whitman probably used the 1822 London edition, but the book was reprinted in New York by Peter Eckler (n.d.); references in this essay are to the latter edition, hereafter cited as FDA.

11 Traubel, II, 445.

12 See *The New Encyclopaedia Britannica* (Chicago: Encyclopaedia Britannica 1974), vol. 17 [Macropaedia], pp 698–702.

13 Testimony of George Whitman, quoted in *In Re Walt Whitman*, edited by his literary executors (Philadelphia: David McKay 1893), p 39.

14 Gay Wilson Allen, *The Solitary Singer: A Critical Biography of Walt Whitman* (New York: Macmillan 1955), p 187.

15 In the Civil War hospitals Whitman observed that nature usually made the final moments of death easy: *Prose Works 1892*, edited by Floyd Stovall (New York: New York University Press 1964), II, 672; quotations from the *Prose Works* are from this edition, hereafter cited as PW.

16 'Sunday Morning,' sec. 5, 'Death is the mother of beauty.'

17 PW, I, 271; see *Encheiridion*, sec. 15 – and index of *Epictetus: The Discourses as Reported by Arrian, the Manual, and Fragments*, trans W.A. Oldfather, Loeb Classical Library, 2 vols (London: Heinemann 1926; repr Cambridge, Mass.: Harvard University Press 1952).

18 See, among others, Jean Catel, *Rythme et langage dans la 1er édition des 'Leaves of Grass' (1855)* (Paris: Les Éditions Rieder [1930]).

19 See Rolleston's letter to Whitman, 16 October 1880, in *Whitman and Rolleston: A Correspondence*, ed Horst Frenz (Bloomington: Indiana University Press 1951), pp 15–16.

20 Johnson and Wallace, p 256.

21 Traubel, III, 4.

22 Cf Allen, *Solitary Singer*, pp 520–1.

23 *Epictetus*, Loeb Classical Library, II, 483; hereafter the references are given in parentheses in the text, preceded by E if they might be confused with Whitman's words.

24 The periods are in Whitman's 1855 text and indicate caesurae; the number of periods varies; these were eliminated in later editions.

25 E, II, 483: things under our control, things not.

26 Published by Whitman in his 1856 *Leaves of Grass*: 'I greet you at the beginning of a great career.'

27 Cf George Whitman's testimony, *In Re*, p 35; and Whitman's whole subsequent career.

28 *The Uncollected Poetry and Prose of Walt Whitman*, ed Emory Holloway, 2 vols (New York: Doubleday, Doran 1921), II, 94; hereafter cited as UPP.

29 UPP, II, 94–5.

30 See Allen, *Solitary Singer*, pp 420–4. See also Roger Asselineau, *The Evolution of Walt Whitman: The Growth of a Personality* (Cambridge, Mass.: Harvard University Press 1960), I, 185 ff.

31 *Walt Whitman's Poems*, ed Gay Wilson Allen and Charles T. Davis (New York: New York University Press 1955), p 176. Joseph Beaver, *Walt Whitman, Poet of Science* (New York: King's Crown Press 1951), pp 55–6, thinks Whitman borrowed the term from astronomy.

32 Sholom Kahn, 'Whitman's Stoicism,' *Scripta Hierosolymitana: Studies in Western Literature* (The Hebrew University, Jerusalem), 10 (1962), 164.

33 *Whitman's Manuscripts: Leaves of Grass (1860), A Parallel Text*, ed Fredson Bowers (Chicago: University of Chicago Press 1955), pp 167–8.

34 Cf George L. Sixbey, '"Chanting the Square Deific" – A Study in Whitman's Religion,' *American Literature*, 9 (1937), 171–95.

35 Whitman's copy is now in the Feinburg Collection at the Library of Congress. William White describes it in *The Walt Whitman Review*, 8:4 (December 1962), 95–[96]. Kahn has examined it, and comments, p 150, n 10.

36 Kahn, p 161.

37 UPP, II, 63–97.

38 *The Communings with Himself of Marcus Aurelius Antoninus, Emperor of Rome, together with his Speeches and Sayings*, trans Charles Reginald Haines (London: Heinemann / New York: Putnam's 1916), p xiii; hereafter cited as M.

39 UPP, II, 64.

40 UPP, II, 65.

41 For interpretation of the symbolical 'I' of this poem, see Gay Wilson Allen, *A Reader's Guide to Walt Whitman* (New York: Farrar, Straus & Giroux 1970), p 173.

BEATTIE / HENRY JAMES: 'THE VOICE OF STOICISM'

1 *The Letters of Henry James*, selected and edited by Percy Lubbock (New York: Scribner's 1920), II, 245.

2 *Henry James Letters*, ed Leon Edel, II (Cambridge, Mass.: Belknap-Harvard University Press 1975), 133.

3 Edel, *Letters*, II, 424.

4 Edel, *Letters*, II, 425.

5 Lubbock, *Letters*, II, 104–5. This letter is quoted and the circumstances that called it forth are related in R.W.B. Lewis, *Edith Wharton: A Biography* (New York: Harper 1975), p 238.

6 Lubbock, *Letters*, II, 124.

7 Leon Edel, *The Middle Years* (Philadelphia and New York: Lippincott 1962), p 366.

8 Guilt over his failure to take a part in the national conflict, unconscious mirroring of his father, envy of his brother William, shrinking from sexuality – these and several other sources of his ailments have been supplied by various analysts. The pain, all the same, must have been real and persistent, its debilitating effect inescapable. Too many to cite are the allusions to it, not only in his letters, but even more in letters by his father, his mother, his brother, and his sister. Invalidism was a constant element of his 'untried years.' He refers to it several times, most notably in the long letter of 20 March 1870 to his brother shortly after hearing of the death of Minny Temple: 'Among the sad reflec-

tions that her death provokes for me, there is none sadder than this view of the gradual change and reversal of our relations: I slowly crawling from weakness and inaction and suffering into strength and health and hope: she sinking out of brightness and youth into decline and death ... She never knew how sick and disordered a creature I was' (Edel, *Letters*, I, 224).

'"Invalidism" is perhaps too strong a word,' Edel suggests (*Letters*, I, 229), 'to describe HJ's recurrent back-ache ... or the constipation which troubled him during these early years ... He himself describes in *Notes of a Son and Brother* how quickly he revived when the war was ended (Chap. IX) and thereafter he led a strenuous life of travel and work for many years until beset by the infirmities of old age.' Beside this, however, might be set numerous allusions to indisposition throughout his life. The absorbing and moving retrospective survey written while he was in California in March 1905 refers in these terms to the middle 1860s: 'I was miserably stricken by my poor broken, all but unbearable, and unsurvivable *back* of those [and still, under fatigue, even of these] years' (*Notebooks of Henry James*, ed F.O. Matthiessen and Kenneth B. Murdock (New York: Oxford University Press 1947), p 320), brackets added by Matthiessen. From the early 1880s might be adduced this impression by Edmund Gosse: 'Stretched on a sofa and apologizing for not rising to meet me, his appearance gave me a little shock, for I had not thought of him as an invalid. He hurriedly and rather evasively answered that he was not that, but that a muscular weakness of his spine obliged him, as he said, "to assume the horizontal posture" during some hours of every day in order to bear the almost unbroken routine of evening engagements' (Edmund Gosse, *Aspects and Impressions* [London: Cassell (1922)], p 27).

In a letter of 23 December 1907 James wrote thus to W.E. Norris: 'I am engaged ... in a perpetual adventure, the most thrilling and in every way the greatest of my life, and which consists of having more than four years entered into a state of health so altogether better than I had ever known that my whole consciousness is transformed by the intense *alleviation* of it, and I lose much time in pinching myself to see if this be not, really, "none of I." That fact, however, is much more interesting to myself than to other people – partly because no one but myself was ever aware of the unhappy nature of the physical consciousness from which I have been redeemed' (Lubbock, *Letters*, II, 86).

9 '... a perfectly insane and abject terror, without ostensible cause, and only to be accounted for, to my perplexed imagination, by some damned shape squatting invisible to me within the precincts of the room, and raying out from his fetid personality influences fatal to life' (from *The Literary Remains of the Late Henry James* [Senior], repr in F.O. Matthiessen, *The James Family Including Selections from the Writings of Henry James, Senior, William, Henry, and Alice James* [New York: Knopf 1961], p 161). William James's hair-raising experience is described in the chapter on 'The Sick Soul' in his *Varieties of Religious Experience*, repr in *The James Family*, pp 216–17. Cf also *The Diary*

of Alice James, ed with intro by Leon Edel (New York: Dodd, Mead 1964), p 104. This is a fascinating book, to be read not so much for its infrequent references to her various forms of illness as because it so engagingly demonstrates the wit and penetration of her mind – 'the life, the power, the temper, the humour and beauty and expressiveness of the Diary' (Henry James to his brother and sister-in-law, Lubbock, *Letters*, I, 214– 17). As well, the Diary exemplifies and enacts Alice James's own special kind of stoicism.

10 *The James Family*, pp 253–5.
11 Edel, *The Middle Years*, p 166; p 361.
12 Ibid, p 166.
13 Edel, *The Master*, pp 434 ff.
14 From Beerbohm's notebook and from conversastion with S.N. Behrman, as quoted in David Cecil, *Max: A Biography* (Boston: Houghton Mifflin 1965), p 211.
15 W. Somerset Maugham, 'Some Novelists I Have Known,' in his *The Vagrant Mood: Six Essays* (London: Heinemann 1952), p 202.
16 Lubbock, *Letters*, II, 16.
17 Maugham, *The Vagrant Mood*, p 202.
18 *Henry James: Letters to A.C. Benson and Auguste Monod*, E.F. Benson (London: Mathews and Marrot 1930), p 87; p 35.
19 *Notebooks*, p 321. These sentences are the climax of his retrospective brooding on Coronado Beach in 1905. Passages such as this lead the reader to wonder how the notebooks escaped the 'gigantic' bonfire at Lamb House in which, late in 1909, James destroyed an immeasurable quantity of letters, manuscripts, and other documents, hoping thus to ensure that the evidences of his private life should irrevocably evade the probings of journalists, biographers, and other searchers after data.
20 Lubbock, *Letters*, II, 91.
21 *The James Family*, p 221.
22 *The Diary of Alice James*, p 104.
23 A.C. Benson, 'Henry James,' in his *Memories and Friends* (London: John Murray 1924), p 203. Another passage describes what seems virtually an acting out by James of his doctrine of social stoicism: 'On another occasion he came down to dine with me at Eton ... He was to have stayed the night, but he excused himself on the score of illness; and when he appeared, it was obvious that he was suffering: he was very pale, and had a gouty lameness which gave him much discomfort. But he talked energetically, and even came with me into the boys' passages to see two or three boys whose parents he knew. He limped distressfully, but he was full of attention and observation ... He ought certainly to have been in bed; and I never saw so complete a triumph of courtesy and genuine interest over bodily pain.'
24 Letter to W.D. Howells, New Year's Eve 1908, Lubbock, *Letters*, II, 119.
25 *The James Family*, pp 253–5.
26 Lubbock, *Letters*, II, 100.

27 *Notebooks*, p 111.
28 Letter of 9 January 1895, *The James Family*, p 336.
29 *Notebooks*, p 188.
30 *Notebooks*, p 179.
31 Edel, *Letters*, II, 424. Compare James's imagery here with that of Marcus Aurelius: 'Be like the headland on which the billows dash themselves continually; but stand fast, till about its base the boiling breakers are lulled to rest.'
32 Letter of 23 December 1906, Lubbock, *Letters*, II, 60.
33 Lubbock, *Letters*, II, 360–1.
34 Henry James, *Notes and Reviews*, ed Pierre de Chaignon la Rose (Cambridge, Mass.: Dunster House 1921), pp 173–87.
35 Henry James, 'Ivan Turgenieff,' *French Poets and Novelists* [London, 1878], intro by Leon Edel (New York: Grosset & Dunlap 1964), p 243.
36 *The Nation*, 21 December 1865, repr in *The Future of the Novel*, Leon Edel (New York: Vintage 1956), pp 75–80.
37 *French Poets and Novelists*, p 89. Consider, too, these remarks: 'Baudelaire is ... a capital text for a discussion of the question as to the importance of the morality ... of a work of art' (p 64). 'His [Théophile Gautier's] native incapacity to moralize ...' (p 52). 'The reason why [Charles de Bernard] remains so persistently second-rate is, to our sense, because he had no morality. By this we of course do not mean that he did not choose to write didactic tales, winding up with a goody lecture and a distribution of prizes and punishments. We mean that he had no moral emotion, no preferences, no instincts – no moral imagination, in a word' (p 196). 'Practically M. Flaubert is a potent moralist ... Every out-and-out realist who provokes serious meditation may claim that he is a moralist' (p 201). 'Moral meaning giving a sense to form and form giving relief to moral meaning ...' ('Ivan Turgenieff,' p 221).
38 'The Art of Fiction' (1884), in *Partial Portraits* (London: Macmillan 1888), esp pp 404–8.
39 *Partial Portraits*, p 406.
40 *The Ambassadors* in The New York ed (New York: Scribner's 1907–9; repr Scribner's 1961–4), XXII, 326–7.
41 *The Spoils of Poynton*, New York ed, X, xv; hereafter cited as SP.
42 'The Beldonald Holbein,' in *The Better Sort* (London: Methuen 1903), p 29.
43 *The Aspern Papers*, New York ed, XII, 72.
44 *The Portrait of a Lady*, New York ed, III, 52–4.
45 *The James Family*, p 594. The quoted words appear in Henry James's essay 'Is There a Life After Death?' in *In After Days: Thoughts on the Future Life* by Henry James, W.D. Howells, and others (1910). The essay is reprinted in *The James Family*, pp 602–14.
46 'The Bench of Desolation,' in *The Finer Grain* (London: Methuen, 1910), p 307.
47 'Broken Wings,' in *The Better Sort*, p 17.

48 Lubbock, *Letters*, II, 140.
49 'A Round of Visits,' in *The Finer Grain*, p 160.
50 *The Golden Bowl*, New York ed, XXIV, 233.
51 *The Wings of the Dove*, New York ed, XX, 329.

DAVISON / A READING OF FRANK NORRIS'S *The Pit*

1 A chapter on *The Pit* is an appropriate contribution to a book in memory of a painstaking Crane scholar who was also an admirer of Frank Norris.
2 See my 'Frank Norris' *The Octopus*: Some Observations on Vanamee, Shelgrim and St. Paul' in *Literature and Ideas in America* (Athens: Ohio University Press 1975), pp 182–203.
3 See *Frank Norris of 'the Wave': Stories and Sketches from the San Francisco Weekly, 1893 to 1897*, ed and intro by Oscar Lewis (San Francisco: Westgate Press 1931), pp 175–80; quotation from pp 177–8. Unless otherwise noted, further Norris citations are from *The Complete Edition of Frank Norris* (Garden City: Doubleday, Doran 1928). Hereafter page references to the *Complete Edition* will be incorporated into the text. *The Pit* comprises vol IX of this ten-volume edition.
4 See vol X, pp 115–47, for 'Lauth.'
5 See vol V for *Vandover and the Brute*.
6 *A Man's Woman*, VI, 104.
7 See also such stories as 'A Memorandum of Sudden Death,' IV, 228–46, for examples of Norris's admiration for stoical courage.
8 'Ten Letters by Frank Norris,' ed Donald Pizer, *Quarterly Newsletter*, 26 (1962), no. 9 [November 1901].
9 Ibid.
10 The title may also refer to 'the abyss that Norris had spoken of as early as *Vandover* – the pit toward which people are hurled as the indulgence of their self-love causes them to attempt to thwart what the novelist calls "the restless forces of nature."' See Warren French's *Frank Norris* (New York: Twayne 1962), pp 115–16.
11 In *The Responsibilities of the Novelist*, VII, 147–52.
12 The strong similarities of Laura Dearborn Jadwin and Curtis Jadwin to Norris's father and mother have been widely discussed.
13 The third volume was tentatively entitled *The Wolf, A Story of Europe*. Norris died of peritonitis before the novel was written.
14 Throughout these writings Norris attacks the pseudo-artist-critics who frequented Greenwich Village during his day. See, for instance, 'Dying Fires' in *The Third Circle*, IV, 113–27.
15 Donald Pizer discusses Joseph Le Conte's influence on Norris in his fine book *The Novels of Frank Norris* (Bloomington: Indiana University Press 1966). See also Robert

Lundy's fine unpublished dissertation 'The Making of "McTeague" and "The Octopus,"' (University of California, Berkeley 1955).

16 Norris makes Corthell sound very much like the arty young ladies in *The Octopus* who attempt to apply a semi-digested mish-mash of critical terms in describing Hartrath's painting. See II, 26–7.

17 Although Corthell's speech is excessive, Norris may have agreed with the spirit of it which is close to Le Conte's views on art. See 'On the Nature and Uses of Art,' *Southern Presbyterian Review*, 15 (1863), 311–48 and 515–48.

18 For an interesting discussion of fact turned into fiction, see Charles Kaplan's 'Norris' Use of Sources in *The Pit*,' *American Literature*, 25 (1953), 75–84.

19 Criticism of *The Pit* has too often been negative. Although Warren French defends *The Pit* as 'more carefully thought out' than *The Octopus*, he attacks its structure by calling it (paradoxically, it would seem) an 'ungainly pile' (*Frank Norris*, pp 107 and 108). Other critics have been less kind. Ernest Marchand feels the novel is lopsided, 'weakened by the overprominence of the love story'; see *Frank Norris, a Study* (Stanford: Stanford University Press 1942), p 35. Charles Walcutt sees Laura 'merely as a foil to set off the great struggle in the pit'; see *American Literary Naturalism, A Divided Stream* (Minneapolis: University of Minnesota Press 1956), p 154. Charles G. Hoffman recognizes that the love story is Norris's main concern but feels it is marred by the expectation of a social message and overshadowed by the effective style of the wheat scenes; see 'Norris and the Responsibility of the Novelist,' *South Atlantic Quarterly*, 54 (1955), 508–15. He also seems unaware of Norris's careful juxtaposition of the love and business plots, so that each one reinforces and comments on the other. More recently Pizer associates *The Pit* with 'Norris's decline' and a reason for 'Norris's career [ending] on a low note' (*The Novels*, p 162). Although he acknowledges Norris's 'method of preparation and composition' (p 162), he feels that neither 'the business nor the love plot ... is really successful ... there seems to be no common theme in the two, and the critic is therefore reduced to describing what Norris perhaps intended rather than whan he achieved' (p 174). William B. Dillingham sees *The Pit* as 'a "chilling descent" from what came before.' It is an 'example of the novel which writes itself, without a strong disciplined hand and a shrewd, watchful eye ... a novel slipping page by page out of control and taking itself along routes which the author originally meant to be only byways'; see *Frank Norris: Instinct and Art* (Lincoln: University of Nebraska Press 1969), pp 121 and 125.

20 See IX, 85–6, for Norris's overt comment on Landry's 'double personality.'

21 Jadwin's near-ruin of Scannel to allow Hargus a revenge (which the old man does not even comprehend) is largely the capricious act of a man who embraces the morality of poetic justice. His paternalism does nothing to alleviate the deplorable condition of those starving in Europe because of inflated prices.

22 The lengths of the Bull careers of both Jadwin and Leiter (April 1897 to 13 June 1898) are exactly the same. Kaplan ('Norris' Use of Sources in *The Pit*') has demonstrated,

however, that Norris altered the sequence of events in Leiter's career to achieve the dramatic effect he sought.

23 Norris uses hair and clothing imagery effectively to externalize the changing facets of Laura's character. See, for instance, IX, 147, 163, 165, 177, 278, and 295–8.

24 It is her daydreams and selfish preoccupations that Laura must transcend in order to mature.

25 *Frank Norris*, p 111.

26 There is hubris behind Jadwin's declaration: '"By God ... if I lay my hands on Scannel – if we catch him in the corner – holy, suffering Moses, but I'll make him squeal!"' (IX, 306).

27 The real horror of Laura's discovery is in her memory. Waiting for Jadwin she notices the note from Mrs Cressler announcing the funeral: 'At this sight, all the tragedy leaped up again in her mind and recollection, and in fancy she stood again in the back parlour of the Cressler home; her fingers pressed over her mouth to shut back the cries, horror and the terror of sudden death rending her heart, shaking the brain itself' (IX, 384).

28 Page describes Laura as being '"just like a stone – just as though she were crowding down every emotion or any feeling she ever had. She seems to be holding herself in with all her strength – for something – and afraid to let go a finger, for fear she would give way altogether"' (IX, 362).

29 Page has always taken an active interest in Landry's business career. Early interested in art and literature, they are reading together books they both enjoy: '"We are reading George Sand aloud and making up the longest vocabulary"' (IX, 399). Although Norris is still poking gentle fun at their semi-naivety, the juxtaposition of their more stable relationship with the Jadwin's early lack of real communication and mutual understanding is no less intentional.

30 Certainly Norris was capable also of portraying Jadwin in the throes of a powerful inner struggle. He had already probed the spiritual growths of Vanamee and Annixter as well as the moral deterioration of Vandover and Magnus. It seems apparent that it was Norris's keen sense of balance, his awareness of the aesthetics of structure that allowed him to let Laura occupy 'the centre of the stage.'

31 Another instance of Norris's structural control is in his circular use of physical setting. As the Jadwins leave Chicago, Laura's last visual impression is the same as at the close of chapter one. But it is an enlightened Laura who once again looks on the impassive 'Board of Trade Building, black, monolithic [in] the drifting veil of rain' (IX, 29 and 403).

SALOMON / SOME STOIC PERSONAE IN THE WORK OF
WILLIAM CARLOS WILLIAMS

1 *Imaginations*, ed Webster Schott (New York: New Directions 1970), p 27.
2 *The Inverted Bell: Modernism and the Counterpoetics of William Carlos Williams* (Baton Rouge: Louisiana State University Press 1974), p 46.

3 This latter point is made by Riddel in *The Inverted Bell*, pp 72–3, who refers, in turn, to Geoffrey Hartman, *Beyond Formalism: Literary Essays, 1958–1970* (New Haven: Yale University Press 1970).

4 (New York: New Directions, 1963), p 140; hereafter cited as P.

5 'Reply to Papini,' in *Collected Poems* (New York: Knopf 1964), p 446.

6 'The Structure of the *Quixote*,' in *Cervantes, A Critical Trajectory*, ed and trans Raymond E. Barbara (Boston: Mirage Press 1971), p 193.

7 'The Structure of the *Quixote*,' p 183.

8 See 'The Structure of the *Quixote*,' p 198: 'The epic-chivalric hero could not allow the meaning of his heroic life to be doubted.'

9 'Pierre Menard, Author of the *Quixote*,' in *Labyrinths: Selected Stories and Other Writings*, ed Donald A. Yates and James E. Irby, trans James E. Irby (New York: New Directions 1964), pp 39–44.

10 *The Necessary Angel: Essays in Reality and the Imagination* (New York: Vintage 1951), pp 9–10.

11 *In the American Grain* (New York: New Directions 1956), p 136; hereafter cited as IAG.

12 See my essay, 'Mock-Heroes and Mock-Heroic Narrative: Byron's *Don Juan* in the Context of Cervantes,' *Studies in the Literary Imagination*, 9 (1976), 69–86.

13 *Beiträge zu einer Kritik der Sprache*, I, 25, quoted in Allan Janik and Stephen Toulmin, *Wittgenstein's Vienna* (New York: Simon and Schuster 1973), p 126; trans by the authors.

14 *Selected Poems* (New York: New Directions 1963), p 3; hereafter cited as SP.

15 *Pictures from Brueghel and Other Poems* (New York: New Directions, 1962), pp 110–20; hereafter cited as PB.

16 *Collected Later Poems* (New York: New Directions, 1967), p 5; hereafter cited as CLP.

17 *The Inverted Bell*, p 93. Riddel has many brilliant things to say about Williams's aesthetic theory. In bringing him under the aegis of structuralist poetics, however, he makes a positive program out of Williams's commitment to the new without being enough aware, as I think Williams was, of the degree to which this commitment was the quixotic strategy of one who, like Joyce, lives in the intractable environment of diminished times (more 'realistic' than 'romantic') and whose doubts are in constant dialogue with his vision. Riddel's strong focus on aesthetic theory tends to neglect the actual nature of Williams's personae. The pain, the struggle, the approaches to despair, the frequent mockery, the incessant anticlimax, and the counter-rhythms of much of Williams's work, including at least the first four books of *Paterson*, are, by and large, ignored by Riddel. Ironically, he makes Williams into the authentic hero of the new world that Paterson and the other personae are always *trying* to be. Paterson is, in effect, a parody of Riddel's own critical dream.

18 'Nature,' in *The Complete Essays and Other Writings*, ed Brooks Atkinson (New York: Modern Library 1940), p 20.

19 *Collected Poems*, pp 300–2.

BACKMAN / DEATH AND BIRTH IN HEMINGWAY

1 Paul Tillich, *The Courage to Be* (New Haven: Yale University Press 1952), pp 12–13, 38–9.
2 Malcolm Cowley, 'Nightmare and Ritual in Hemingway,' in *Hemingway: A Collection of Critical Essays*, ed R.P. Weeks (Englewood Cliffs, NJ: Prentice-Hall 1962), p. 40.
3 Ibid, p 41.
4 Ernest Hemingway, *The Short Stories of Ernest Hemingway* (New York: Scribner's [Modern Standard Authors] 1953), p 88. This edition is used for all quotations from Hemingway's short stories.
5 Samuel Beckett, *Waiting for Godot* (New York: Grove Press 1954), p 57.
6 It should be apparent that I am much indebted to Philip Young for his germinal research on the war trauma in Hemingway: *Ernest Hemingway: A Reconsideration* (University Park: Pennsylvania State University Press 1966).
7 Ernest Hemingway, 'Three Shots,' *The Nick Adams Stories* (New York: Scribner's 1972), p 14.
8 Sandor Ferenczi in *Thalassa: A Theory of Genitality* (New York: Norton 1968) and Otto Rank in *The Trauma of Birth* (New York: Robert Bruner 1952) develop the theory of man's innate need to regress to the intrauterine state and relive the birth trauma. Ferenczi, moreover, relates the intrauterine existence of the higher mammals to the aboriginal piscine period and relates birth itself to the transition from the aquatic to the terrestrial existence of our animal ancestors; see pp 45 ff.
9 *A Farewell to Arms*, p 30, in *Three Novels of Ernest Hemingway: The Sun Also Rises, A Farewell to Arms, and The Old Man and The Sea* (New York: Scribner's 1962). This edition is used for quotations from these novels.
10 Edmund Wilson, 'Hemingway: Gauge of Morale,' in *The Wound and the Bow: Seven Studies in Literature* (New York: Oxford 1947), p 239n.
11 Carlos Baker, *Ernest Hemingway: A Life Story* (New York: Scribner's 1969), p vii. I am indebted to Baker's biography in many ways: to its patiently amassed factual details and to the sane, judicious portrait of Ernest Hemingway.
12 Georges Schreiber, *Portraits and Self-Portraits* (Boston: Houghton Mifflin 1936), p 57; repr in *Essay Index Reprint Series* (Freeport, NY: Books for Libraries Press 1969). Young was the first to call attention to this quotation; see Young, pp 134, 166.
13 Ernest Hemingway, *Death in the Afternoon* (New York: Scribner's 1932), p 82.
14 *For Whom the Bell Tolls* (New York: Scribner's 1940).
15 Ferenczi has noted correspondences between orgasm and the intrauterine situation; see Ferenczi, pp 35–6, 42, 43.
16 Tafalla is also the home of the young father who was fatally gored in Pamplona in *The Sun Also Rises* and who left behind a wife and two children. The waiter in the cafe comments: 'Badly cogido through the back ... A big horn wound. All for fun. Just for fun. What do you think of that?' (*The Sun Also Rises*, pp 197–9).

17 Ferenczi, p 47.

18 *Islands in the Stream* and *The Dangerous Summer* reveal the serious trouble Hemingway was experiencing in writing and completing works in the last decade of his life. Like the fragmentary works of Mark Twain in the last years of his life, they testify to the breakdown of the artist and reflect psychic disturbance.

19 Melvin Backman, 'Hemingway: The Matador and the Crucified' in *Hemingway and His Critics: An International Anthology* (New York: Hill and Wang 1961), p 256.

20 The crucifixion, Otto Rank has said, 'corresponds to a painfully emphasized return to the womb, after which follows quite consistently the resurrection, namely, birth and not rebirth. For here it is also a question of nothing but a repetition and reproduction of the process of birth, ethically and religiously sublimated in the sense of a neurotic overcoming of the primal trauma' (Rank, p 137).

21 'A Way You'll Never Be,' in *The Short Stories of Ernest Hemingway*, p 414.

22 Baker, pp 563–4.

MacMILLAN / STOIC HUMANISM IN FAULKNER'S *A Fable*

1 William Faulkner, *A Fable* (New York 1954); all references are from this edition, hereafter cited as F.

2 Faulkner published *Intruder in the Dust* (1948), *Knight's Gambit* (1949), *Collected Stories* (1950), *Requiem for a Nun* (1951), and *Notes on a Horsethief* (1951); he received the Nobel Prize for Literature on 10 December 1950 and was created a Member of the French Legion of Honour in October 1951. For this period of Faulkner's life see Michael Millgate, *The Achievement of William Faulkner* (New York 1963), pp 42–51; Malcolm Cowley, 'Introduction,' *The Portable Faulkner*, rev ed (New York 1967), pp vii–xxxiii; and especially Joseph Blotner, *Faulkner: A Biography*, 2 vols (New York 1974), II, 1014–1526.

3 Malcolm Cowley, *The Faulkner-Cowley File: Letters and Memories 1944–1962* (New York 1966), p 128.

4 *The Faulkner-Cowley File*, p 105.

5 William Faulkner, *Faulkner in the University*, ed F.L. Gwynn and J.L. Blotner (New York 1965), pp 25–6.

6 Cf Malcolm Cowley, 'The Solitude of William Faulkner,' *The Atlantic Monthly*, 193 (June 1966), 101; William Faulkner, *Faulkner at Nagano*, ed R.A. Jelliffe (Tokyo 1966), pp 23, 46–7; Jean Stein, 'William Faulkner: An Interview,' *Paris Review* (1956), pp 28–52, repr in *William Faulkner: Three Decades of Criticism*, ed F.J. Hoffman and O.W. Vickery (New York 1960), pp 67–82; quotation on pp 74–5. See also *Faulkner in the University*, p 62; and J.B. Meriwether, 'A Note on *A Fable*,' *Mississippi Quarterly*, 26 (1973), 416–17.

7 For all Faulkner's major speeches, see *William Faulkner: Essays, Speeches, and Public Letters*, ed J.B. Meriwether (New York 1965).

8 'The Stockholm address was, I hoped, exactly what it said. I wished to use that moment to speak to the young writers ... to remind them that the things to work toward, to write about, were the verities which later [they] would never be ashamed of ... and that the poet's duty is not just to record his triumphs and his defeats but to remind him always that his triumphs are truly [the] triumphs ... of all men' (*Faulkner at Nagano*, p 66).

9 *Faulkner at Nagano*, pp 156–60.

10 *Faulkner in the University*, p 62.

11 Cf *A Fable*, pp 9, 22, 48, 119, 180 ff, 198, 199, 200, 201, 202, 203, 205, 206, 222, 236, 239–42, 263, 291, 344, 347, 350, 352, 354, 399, 435–7.

FUCHS / SAUL BELLOW AND THE EXAMPLE OF DOSTOEVSKY

1 Irving Howe, 'Dostoevsky: *The Politics of Salvation*,' in *Politics and the Novel* (New York: Meridian 1957), p 51.

2 V.S. Pritchett, review of Alfred Kazin's *Bright Book of Life*, in *New York Times Book Review*, 20 May 1973, p 3.

3 Philip Rahv, 'The Legend of the Grand Inquisitor,' in *The Myth and the Powerhouse* (New York: Farrar, Straus and Giroux 1965), p 159.

4 Fydor Dostoevsky, *The Idiot*, trans Constance Garnett (New York: Modern Library 1935), p 208. Quotations from Dostoevsky's novels are from the Garnett translations (Modern Library editions, though the Garnett translations of Dostoevsky's *The Double* [hereafter cited as D] and *The Eternal Husband* [hereafter cited as EH] are in *The Short Novels of Dostoevsky* [New York: Dial Press 1951]). In the case of *Notes from Underground*, however, I have used the Matlaw translation (New York: Dutton 1960). The Bellow editions from which I have quoted are as follows: *Dangling Man* (New York: Meridian 1960); hereafter cited as DM; *The Victim*, (New York: Signet NAL 1965); hereafter cited as V; all other quotations from Bellow are from the Viking editions of his works.

5 Saul Bellow, 'Cloister Culture,' *New York Times Book Review*, 10 July 1966, p 45.

6 Dostoevsky, *The Brothers Karamazov* (1960), p 300; hereafter cited as BK.

7 Dostoevsky, *The Possessed* (1959), p 705.

8 Ibid, p 427.

9 *Notes from Underground*, p xiii.

10 *Crime and Punishment* (1956), pp 354 ff.

11 Ibid, p 411.

12 *The Possessed*, p 268.

13 Raymond Aron, *The Opium of the Intellectuals* (New York: Norton 1962), p 80.

14 Ibid, p 96.

15 Ibid, p 100.

16 R.W.B. Lewis, 'Lionel Trilling and the New Stoicism,' review of Lionel Trilling's *The Liberal Imagination*, in *Hudson Review*, 3 (1950), 317.

17 *Herzog* (New York: Viking 1964), p 163.

18 Edward Shils, 'Daydreams and Nightmares: Reflections on the Criticism of Mass Culture,' *Sewanee Review*, 65 (1957), 587–608 passim; 'The Theory of Mass Society,' in *America as a Mass Society*, ed Philip Olson (Glencoe: Free Press 1963), pp 30–47 passim; 'Social Sciences and Law,' in *Great Ideas Today* (Chicago: Encyclopedia Britannica 1961), pp 245–89 passim.

19 Shils, 'The Concept and Function of Ideology,' *International Encyclopedia of Social Science*, VII (New York: Macmillan and Free Press 1968), 66–76 passim; 'Ideology and Civility: On the Politics of the Intellectual,' *Sewanee Review*, 66 (1958), 450–80 passim.

20 Dennis Wrong, 'Reflections on the End of Ideology,' in *The End of Ideology Debate*, ed Chaim L. Waxman (New York: Funk & Wagnalls 1968), p 123.

21 Bellow, unpublished *Notebooks*, C.2.7, p 6, untitled draft for a lecture on the novel.

22 Dostoevsky, *The Diary of a Writer*, trans Boris Brasol (New York: Scribner's 1949), p 787.

23 Philip Rahv, 'Dostoevsky in *The Possessed*,' in *Image and Idea* (Norfolk: New Directions 1949), p 90.

24 Nicholas Berdyaev, *Dostoevsky* (Cleveland/New York: Meridian 1964), p 25.

25 Ibid, p 40.

26 Arnold Hauser, *The Social History of Art* (New York: Vintage 1958), IV, 152.

27 George Steiner, *Tolstoy or Dostoevsky* (New York: Vintage 1961), p 154.

28 Rahv, 'Dostoevsky in *The Possessed*,' p 101.

29 Herbert Gold, review of *Henderson the Rain King*, in *The Nation*, 188 (21 Feb. 1959), 172.

30 Berdyaev, *Dostoevsky*, p 21.

31 Edward Wasiolek, *Dostoevsky: The Major Fiction* (Cambridge, Mass.: MIT Press 1964), p 54.

32 Berdayev, *Dostoevsky*, p 113.

33 The one mitigating factor in Pytor Verkovensky's dossier is his father's relationship to him as a child. Stepan Verkovensky, a caricature of the airy, literary, liberal, may think fondly of Pytor, 'the fruit of our first still unclouded happiness,' but on the death of his wife, as the MacAndrew translation has it, 'the fruit of their happiness was immediately packed off to Russia and his education entrusted to some distant relative residing in a remote backwater' (*The Possessed* [New York: Signet NAL 1962], p 13). Similarly Fydor Karamazov disposes of his own, with results even more patricidal in intention. Though there seems to be no evidence of it, Dostoevsky may have wryly contemplated, in a book he knew well, the spectacle of western egotism in Rousseau's *Confessions* a book whose self-analytical hero abandons his five children and goes on to write a book, a great book, about child rearing.

34 Konstantin Mochulsky, *Dostoevsky: His Life and Work* trans Michael A. Minihan (Princeton: Princeton University Press 1973), pp 623–4.

LAWSON / *The Moviegoer* AND THE STOIC HERITAGE

I wish to acknowledge the assistance of the General Research Board of the University of Maryland in the preparation of this paper.

1 Walker Percy, *The Moviegoer* (New York: Noonday Press 1967), p 78; hereafter cited as M.

2 Thomas E. Keys, 'The Colonial Library and the Development of Sectional Differences in the American Colonies,' *Library Quarterly*, 8 (1938), 374.

3 See Thomas Franklin Mayo, *Epicurus in England (1650–1725)* (Dallas: Southwestern Press 1934), pp 110–11, for the alliance of stoicism with the Platonic idealists, the Royal Society, and the Cartesian rationalists.

4 John Melville Jennings, 'Notes on the Original Library of the College of William and Mary,' *Papers of the Bibliographical Society of America*, 41 (1947), 265.

5 John Melville Jennings, *The Library of the College of William and Mary in Virginia, 1693–1793* (Charlottesville: University Press of Virginia, 1968), pp 47–8.

6 Mayo, pp 110–11, argues that Anglican Christianity had little difficulty in accepting nearly all stoic beliefs as relatively harmless departures from orthodoxy.

7 Jennings, *The Library*, p 30, points out that 'Three of the six private book collections analysed by Louis B. Wright in his *First Gentlemen of Virginia* were owned by members of the college board of visitors [of the College of William and Mary] – Ralph Wormeley II, Robert ('King') Carter, and William Byrd, II.' If Wright can generalize broadly upon the reading and other tastes of a class from six examples, then it seems not entirely out of line to suggest here that the thinking of that class was coloured by particular books found in its libraries.

8 George K. Smart, 'Private Libraries in Colonial Virginia,' *American Literature*, 10 (1938), 51.

9 John Rogers Williams, 'A Catalogue of Books in the Library of "Councillor" Robert Carter,' *William and Mary College Quarterly*, 11, 1st series (1902), 23.

10 John Spencer Bassett, *The Writings of Colonel William Byrd* (New York: Doubleday, Page, 1901), appendix A, pp 413–43.

11 Louis B. Wright, *The First Gentlemen of Virginia* (San Marino, Calif.: Huntington Library 1940), p 233.

12 William D. Houlette, 'Sources of Books for the Old South,' *Library Quarterly*, 38 (1958), 195.

13 Lester J. Cappon and Stella F. Duff, *Virginia Gazette Index* (Williamsburg: Institute of Early American History and Culture 1950), II, 1022.

14 See *Virginia Gazette*, 13 November 1768; 21 November 1768; 11 April 1769.

15 The stoics were being read in other Southern colonies as well. For Maryland see Joseph T. Wheeler, 'Reading Interests of the Professional Classes in Colonial Maryland, 1700–1776,' *Maryland Magazine of History*, 36 (1941), 201; for North Carolina see J.B. Grimes, *North Carolina Wills and Inventories* (Raleigh: Edwards and Braughton 1912), pp 559, 562–4; and S.B. Weeks, 'Libraries and Literature in North Carolina in the Eighteenth Century,' *Annual Report of the American Historical Association* (1895), p 205.

16 'Catalogue of the Library of Daniel Parke Custis,' *Virginia Magazine of History and Biography*, 17 (1903), 404–12, esp p 409.

17 Genevieve Yost, 'The Reconstruction of the Library of Norborne Berkeley, Baron de Botetourt, Governor of Virginia, 1768–1770,' *Papers of the Bibliographical Society of America*. 36 (1942), 119.

18 Eleanor Davidson Berman, *Thomas Jefferson Among the Arts* (New York: Philosophical Library 1947), p 271.

19 Andrew A. Lipscomb, ed, *The Writings of Thomas Jefferson*, Memorial ed (Washington 1903), V, 85.

20 Elizabeth Cometti, *Jefferson's Ideas on a University Library* (Charlottesville: University Press of Virginia 1950), p 30.

21 Lipscomb, XV, 219.

22 Lipscomb, XV, 221.

23 Anson Phelps Stokes, *Church and State in the United States* (New York: Harper 1950), I, 136.

24 Stokes, I, 82–3.

25 Lipscomb, XV, 220. Nor was Jefferson's classification to William Short merely one of those statements so influenced by friendship that it is tailored to please the person for whom it is intended. Over fifteen years before Jefferson had employed the same assignment of values in writing to Dr Benjamin Rush. The purpose of the letter was to urge Dr Rush to write a book that Jefferson would have written himself had his life not been given over to public service. He had gone so far as to prepare a 'Syllabus of an Estimate of the Merit of the Doctrines of Jesus, compared with those others.' In the letter he announced: 'To the corruptions of Christianity I am, indeed, opposed; but not to the genuine precepts of Jesus himself. I am a Christian, in the only sense in which he wished any one to be; sincerely attached to his doctrines, in preference to all others; ascribing to himself every *human* excellence; and believing he never claimed any other.' Then he explained why, despite the nobility of classical philosophy, the doctrines of Jesus were essential:

'Let a just view be taken of the moral principles inculcated by the most esteemed of the sects of ancient philosophy, or of their individuals; particularly Pythagoras, Socrates, Epicurus, Cicero, Epictetus, Seneca, Antoninus.

I. Philosophers. 1. Their precepts related chiefly to ourselves, and the government of those passions which, unrestrained, would disturb our tranquility of mind. In this branch of philosophy they were really great.

2. In developing our duties to others, they were short and defective.'
See Lipscomb, X, 380–2.

26 Adrienne Koch, *The Philosophy of Thomas Jefferson* (Gloucester: Peter Smith 1957), p 4.

27 Jay B. Hubbell, *South and Southwest* (Durham: Duke University Press 1965), p 235. James McBride Dabbs, *Who Speaks for the South?* (New York: Funk and Wagnalls 1964), p 127, expands on the reasons for the popularity of stoicism in the South during the nineteenth century: 'For several reasons, Stoicism found a rich soil in the ante-bellum South. First, because of the rising individualism of the Western World, of which the South was a part, an individualism which coincided with and was in part the cause of the decay of the inclusive community life of the Middle Ages. Second, because of the existence of slavery, increasingly under moral attack, impossible to defend in the humanitarian air of the nineteenth century and within a Christianity increasingly concerned about life in the world, but easy to defend by the Stoic doctrine that a man's worldly condition does not matter. Third, because of the growing doubt within the minds of Southern leaders, a sense of the coming eclipse of the nation, a fear of the possible breakdown of the social and economic order of the South. In such a mood a man, if he were a Stoic, could retire to the inviolable castle of his own soul and watch with stern composure the playing out of the game.'

28 Douglas Southall Freeman, *R.E. Lee* (New York: Scribner's 1935), IV, 464.

29 Freeman, III, 237.

30 Freeman, IV, 464.

31 'Fortunate and prosperous wickedness is called virtue' (New York: Belford Company 1890), frontispiece.

32 William Styron, *Lie Down in Darkness* (New York: New American Library 1951), p 12; hereafter cited as LDD.

33 William Alexander Percy, *Lanterns on the Levee* (Baton Rouge: Louisiana State University Press 1973); hereafter cited as LL. In 'Walker Percy's Southern Stoic,' *Southern Literary Journal*, 3 (1970), 5–31, I have attempted to demonstrate Walker Percy's reaction to his 'Uncle Will' in both *The Moviegoer* and *The Last Gentleman*, his second novel, without addressing the extent to which the older Percy exemplified the stoic heritage.

34 *The Commonweal*, 44 (6 July 1956), 342–4; hereafter cited as SS.

35 *Being and Time*, trans John Macquarrie and Edward Robinson (New York: Harper and Row 1962), pp 179–82.

36 I have attempted to deal with the nature of Jack's existential quest in 'Walker Percy's Indirect Communications,' *Texas Studies in Literature and Language*, 11 (1969), 867–900.

Notes on Contributors

GAY WILSON ALLEN, Emeritus Professor of English, New York University, and Visiting Professor of English at Harvard (1969–70), has accomplished both a prodigious bibliography and a highly acclaimed reputation in American scholarship. Professor Allen's major publications include *The Solitary Singer: A Critical Biography of Walt Whitman* (1955); *William James, a Biography* (1967); and *The New Walt Whitman Handbook* (1975). He is the General Editor of *The Collected Writings of Walt Whitman*, in process of publication by New York University Press, and is finishing a biography of Ralph Waldo Emerson.

MELVIN BACKMAN, Professor of English and Chairman of the Department (1973–6) at C.W. Post College, Long Island University, has published widely on Ernest Hemingway and William Faulkner. Among his principal studies are *Faulkner, the Major Years: A Critical Study* (1966); 'Hemingway: The Matador and the Crucified,' *Modern Fiction Studies* (August 1955), often reprinted, and translated into French; and 'Sutpen and the South: A Study of *Absalom, Absalom!*' *PMLA* (December 1965), also reprinted. 'Addie Bundren and William Faulkner' will be published in *Twentieth Century Studies* and in *William Faulkner, the Unappeased Imagination: A Collection of Critical Essays*. Professor Backman is preparing a study of Walt Whitman.

MUNRO BEATTIE, Emeritus Professor of English, has been associated with Carleton University since its foundation in 1942, and he was Chairman of the Department of English 1947–69. He has contributed four chapters to the *Literary History of Canada* (1965; second edition 1976); 'Archibald Lampman' to *Our Living Tradition* (1957); 'The Many Marriages of Henry James' to *Patterns of Commitment in American Literature* (1967); and has co-authored *Composition for Canadian Univer-*

sities (1964). Professor Beattie is now completing *Henry James as an Observer of English Society*.

PETER BUITENHUIS, Chairman and Professor, Department of English at Simon Fraser University, has taught at McGill, University of California (Berkeley), University of Toronto, and Yale University. He has published *The Grasping Imagination: The American Writings of Henry James* (1970); *Hugh MacLennan* (1969); *Five American Moderns* (1965); and is currently engaged in studies in Canadian literature and literature of the First World War.

RICHARD ALLAN DAVISON, Professor of English at the University of Delaware, has more than thirty publications on John Webster, Hawthorne, Melville, Whitman, Crane, Norris, Hemingway, R.P. Warren, and Albee to his credit. He edited *Merrill Studies in the Octopus* (1969); and contributed 'Frank Norris' The Octopus: Some Observations on Vanamee, Shelgrim and St. Paul' to *Literature and Ideas in America* (1975). Books on Frank Norris and Frank, Charles, and Kathleen Norris are in process.

DANIEL FUCHS, Associate Professor of English at the College of Staten Island, City University of New York, has also taught at the University of Chicago, and has twice been Senior Fulbright Lecturer: Nantes (1967–8) and Vienna (1975–6). He has published *The Comic Spirit of Wallace Stevens* (1963), and articles on Hemingway, Wallace Stevens, and Saul Bellow. He is working on *Saul Bellow: Vision and Revision*, of which 'Saul Bellow and the Example of Dostoevsky' will be a part.

PATRICK HAYMAN has lived in New Zealand and England and in the post-war period was associated with Peter Lanyon, Ben Nicholson, Terry Frost, and Barbara Hepworth in the artistic colony at St Ives. In 1958 he founded *The Painter and Sculptor* and edited the journal until its demise in 1963. Hayman belongs to the essentially English school of visionary painters. His artistic forbears include Samuel Palmer and William Blake: he is represented in the collections of The Art Council of Great Britain, The Contemporary Art Society, The National Gallery of Modern Art (Edinburgh), the Calouste Gulbenkian Foundation, and the National Gallery of South Australia.

GEORGE JOHNSTON taught at Mount Allison University and, since 1950, has been at Carleton University. He was granted an LL D (*honoris causa*) from Queen's University in 1971. Professor Johnston's three books of poetry are *The Cruising Auk* (1959), *Home Free* (1966), and *Happy Enough* (1972); he has also translated Old

Norse, Faroese, and modern Icelandic sagas in *The Saga of Gisli* (1963), *The Faroe Islanders' Saga* (1974), and *The Greenlanders' Saga* (1976). A collection of short stories is soon to be published.

LEWIS A. LAWSON, Professor of English at the University of Maryland, was Fulbright Lecturer at the University of Copenhagan (1971–2). His major publications include 'Walker Percy's Indirect Communications,' *Texas Studies in Literature and Language* (1969), 'William Faulkner,' in *The Politics of Twentieth-Century Novelists* (1971), and 'Rabbit Angstrom as a Religious Sufferer,' *Journal of the American Academy of Religion* (1974); and his recent scholarship examines Walker Percy's use of Heidegger and Sartre.

DUANE J. MacMILLAN, Associate Professor of English at the University of Saskatchewan, has published '*Pylon*: From Short Stories to Major Work,' *Mosaic* (1973). He has edited a special Conrad Aiken issue of *Notable works and Collections* (University of Saskatchewan Library). *The Stoic Strain in American Literature: Essays in Honour of Marston LaFrance* is his first major work. Essays on Faulkner, Aiken, Dreiser, and Hemingway are forthcoming.

TOM MIDDLEBRO', Associate Professor of English at Carleton University, has published a number of articles on Dickens, A.M. Klein, William Morris, and George Orwell. He lectured for several years at the University of Saskatchewan, but since 1963 has been at Carleton: his present interests lie in studies of nineteenth-century British fiction and critical prose, and in Canadian literature.

ROGER B. SALOMON, Professor and Chairman of English at Case Western Reserve University, has also taught at Mills College and Yale University. Among his major publications are *Twain and the Image of History* (1961); 'Escape from History: Mark Twain's Joan of Arc,' *Philological Quarterly* (1961); 'Realism as Disinheritance: Twain, Howells, and James,' *American Quarterly* (1967); 'Mark Twain and Victorian Nostalgia,' *Patterns of Commitment in American Literature* (1967); and 'Mock-Heroes and Mock-Heroic Narrative: Byron's *Don Juan* in the Context of Cervantes, '*Studies in the Literary Imagination* (1976). Professor Salomon is a contributor to an edition of *The Prince and the Pauper* for the forthcoming Iowa-Berkeley Works of Mark Twain and is currently making a study of the mock-heroic sensibility in more recent times.

MILTON R. STERN, Distinguished Alumni Professor, University of Connecticut, has taught at the University of Illinois (Urbana), University of Wyoming, Smith College, and was the Fulbright-Hayes Professor at the University of Warsaw (1964–5). *The Fine Hammered Steel of Herman Melville* (1957) and *The Golden Moment: The Novels of F. Scott Fitzgerald* (1970) number among his major publications, as do his editions of *Discussions of Moby-Dick* (1960), *Typee and Billy Budd* (1958), and (with S.L. Gross), *American Literature Survey*, 4 volumes (1962; revised and expanded 1968, 1975).